Social Research

A Simple Guide

Morley D. Glicken

Boston ■ New York ■ San Francisco
Mexico City ■ Montreal ■ Toronto ■ London ■ Madrid ■ Munich ■ Paris
Hong Kong ■ Singapore ■ Tokyo ■ Cape Town ■ Sydney

Series Editor: *Patricia Quinlin*
Editorial Assistant: *Annemarie Kennedy*
Editorial-Production Administrator: *Joe Sweeney*
Editorial-Production Service: *Colophon*
Composition Buyer: *Linda Cox*
Manufacturing Buyer: *JoAnne Sweeney*
Cover Administrator: *Kristina Mose-Libon*
Text Composition: *Modern Graphics*

For related titles and support materials, visit our online catalog at
www.ablongman.com.

Between the time Website information is gathered and then published, it is not
unusual for some sites to have closed. Also, the transcription of URLs can result in
unintended typographical errors. The publisher would appreciate notification
where these errors occur so that they may be corrected in subsequent editions.

Library of Congress Cataloging-in-Publication Data

Glicken, Morley D.
  A simple guide to social research / Morley D. Glicken.
    p. cm.
  Includes bibliographical references and index.
  ISBN 0-205-33428-8 (alk. paper)
    1. Sociology—Research—Methodology. 2. Social sciences—Research—
Methodology. I. Title.

HM571 .G57 2002
300'.72—dc21

                                                                    2002018686

Printed in the United States of America

10 9 8 7 6 5 4 3 2 1   09 08 07 06 05 04 03

This book is dedicated to my parents, Rose and Sam Glicken, who walked across Europe so that they could come to the United States and have a safe haven in which to raise their children. Their love of knowledge, their sense of humor, and their desire to make the world a better place to live in were inspirations to me and throughout the writing of this book. They were very special people with the tough but tender immigrant will to survive and persevere. Not a day goes by that I don't miss them.

CONTENTS

4 The Research Proposal 54

PREFACE

Who said that research can't be fun or that it has to be so deadly serious that your research books weigh twelve pounds and are about as interesting as reading Martian? Well, nobody ever said that, although, to be honest, a lot of research is written in a language so unnecessarily technical that most of us can't understand it. This overly technical way of writing often seeps into the research texts that many students find cumbersome and difficult to understand. Like you, I get bored and confused reading research books. Some of them read like the instruction booklets you get when you're putting together a bike or a piece of furniture; the work isn't complicated but the instructions certainly are.

I'm a former dean of a school of social service work, but in another life, in a place far, far away (California), I was a professor of social work in graduate research. Most of my students came from the social sciences and had majors in psychology, sociology, or criminal justice. Sometimes they came from fields a bit apart from social work, but all of my students took courses in research methods. On the first day of my research class when I asked them what they remembered about research, they usually remembered nothing. Just the word *research* brought groans from my students. "What?" they'd ask me, "we have to take research? We're here because we're warm and fuzzy and we want to help people. Who cares about research?" And then I'd have to explain to them how important research is, that it helps us know what works and what doesn't work, and that it makes people's lives better. Silence. Disbelief. They weren't convinced at all. "Give us another course in therapy," their eyes would say to me, "and let's forget this research nonsense."

Research. It's no one's favorite subject. And research books? My own daughter, who graduated with a degree in sociology, calls the books she had to read, "akin to living the rest of my life in North Dakota on the worst winter day since the dinosaurs became extinct." Now that hurts. "Why?" I asked her, "Why don't you like research?" "Because, Dad," she said with a groan, "it's so useless and it's b-o-r-i-n-g." My own daughter! Painful.

I thought about that for a while. To be honest, I disliked research until I started teaching it, and then it took a while for the light to go on. I taught research in the same way it was taught to me . . . mind numbingly technical and unexciting. And the books I assigned to my students. Ugh! *I* couldn't even read them. But after a while, when I started seeing the way the course *could* be taught, when I took away the confusing language and the unnecessarily technical terms and pared the subject down to its basics, it really became interesting and, dare I say it? Fun. *Really* fun.

So I decided to write a book in the same way I teach research. I decided that it would be easy to read, funny, not serious, interesting, short, non-technical, relevant to the real world we all live in and, not once (and this is a promise) would I mention rats or mice running through a maze. If I gave examples, I promised myself, I would use material from the real world. In the real world we have to make decisions, important ones, based on such limited information that we often wonder why we're being put on the spot. Need an operation? Try to get accurate data about the success rate of a surgery from a specific doctor. Need to buy a car? Try to figure out the confusing and contradictory information about repair rates and crash impact studies. That's the real world where what we know about research can help us make important life decisions.

So here we go, friends, students, countrymen, a research book that you can actually read, understand, and use in your courses. Maybe you can even use the material in your life because, along the way, I'm going to stop and give you advice. I'll tell you things about me, and I'll talk a bit about food since I'm always on a diet. If you laugh or think I'm adolescent, good deal. It will just make the book more fun to read. And if I get really silly, really dumb, just remember these wise words my daughter told me on the occasion of my last insipid joke: "Dad," she said, "you have the best mind ever to stay in the sixth grade. Sometimes it scares me to see a grown man act so silly, and sometimes I fear for my own future. Will I become like you? I can't even imagine waking up in the morning with the actual *need* to say funny stuff. Don't you feel tired and irritable in the morning?" Nope, I don't. In fact, I wrote this book from 5:00 to 7:00 A.M., mostly in California, but some of it in Texas and Michigan. It was fun to write, and I hope you find it fun to read and useful.

I should tell you that I joke a lot about North Dakota in this book. That's because I come from North Dakota, and I'm very proud to have survived twenty-two winters of 40° below weather, wind chill factors over 100 below, and the assorted floods, tornados, thunderstorms, windstorms, blizzards, grasshopper attacks, visits by aliens, long underwear shortages, addictions to Norwegian foods like lutefisk and lefsa, and the complete and utter feeling of isolation that comes from living three miles from the Arctic Circle. For all you brave and tender souls from the country of the tundra, may the grass grow warm under your feet as you make the long and sometimes incredibly cold journey through life. I'm proud of you.

ACKNOWLEDGMENTS

I have been blessed with the help of some wonderful people while preparing this research book. Thanks must first be given to Karen Hanson of Allyn and Bacon who e-mailed me a contract for the book after seeing the prospectus for only a few hours. I thought a funny, easy-to-read, slightly irreverent book on research would be a great idea and she agreed. Thanks, Karen. Alyssa Pratt of Allyn and Bacon helped a great deal by providing supportive, calming, and reassuring feedback. All authors are a little neurotic, and I'm as bad as most. Thanks, Allysa. Patricia Quinlin and Anne Marie Kennedy, my new editor and her assistant at Allyn and Bacon, have also been helpful, thank you.

My wonderful student assistant, Megan Dwyer, of Central Michigan University, helped edit and locate references. She is the best, and this book would never have been completed without her help. Renee Bibby, my faithful editorial assistant, gave me feedback that was thoughtful and wise, and she helped do the graphics that are beyond my primitive competencies. Allen Sacket, MSW, my former graduate student at California State University, San Bernardino, read the manuscript when it was in very rough shape. His comments were very helpful as were those of my daughter, Amy Glicken. Thanks, Allen and Amy. Joseph Greene, MSW, another former graduate student at California State University, San Bernardino, helped write and edit a good deal of the material in Chapters 11 and 12 (Sadistic Statistics, Parts I and II). The process of writing about statistics is more masochistic than sadistic: Joseph did a wonderful job, and I thank him for his much appreciated and enthusiastic work. We may have paid the rent at Jazz and Java, a coffee house in Redlands, California, where we frequently met to discuss our work.

Most of all, I would like to thank my past and present students who helped me refine my ideas for the book and who appreciated a good laugh even when the material I was presenting was often not very funny. No one can teach without students, and mine have been the best.

While the material presented in this book is sometimes silly to a fault, I believe in the scientific method, and I value research. Our country needs objective thinking as we face a moment in our history of serious social upheaval. To that purpose, all academics who write research books to help students critically understand the scientific method deserve a great deal of credit. I want to pay tribute to the many published research books I consulted and to their authors. This book would not have been possible without them.

Thanks to those who reviewed early drafts of the manuscript: Dr. Ron Cisler, University of Wisconsin, Milwaukee; Marcie Goodman, University of Utah; and Jacquelyn Gyamerah, The Ohio State University.

Finally, to my parents, Rose and Sam Glicken, who raised us in an atmosphere of thoughtful, progressive, and enlightened concern for the social issues of our time, and who dealt with bigotry and anti-Semitism in a way that taught us to hate the behavior but to love the people: Thank you, Mom and Dad, for your faith in me and for your encouragement. I miss you both.

1 Why Bother Learning Research?

Introduction

Most of my graduate students in social work enter the program thinking that research isn't relevant to their future work in social service agencies. Their argument is that they intend to be professional helpers and they can't see what possible good research might be in their direct work with people.

In a way, it's a very good argument. Research is a rational approach to problem solving. Most problems encountered by social scientists are fundamentally irrational in nature. Why, for example, does one person who experienced sexual abuse as a child grow up and lead a productive and healthy life without any of the emotional problems often seen in adult victims of child abuse, while another person has many of these problems? No one can say for sure. Might the answer be bad environments or differences in innate resilience that allow one abuse victim to cope with the abuse more adequately than another person? Perhaps the answer is good therapy at an early age, or the benefits of a genetic makeup that allows the traumatized child to successfully heal? No one really knows for sure and, more to the point, how could we ever know? The issue of why some people do well and others do not has confused us since time began. But social workers essentially work with the people who *don't* do well. Why then, my students wisely ask, should they use something as rational as research to try to explain something that isn't rational? The people we see in social work are often hurt beyond repair. What good is research going to do?

Well, and this is an ongoing discussion with my students, research can help in many ways. It can also help us find the best treatment approaches for working with our clients. It can also help us determine whether we are effective in our work. Research can make us sophisticated consumers of a growing body of knowledge about helping approaches with troubled people that may someday make our work much more objective and scientific.

Social scientists and people in the applied helping professions sometimes argue that being able to help others (it is often called the *helping impulse*) is something that we are born with, and that education can only serve to shape our inate helping abilities and give them direction. But the reality is that we can have a long history (perhaps since childhood) of people seeking us out because of our listening and advice giving abilities and still not help people. Like any method, effective counseling, therapy, or case management (we call it lots of things these days) comes from objective knowledge. If you are not consulting the research literature about the clients you work with, how can you (or anyone) know that you are providing the best help possible?

Clients can never be certain that the help they are getting from us is going to be beneficial if all we do is intuitively provide help which may, in the final analysis, do the client more harm than good. There is considerable evidence that people in the helping professions do a great deal of harm. In fact, looking at research studies from the 1970s back to the 1920s, most social researchers have concluded that one-third of clients improve in treatment, one-third stay the same, and one third (a third!) get worse as a result of treatment (Bergin, 1978).

We never think that the help we provide may result in harm because our intentions are good. In California, where I lived for twelve years, the education establishment rejected the use of phonics for many years under some deluded belief that other methods were better. These other approaches were often more creative and appealed to our emotions, but they just didn't work and many children in California suffered the consequences of poor reading skills. The research to support the non-phonics approach to reading is appalling. It isn't research at all, it's testimony, opinion, and idealistic beliefs (Palmaffy, 1997, p. 32). The many problems facing our society where research might help give us direction are, unfortunately, often decided on by emotional reflection and political correctness rather than by objective analysis. Carol Meyer (1970) notes that in many cases, social research results are ignored whenever they conflict with social or political beliefs.

It's bad enough that research plays such a limited role in the social policy and treatment decisions we make, but does the same problem exist in a hard science field like medicine? Seemingly it does. Consider heart problems. Heart disease is still the primary killer of people in America. The four major approaches to treating heart problems have been by-pass surgery, angioplasty, a more complex type of angioplasty involving the removal of plaque, and a very low-fat diet combined with exercise. We all know that by-pass surgery is very dangerous. A person is placed on a machine to do his or her breathing as veins are removed from the leg to replace the arteries in the heart clogged with plaque. Many things can go wrong. If the surgery lasts too long, brain damage might result. Infections to the heart following by-pass surgery are fairly common, requiring the surgeon to re-open the chest cavity and do more work. The surgery can do psychological damage: many by-pass patients develop a sense of fragility that keeps them from returning to work and to the many areas of life needed for people to stay healthy and optimistic. This may include fear of sexual activity because it might cause a heart attack. Give up sex? I hope not.

Until recently, there have been no real studies of the effectiveness of any of the four techniques. However, in the past few years it has been discovered that one technique is about as effective as another (Gorman, 2001). If that's the case, why would anyone choose by-pass surgery if exercise and a very low-fat diet are just as effective? What prevented the medical establishment from doing this type of research a long time ago? Pity the poor heart patient who had a by-pass procedure who might have done just as well with diet and exercise. Perhaps you can see a parallel to this example when helping professions provide social and psychological treatment by intuition and personal bias. The results are disastrous. Children get taken from parents only to be placed in abusive foster homes. People who might otherwise function normally with an effective social support system are placed on powerful psychotropic medications that alter their ability to function and cloud their minds. The elderly who function best when they are helped to live in their own homes are placed in nursing homes where their quality of life and their life expectancy are reduced. The helping professional who provides service on the basis of intuition, personal bias, or folk wisdom (shared beliefs that are frequently incorrect) is going to hurt someone.

Keeping up with the most current research is absolutely essential for social scientists and helping professionals. The advent of the Internet allows easy access to the most recent social and psychological research whose findings, if read and understood, may actually save lives. Intuition may be fine for buying stocks or falling in love (although, as most of us know, it isn't fine at all), but in the real world of the social scientist, intuition may neither help us understand issues that confront us nor serve to provide needy people with the most effective service possible.

What are some of the issues that confront social scientists? I can think of a number of them and maybe you can think of some, as well. For a starter, why do people of color experience more police harassment and arrests? Is the three-strikes law actually lowering the crime rate or is it the very good economy we currently enjoy? Are native-born Americans becoming dependent on immigrant labor to do the necessary work some of us would rather not do for ourselves? In fact, was it foreign-born workers who drove the wonderful economy we experienced for so many years? If native-born Americans are becoming less productive [and Robert Bly (1996) says that our laziness is a result of an extended adolescence that gives many Americans a sense of entitlement and makes them believe that someone will take care of them if they fail in life], what does that say about American society? Why is it that so few people are involved in the voting process? Is it because of bad candidates or is it because of a lack of concern? And if people don't vote because they just don't care, what does that say about the state of our democracy? Why are so many people risking the savings they have set aside for retirement by buying stock in companies with no earnings and no possible future earnings for many years to come? One could go on and on. The important questions we can study in the social sciences, large and small, are endless.

The Excitement of Discovery

For many years, I taught in a public university in the very far eastern area of Los Angeles. (An area someone jokingly called the Inland Empire, although its relationship to an empire is laughable. It's a hot, dry place, not very attractive, with heavy smog and high winds.) Most of the students who attended my university came from economically poor backgrounds. Many were first-generation college students. Unfortunately, many of our students had poor high school educations that resulted in poor writing and math skills. Over 80 percent of our newly admitted freshmen students needed remediation in math, and over 60 percent needed remediation in writing. As an instructor, I observed my students' initial resistance to research and the difficulties they had with some of the more abstract concepts. Sooner or later, however, the resistance faded and many of the students became hooked on research.

Perhaps this happened because in our graduate social work program, students were required to do an actual piece of original research. Everyone prepared a research proposal with an extensive literature review, ran their data, analyzed their data, and perhaps, for the first time in their lives, statistics made sense. The data they collected and analyzed often confirmed their hypotheses and they could now see the utility of research. Maybe the literature review found material that was eye opening. I don't know why for certain, but at some point, many of our students began to like research. All of them? Nope. Many of them? Yup.

There is certainly something very exciting about the quest for knowledge and the desire for truth. Intuition, gut feeling, and opinion are still important parts of the human experience. They can be very useful in some circumstances. But for my money, getting the best information available makes my life much more predictable and, with it, much more successful. We live in a world where we make important choices everyday. Should we make those choices based on intuition and emotion, or should we make them in the most rational and objective way we can? Research offers objectivity and rationality. Intuition offers us a carefree and emotional way of choosing what may, in certain instances, work for us. I don't know a rational way to choose a mate for life, however when it comes to medical decisions, I'm going to choose science and research findings every time. Let's consider this question by discussing the difference between thinking that is intuitive, or inductive, and thinking that is rational, or deductive.

Knowledge Is Knowledge, or Is Some Knowledge Better: Inductive and Deductive Reasoning

Deduction

If I had grown up in a fully assimilated American family instead of an immigrant family and you had come to our home for dinner, you would have easily followed the conversation. Your frame of reference would have been based on similar ways of communicating. You would have probably felt comfortable in your ability to understand or *deduce* the meaning of the conversation. Your ability to use deductive reasoning which follows a precise and orderly series of judgments would have lead you to rational conclusions about the conversation. **Deductive reasoning** follows a precise and orderly path leading to logical conclusions. When you think about deductive reasoning, you might want to think about the scientific method used in research designs that set out to prove hypotheses and try to establish cause-effect relationships. This type of reasoning is evident in quantitative research that tests hypotheses and uses data collection and analysis to determine connections between variables.

Induction and Inference

But I didn't grow up in a fully assimilated American family with easily understood ways of communicating. Instead, my parents spoke in metaphors. If you did something my parents didn't like, they might respond by saying something like, "The tree only bears the fruit tough enough to last." Huh? I made that one up, by the way, but in my family you learned through indirect communication. No one ever said, "Don't do that or you'll get into trouble." Instead, my parents used parables, proverbs (many of them fractured), and statements about other people who had done something bad and were subsequently visited by the plague. My mother might say, "You know your cousin Jimmy, the one who talks back to his parents? Well, one time he said something really awful to his mother and you know what happened? On the way to school he fell and broke his arm." Silence. No need to explain. You talk back to your mother and see what happens to you?

When I listened to my parents talk, I inferred the meaning of the messages they were giving me through their tone of voice and the metaphors they were using. This is inductive reasoning, in a way, because I grew up knowing my parents' patterns and the underlying meaning of their communication. I learned to intuit meaning from a long history of contacts with them. Is this unscientific? Not at all. It may be unclear to others, but to me it made a lot of sense. Their English was poor; I was much more fluent in the language and so, in their mother tongue, they gave me moral messages that were quite clear to me but very unclear to others. That was their point.

To make meaning clear to others would have been to expose the secret language of communication of a family that was fearful of outsiders. Like many immigrants, they thought family was the last bastion of privacy in an invasive and often dangerous world. In the ghettos of Europe, they had learned a way of communicating that was clear to those in their immediate world but unclear to the officials and government representatives whom they perceived as a threat to their safety.

Induction is considered less scientific than deduction because with it there is no purely logical and concise way to collect information. This forces us to develop very creative and indirect ways of collecting needed data. I think I could explain to an outsider the inferred meaning behind the statements my parents made to me. To do this would require very intensive training in sub-textual or indirect communication (the difference between what is said and what is meant). The head shake, the glance at the door, the look upward to heaven when my parents spoke: all of these non-verbal messages were readily meaningful to me. The glance at the door meant that they were fearful of outsiders hearing our conversation. The glance up at heaven meant that whatever they said was reinforced by the power of their belief that God would agree with them. I knew that, but others couldn't possibly know. To know as much as I did would require others to engage in inductive methods of collecting and analyzing data usually suited to qualitative or subjective approaches to conducting research. In this difference between the rational and the more intuitive, you may see the beginnings of the dialogue researchers have with one another about how best to organize information that may not lend itself to objective analysis. Can one organize social and cultural issues in a rational way to make a study highly objective? And if we do so, will we capture the subtle differences and the uniqueness of a situation sufficiently to accurately report what really took place? Many people believe that this very attempt to construct a rational explanation by-passes the social reality of what actually may have happened. They believe that intuitive methods often find the subtleties that form effective explanations, and that certain social issues are better studied using inductive reasoning. We will discuss this issue more fully in Chapter 2 when we consider post-modernism and the paradigms that permit less rigidly objective research studies.

Which Approach Is Better?

Deductive reasoning is scientific in nature. It assumes that information can be collected in a precise and orderly way and that events unfold rationally. Because we follow a series of steps to collect and analyze data and because all of the steps are done under precise rules related to scientific inquiry, the results should give us better information than would inductive reasoning. This certainly may be the case for more concrete issues where number counting is essential and accuracy of data is crucial. But when it comes to cause-effect relationships, all social researchers can readily see problems in using deductive reasoning alone. Deduction may help us to see connections in the physical world where events unfold in a mostly rational way, but in the social world, events unfold chaotically and at random. While we may try to study the social world so that we can understand it, the reality is that quite often, we can't. Using quantitative approaches to social science issues may provide voluminous data. We may move from a non-specific understanding to a more specific understanding of events, but do we really grasp the subtleties that may be much more important in understanding complex social issues than the voluminous quantitative data we've collected and analyzed? That's the problem facing the social scientist.

It is one reason why so many researchers have begun advocating for qualitative approaches to research. These researchers believe that inductive reasoning and the research studies that come from more subjective ways of thinking really do provide beginning answers to questions that help us understand the chaotic, complex, and unpredictable world we live in. This willingness to look at the subtleties of behavior will hopefully excite new research students (you, that is), because it opens the door to a large range of research methods, many of them much less objective than those used in the past. Inductive reasoning may be less scientific, but it also helps us understand some complicated interactions in the social world for which quantitative research may be inadequate. Why? Because the very rules that apply to the deductive method of reasoning often restrict the researcher and limit the level or degree of inquiry.

Why do soccer fans in England riot so often? Well, because they're often drunk. But why are they drunk so often? Well, because they're full of hostility at being poor, so they act out at soccer matches. I've just suggested two hypotheses to explain soccer riots in England. To test these hypotheses, I would try to count the number of people who come to soccer matches drunk. I would also try to get a measure of the socio-economic class of these people and then see if there is a relationship between drinking, socio-economic class, and acting-out behavior at soccer matches. Both are very good ideas and are examples of deductive reasoning. I think I know the answer to the problem, so I've developed several hypotheses that I plan to test. I just have to come up with a research design that allows me to measure the three variables I've just mentioned: drinking, lower socio-economic class, and acting-out behavior at soccer matches.

Inductive reasoning suggests a very different set of hypotheses. Because I really don't know that there is a connection between drinking, socio-economic class, and rioting, perhaps a better idea would be to study the behavior of soccer fans and see if I can identify the reasons for the riots. Using this approach, I might sit in the stands with the rowdy fans who have rioted in the past (me and maybe fifteen other brave researcher souls) and observe the behavior of the fans most likely to riot. For certain, I would have a research protocol (a list of behaviors to look for) but, in essence, I would have no hypothesis. I would wait to find out what happened when the fans got together. My research team would meet before the soccer match and decide how best to observe and collect information. We might concentrate on specific behaviors this initial time because we can always go to another soccer match and observe other behaviors (although risk of bodily harm in an English soccer riot would make that decision troubling). From our study, we might be able to understand the progression of behaviors that lead to rioting by noting the instigators, the language used to influence others to riot, the behavior of fans as they begin to riot, and many other behaviors that might help us predict and control future riots. We certainly could not generalize to other situations or show a cause-effect relationship using this approach, but a less objective study using the inductive method might be much more helpful in understanding and controlling riots in the future than a deductive approach.

The difference between inductive and deductive reasoning is that **deductive reasoning** follows orderly lines of thought that include hypothesis testing while **inductive reasoning** is far more subjective and may follow creative but not necessarily objective ways of trying to answer questions that concern the social scientist.

The Scientific Method

Even though I've just made a case for a less objective approach to research, that does not eliminate the need for rules to guide any study we may do. Research is a scientific way to approach information and knowledge. Consequently, these are some rules we all try to abide by in social research.

1. *We Need to Be Able to Accurately Describe What We Plan to Do.* All research comes with a mandatory expectation that we clearly describe the way we intend to conduct our study and that the procedures used are judged by rules of objectivity. That is, the more objective the study and the more the rules of the scientific method are followed, the more we are inclined to accept the findings. Every time we have an automobile problem in America, you begin to understand that what the researcher planned to do was never as clearly stated as the findings would have us believe. Do SUV's roll over because of weight distribution and bad driving, or because the tires are flawed? That seems to be a pretty simple question, but remember that the people who do the research (the auto manufacturer) have an agenda. That agenda is not to provide accurate and meaningful information, but to sell a product. Consequently, the car manufacturer finds that the car is safe but blames the tires for rollovers. The tire manufacturer finds the tires safe but

the car design unsafe. How can that be? It's because the tire manufacturer set out to prove that the *tires* were safe, while the car manufacturer set out to prove that the *car* was safe. Neither intended to find the real reason for SUV rollovers. The lack of clarity in the description of what was intended in the research study leaves the consumer confused. Because of that confusion, as in the recent case of the Ford Explorer equipped with Firestone tires, Ford Explorer and Firestone tire sales have declined dramatically because consumers trusted neither pieces of research.

2. *We Need to Be Able to Describe What We Actually Did.* All research comes with a mandatory expectation that we accurately describe what actually happened during the study. The admission of any deviation from our plan is very important because it allows for a thorough evaluation of our study by others. The scientific method demands that we are truthful about any problems encountered during the study. This includes any changes in the procedures used and any flaws in the design or the sampling approach that came to light once the study was initiated. The scientific method is therefore scrupulously honest. If others can't **replicate** an original study (do the study over again in the same way that it was originally done), most of us would be unwilling to accept the original findings. Consequently, to permit the study to be replicated, the researcher must share every piece of data and information available with other researchers. If a study is replicated and the findings vary from the original study, we would wonder if the original findings were justified in the first place, or we could logically ask if the replicated study used exactly the same procedures and methods as the first study. If not, a third study might need to be done. By sharing information, we always have a way to judge the accuracy of any piece of social research.

3. *We Need to Indicate the Safeguards We've Used to Protect Our Study from Incorrect Collection of Data and Distorted Results.* We have all too many examples of researchers not informing us of conflicts of interest or shortcuts taken during their studies. These conflicts, as in the case of drug companies paying researchers to test medications who then publish the results of their research in journals without disclosing the fact that the research was paid for by the drug companies, stretch their credibility and increase our cynicism. We all suspect that paying someone else to, hopefully, come up with good results, may bias the study. Furthermore, all too many studies indicate positive outcomes when none should be found because researchers desperately want to publish findings that may benefit their career.

Consequently, as will be discussed in an entire chapter on ethics (Chapter 13), researchers have agreed to use safeguards that first require the researcher to receive approval for their research study from an **institutional review board**. This board, sometimes referred to as a **human subjects review board,** determines whether the research violates the civil rights of subjects and is ethically conducted, and assures protections of the research subjects. The board is also responsible for recommending sanctions against researchers who violate ethical standards. While this isn't a perfect solution and violations of ethical procedure continue, it does suggest a procedure to follow and a way of punishing researchers for violating ethical principles. Hopefully, this serves as a cautionary process to keep researchers absolutely ethical.

4. *We Need to Indicate the Limitations of Our Study to Protect Others from Thinking that We've Found out More Than the Study Warrants.* The scientific method limits what we can say about our findings. We can only report what we have found. We can speculate, of course, but that's the extent of the leeway given the researcher adhering to the scientific method. We can't bake our data (make more of it than is warranted) and, for certain, we cannot indicate cause-effect relationships when none have been found. Additionally, we cannot suggest that the results can be generalized to other people, places, or events when, in fact, that isn't the case. The scientific method doesn't promise a single truth but always leaves the door open to new findings and new studies. In a sense, all research should encourage new research and a continuation of the scientific effort. Without a continued desire to gain new knowledge, we stagnate. Imagine a world without computers because someone decided that everything we ever needed to know about communications had already been discovered with the invention of the radio and the typewriter.

5. *We Need to Describe the Procedures We've Used So That Other Researchers Can Check on Our Findings by Replicating the Study.* Being able to replicate (do the exact same study again) is an important part of the scientific method. How else can we check the accuracy of the findings of a research study unless we can independently recheck the results by doing the study over again? This is particularly important in the social sciences where conditions vary and findings are susceptible to shifting opinions, attitudes, and thinking about the issues we study everyday. If we conduct an attitude poll one day and a week later some world event occurs that affects the very attitude we've just studied, our findings may become obsolete. Social researchers are aware of this and accept it, but competing surveys (voter surveys, for example) should all come up with the same findings if they use the same procedures. Often the procedures used are less about finding truth and more about public relations. The pollsters almost never describe their methods, and the unsuspecting public may be suddenly attracted to a political candidate whose popularity polls show a great surge where none really exists.

Science expects that the ability to continually revisit an issue will eventually produce some level of knowledge. When researchers hide procedures because they are poorly conceived, the reality is that we can't replicate the original study. As a result, the findings from the initial study may do considerable harm. Sadly to say, some social researchers make it difficult to find out what they did to produce their findings. My research students in California contacted researchers continually to ask for additional information about an instrument or about findings in a published study, only to get vague answers, or no answer at all. If the researcher is on the level, he or she will share information with others. It's the only way we have of replicating a study to see if the original researcher was correct in his or her conclusions. If we can't replicate a study, we have to be suspicious about the original findings.

Is the Scientific Method the Only Way to Approach Knowledge?

Have you ever had an intuitive (gut) feeling that something is going to happen and it did? We all know that the human condition is so infinitely complex that there must be room for intuition and subjective reasoning. Belief in God forms a basic belief structure of many people. Is it unscientific to believe in God or to have a deeply spiritual relationship with the world? Absolutely not. The scientific method must be open to a range of perceptions, beliefs, attitudes, and life experiences. It must be willing to accept that people view the world in ways that are individually meaningful, and it must be willing to devise research strategies that permit alternative ways of viewing events. If it doesn't permit alternative ways of viewing events, then science becomes rigid and the information we collect may have limited meaning.

All possible forms of viewing the world and the social events that form our society are worthy of consideration even if, at first glance, they don't seem orderly or scientific. Science should not be used to create cynicism or a rigid orthodoxy by which we judge the beliefs of others. Science offers an objective way of viewing the world, but is it the only way?

Many famous scientists have had wonderfully creative breakthroughs while in the midst of dreams or during religious epiphanies. Creativity is infinitely complex and the insights developed to explain human behavior can be unstructured, intuitive, and illogical. Einstein imagined the theory of relativity. He didn't actually measure time warp, but he constructed a three-dimensional view of time and space in his mind that was later proven to be correct. We should never attack other forms of viewing the world as unacceptable just because the scientific method wasn't used. Before empirical strategies for collecting data in the social sciences were devised, people made astonishing leaps of intuitive understanding of people and societies through their observation of events and their own perceptions of what they saw, felt, and believed. Most early social scientists were observers, not empirical scientists. People like Marx, Weber, and De Tocqueville have frequently been correct in many of their observations about societies, organizations, and political processes even though they used an inductive approach to creating views of the world that have stood the test of time. The moral of the story is that we should remain open to all forms of knowledge. Science should not make us cynical. Rather, it should increase our willingness to see the world in a complex and infinitely interesting way, leaving us to believe in all of the cosmic possibilities open to us for exciting and mind-enhancing discoveries.

Creativity and Science

I won't disagree that some researchers have a fairly standard way of thinking a problem through, but some creative insights come in flashes. The process of creating can be serendipitous and unstructured. I don't agree with the people who say that we have to outline our ideas in an orderly fashion. I agree that we should write our thoughts down as inspiration hits us, but most research comes to us in very intuitive and unplanned ways. It might be helpful to write down the ideas that cruise through our minds and begin to make sense out of them, but going through a logical process of ordering ideas before the ideas have gelled sometimes limits creativity. My way of handling this process is to set myself thinking assignments meant to develop additional ideas until the whole process makes sense to me. Then I write it down in an orderly way. Some of your instructors won't agree with me because they think students need the discipline of outlining an idea from start to finish as a first step in the research process. I can't disagree with them since many new researchers haven't experienced the progression of thoughts that accompany an initial idea. If that's the case with you, then here is an outline to follow as you develop your ideas for a research study. Chapter 4, which deals with developing a research proposal, explores the issue of outlining your ideas in much more detail.

A Way of Processing Ideas

1. *Think about a Subject That Excites and Interests You.* This is generally a good idea unless the subject is too personal or so hurtful to you that you can't be objective. A colleague of mine did his doctoral dissertation on conservatorship, the process of having someone take care of your financial holdings if you are legally deemed to be physically or emotionally unfit. It turns out that his father was deemed unfit by a sibling who managed, but then misspent, all of the father's money. My friend researched the issue of conservatorship and discovered that people are frequently found to be unfit. Further, he discovered that the legal decision upon which the determination of competency was made rested largely on the testimony of the family member with the most to gain financially. My friend had been out of the country when a competency hearing was held without his knowledge, and his elderly father was found to be incompetent based on the testimony of a troubled sibling. By the time my friend learned of the competency hearing and returned home, his elderly father had committed suicide. The subject of legal competence and the terrible repercussions of a badly done competency hearing haunted my friend for years. When he finally began work on his doctorate, he chose conservatorship as the topic of his dissertation. He concluded that courts are scandalous in the way they deal with competency issues and conservatorship. Furthermore, he found that the conservators chosen to manage the money and property of those deemed incompetent often mishandled the money, leaving elderly and physically or emotionally impaired people penniless. Was this too personal an issue for him to do research objectively? Perhaps. Did my colleague have a strong desire to do the research? Yes. There is a fine line between interest in a subject and objectivity but one worth exploring as you consider a research topic.

2. *Go to the Research Literature and Study the Problem in Detail.* Once you have clarity about your initial idea, do an in-depth literature search so that you understand how others have approached a similar problem. If the problem has been studied in great depth, are there side issues or smaller aspects of the problem that might permit a suitable study to take place? You may also benefit from reading studies in which the researchers point out areas of inquiry remaining to be studied. This often takes place at the end of many published journal articles and research reports. As you will note throughout this book, most beginning research students fail to take advantage of published research studies when developing their proposals. A weak literature review is always an indication of a weak research proposal. Seeing what others have done can only serve to make you a more enlightened and efficient researcher.

3. *Seek Help in Narrowing the Idea down So That It Is Manageable.* Many new research students make the mistake of wanting to study an issue that is just too broad to research in a limited amount of time. Talking to your instructor or to someone familiar with the issue you wish to study can be very helpful. Most studies can be narrowed in focus to make them doable. For example, a student of mine wanted to study the relationship between having been placed in a group home as a child (what we used to call an orphanage) and whether the group-home experience lead to emotional problems in adulthood. The subject is pretty broad by anyone's standards. We discussed the difficulty of selecting a sample and of knowing whether it was the group home experience that caused the problems in adulthood or whether it was the abusive or neglectful situations that led the child to being placed in a group home in the first place. We also discussed the problem of separating a positive group-home experience from a harmful one. After several discussions, the student decided to consult the literature and found a fascinating study on exactly what she wanted to do. In fact, she found 50 fascinating studies. Disappointed, she spoke to a group-home supervisor who encouraged her to study the adult aspirations of children currently placed in a group-home, an entirely doable project that still tapped into her interest area but had not been done, so far as she could tell, by anyone else.

4. *Start out with a Problem Formulation and Progress.* All research derives its legitimacy from first having been presented as a research problem. That is, you must indicate what the problem is that you hope to study, why it is a problem you think worthy of study, what other people have said about the problem, and how you intend to study the problem. This is often called the *problem formulation.* I have an entire chapter (Chapter 3) devoted to problem formulations. Their importance is in the ability of the researcher to answer the questions what, why, and how. What is the problem? Why is it a problem worth studying? How will the study be conducted? If you are able to answer these questions in a two- or three-page statement, you really are on your way to doing a research study.

The Three Reasons for Doing Research

Why should we do research in the first place? Generally speaking, there are three reasons for doing research. They are: to explore, to describe, and to explain events, people, and situations.

Exploratory Research

Exploratory research tries to break new ground by delving into new ideas. Its purpose is not to provide an overwhelming amount of information or to show cause-effect relationships, but rather to discover new areas to study and to provide very general forms of information. An area of exploratory research might be a topic about which there is little information. It may be a new idea because the issue is new. Take, for example, early research on the use of the Internet. Before many people were even aware of the Internet (and there really was such a time before browsers, servers, and e-mail were part of our everyday world), researchers were already trying to find out information about the people who used the Internet. They had a hypothesis that the Internet would be an important part of our lives well before many people were actually using the Internet. At its earliest point in time, this was exploratory research because the Internet was so new to us that no one had done any substantive research.

Descriptive Research

Descriptive research takes the information we already know and adds to it. In descriptive research, we already have a body of knowledge, although it may be limited. Using that limited body of knowledge, we can produce additional knowledge at, hopefully, a higher level of importance. Using the prior example, we've had the Internet around for a while now. People are acclimated to its use, and researchers have done some fairly evolved studies centered around its use. What we don't know is whether the Internet is adding to a generalized feeling of isolation or whether it actually brings people together. I looked at a dating site not long ago that proudly proclaimed 110,000 members, but only 49 marriages. That certainly can't be a good sign because a scan of the members showed that many of them were interested in getting married. One could imagine doing a descriptive research study to find out why so few people using that dating service actually got married. Other research questions might relate to how many people meet one another and date through contacts they've made using the dating service. As people continue to use the dating services on the Internet, might they become disaffected by the lack of success in finding people to connect with? Might this lead to even greater feelings of isolation? These questions would be examples of descriptive research topics.

Explanatory Research

This type of research uses the considerable amount of information available to researchers from prior research studies and from that information tries to provide meaningful and accurate conclusions. Again, using the Internet as an example, let's assume that an overwhelming number of studies have been done about the Internet and the way people use it. An explanatory piece of research would bring these studies together by summarizing and evaluating the major issues raised, the major findings, and their overall meaning for the consumer of the research.

Pure and Applied Research

Pure research is done out of a desire to find truth. There is little if any interest in its application to a social problem. Knowing something about small-group interaction might be an example of pure research. The issue is important but the application is a little unclear. Often pure research has an impact on application but the reason it is done relates primarily to the desire to gather data and to create theories of behavior.

In **applied research,** the reason for doing a study is to use the results in some practical way. Small-group theory might help us run more effective treatment groups, or the information about small groups might be applied to understanding how people living in group situations interact with one another. For example, how does a group of 6 to 8 prisoners interact? The purpose of the study is not to collect information for its own sake, but to apply that information to some practical issue facing the social scientist. In this case, we might want to know the optimum manageable size of a living arrangement for prisoners based on their level of violence, their ability to cope with people by race and ethnicity, and their need for privacy. Perhaps we could take personality profiles of prisoners and test our ability to match prisoners to achieve a good fit among a group of prison inmates living together. Most social science research is applied because much of what we are funded to do by government and by foundation funding sources is to find out how we can do things better.

I have just completed a book on violence (Glicken and Sechrest, 2003). Much of the book is a compilation of research studies on understanding and treating violent behavior. I'm not certain about the exact number, but we've included approximately 200 studies in the book. Almost every study is in the applied area of social research. Most of the research suggests the difficulty in both understanding and treating violent behavior. Small- and large-scale efforts to treat violence have not always been successful, and we've concluded that violence is a complex problem requiring much more in-depth analysis. The value of these applied studies is enormous. Anyone with a hypothesis regarding the cause and treatment of violent behavior can find the same sources we found and ground themselves in the failed, semi-successful, and successful efforts of the past 40 years of applied social research. There is, thanks to a large body of research, no reason to assume that boot camps prevent violence or that three-strike laws reduce violent crime. In fact, a good deal of research suggests that longer prison sentences, more prisons, and tougher sentencing laws fail to have a lasting impact on violent people. Most researchers believe that violence is the result of violent family lives where children are socialized or traumatized into violence by the violent behavior of adults. The relationship between violent behavior and having been abused as a child is very compelling and tells us that early intervention in child abuse is the best prevention of future violence.

This discussion of violent behavior is an example of how social science research helps us understand issues that affect our daily lives. However, before the applied research took place, theoretical researchers were trying to understand the origins of violent behavior. Their research led the way to the applied research that followed.

Summary

Research in the social sciences has a significant impact on the way our society works. At its most elegant, social research can help provide direction to very complex social issues. In this chapter, we discussed the relevance of research to the social sciences with special attention paid to the applied social sciences. Further chapters consider the more technical aspects of social research. The next chapter explores the ways of looking at the research process through the use of research paradigms.

REVIEW QUESTIONS

1. With what type of research problems might deductive thinking be most appropriate?

2. Exploratory research sounds like the type of research many students might want to do. Can you think of some reasons exploratory research might be more difficult to do than descriptive or explanatory research?

3. In thinking about a research problem you might want to study, jot down a list of ideas that might help you narrow the topic to a manageable scope.

4. Inductive reasoning sounds unscientific. Do you have some doubts about it? What are they?

5. Believing in the results of research studies has become more and more difficult. Can you think of some reasons why we've become so skeptical of research?

REFERENCES

Bergin, A. E. (1978). *Handbook of psychotherapy and behavior change.* New York: Wiley.

Bly, R. (1996). *The sibling society.* Reading, MA: Addison-Wesley.

Glicken, M., & Sechrest, D. (2003). *The role of the helping professions in treating and preventing violence.* Boston: Allyn & Bacon.

Gorman, C. (2001, January 15). Rethinking treatments for the heart. *Time, 157(2),* 60–85.

Meyer, C. (1970). *Social work practice: A response to the urban crisis.* New York: The Free Press.

Palmaffy, T. (1997). See Dick flunk. *Policy Review, 86,* 32–40.

ADDITIONAL READINGS

Adorno, Theodor W. (1976). The logic of the social sciences. In Adorno et al. (Eds.), trans. Glyn Adey and David Frisby, *The positivist dispute in German sociology* (pp. 87–104). New York: Harper & Row.

Alford, R. (1998). *The craft of inquiry: Theories, method, evidence.* New York: Oxford University Press.

Babbie, E. (1998). *The practice of social research,* 5th ed. Belmont, CA: Wadsworth.

Babbie, Earl. (1990). *Survey research methods,* 2nd ed. Belmont, CA: Wadsworth.

Babbie, Earl. (1998). *The practice of social research,* 8th ed. Belmont, CA: Wadsworth.

Greer, S. (1969). *The logic of inquiry.* Hawthorne, NY: Adine.

Keat, R., & Urry, J. (1975). *Social theory as science.* London: Routledge and Kegan Paul.

Sayer, A. (1992). *Method in social science: A realist approach,* 2nd ed. New York: Routledge.

RECOMMENDED INTERNET SITES

Action Research International
    <http://www.scu.edu.au/schools/gcm/ar/ari/arihome.html>

Association of Social Work Boards
    <http://www.aasswb.org>

Current Research in Social Psychology (Online Journal)
    <http://www.uiowa.edu/~grpproc/crisp/crisp.html>

National Association of State Information Resource Executive's StateSearch
    <http://www.nasire.org>

The Complete Social Worker Guide to Using the Internet
    <http://www.geocities.com/Heartland/4862/cswhome.html>

2

A Way of Viewing the Research Process: Research Paradigms

Introduction

Most researchers begin thinking about a study by considering which research paradigm they will use to guide their research. A **paradigm** in research might be thought of as a model that helps us define and organize our thinking. In social research, it is useful to view the research process as a series of options, or choices that depend on our way of viewing the entire process of studying a problem. Choosing a research paradigm helps the consumer know which set of rules the researcher used in evaluating his or her work. It also gives the researcher a research philosophy to follow, or what some people call a **frame of reference**.

At this stage in your understanding of social research, the use of a research paradigm may appear to be unnecessarily complicated. In reality, however, before you can begin a study you need to explore your own thinking about what research means to you. For some people, this is a passionate issue because it defines our philosophy of research. If you think about research as a way of approaching truth, then the way we view the role of research is a way of approaching the gathering of meaningful knowledge that, in a sense, represents truth. As you will see in this chapter, there is a considerable difference of opinion about the role of research and the way in which we should conduct the gathering of meaningful information. It is more than a difference of opinion about how best to gather information. It is the researcher's set of convictions about the role of research, how it fits into the world of ideas, and how it affects society and the way we live our lives. This tension in the philosophy of science is included in the following discussion of research paradigms.

In social research, there are four commonly used paradigms: the positivist, post-positivist, constructivist, and critical theory paradigms. In this chapter, each paradigm and its related assumptions and methodologies will be discussed.

The Four Paradigms

The Positivist Paradigm

In positivist research, the assumption is that problems in the social sciences can be studied in a highly objective and scientific way, a way that approximates studying problems in the hard (physical) sciences. When a study is completed using the positivist paradigm and the methodology is very well controlled for, the researcher may have the ability to tell the consumer that there are meaningful connections or relationships among variables.

Because the positivist paradigm uses statistics in the form of measurable data that can be analyzed and from which assumptions about issues can be made, positivist approaches are often called **quantitative** or **empirical** and are judged by very strict rules that we will discuss throughout this book.

Social research has tried very hard to use the positivist paradigm over the years to gain some level of acceptance in the scientific community. Unlike research in the hard sciences, the development of positivism in the social sciences has had a more difficult road to travel. Studying anything to do with the social, cultural, and emotional condition of people is very difficult because people are constantly changing and their behaviors are continually in flux. Often, the same thing is true in the hard sciences, but social researchers may feel the strong need to prove themselves without considering the many flaws that sometimes affect research in the hard sciences.

In medical research, for example, the researcher studying the relationship between cigarette smoking and lung cancer has a primary way of using the positivist approach. He can expose lab animals to cigarette smoke over a period of time to determine if the occurrence of lung cancer is higher in lab animals exposed to cigarette smoke than it is in those free of cigarette smoke.

Simple? Not really. Lab animals aren't people. What if there is some small but important flaw in the research? Perhaps the concentration of smoke for lab animals was disproportionate to their body weight? Perhaps the lab animals were given a significantly higher dose of smoke than humans would normally experience smoking. Remember the saccharine scare of a few years ago? Saccharine was given to rats in 200 to 300 times the amount humans would normally use and it was found to cause cancer. When the amount of saccharine approximated the actual amount that humans might use, the threat of cancer was dramatically reduced. These mistakes take place daily in the hard sciences. Perhaps you can think of other serious mistakes in the medical field brought about by flawed research. Read your newspaper. The mistakes are reported almost daily.

Another way of finding a relationship between smoking and lung cancer using a positivist paradigm might be to look back in time and see how many smokers versus nonsmokers developed lung cancer. By doing this, perhaps we could correlate the amount of smoking to the development of lung cancer. Easy? Not exactly. Aren't there other causes (also called **intervening variables**) of lung cancer in addition to smoking? Might diet play a part? How about levels of stress and the physical environments people live in? What about the age at which a person begins smoking, or people who drink and smoke in combination? Are people who smoke more likely to have lower thresholds for stress and anxiety? How do we explain that in some countries, notably Japan, where smoking is very prevalent (65% of the population smoke in Japan as opposed to 30% in America), the incidence of lung cancer is considerably less than in America, and that life span for smokers is far longer (Bezruchka, 2001, p. 14)? Remember that parts of Japan have very high levels of air pollution and crowding. Stress in Japan, from what one reads, has to be as prevalent and as serious as it is in the United States. Might there be problems of accurate reporting by smokers? Might the type of smoking done alter the results (not everyone inhales deeply, for example)? You can see that even in the physical sciences, controlling for every conceivable variable to explain an outcome can be mind-boggling. Often the results of research in the physical sciences leave many questions unanswered, forcing consumers to ponder what they should and should not believe.

As you can see, the positivist approach isn't easy to use in the physical sciences. So many things can go wrong in any research study that researchers often have to give up a promising line of inquiry because the study has become contaminated by a number of small flaws. In the social sciences, positivism is particularly difficult. To use the positivist approach, one must control for errors made when choosing participants for a study (sampling approach to a research design), use a valid and reliable instrument, use correct statistics, and develop a research design that is relevant to the problem being studied. To illustrate this, let's consider the effectiveness of some type of treatment intervention used to help a person with an emotional problem related to a situational crisis. It should be easy enough to take some element of behavior and do a before-and-after measure of whether people receiving that treatment are better or worse as a result of the treatment. We'll use depression as the example of an emotional problem.

Let's take a sample (1%) of everyone going to a public community mental health clinic in America who is seen in psychotherapy by a therapist with a clinical license. Let's use depression as our primary diagnosis, and let's give our sample the Glicken Depression Inventory, also known as the GDI (happily, there is no such instrument) before treatment, after treatment is completed, and perhaps twice more after treatment ends to determine whether the depression remains improved over time. If clients are less depressed a year after treatment, as indicated by the scores on the GDI, should we congratulate ourselves and tell the world that mental health intervention really helps people with depression?

Not really. Without a **control group,** a comparison group who are se-lected randomly but do not receive treatment, how do we know that those receiving help might not have gotten better by themselves? Even with a control group, how do we know for certain that the control group hasn't received some type of informal help from friends, ministers, teachers, and so on? Furthermore, without some idea about how well our treated de-pressed clients are actually functioning in their lives (on the job, in school, in their relationships with others), of what value are the test scores? A bet-ter score on any psychological instrument doesn't tell us whether people are going to work, paying their taxes, supporting their families, or comment on any of the many real-life behaviors that a test is unable to measure. And finally, how do we know, as in the case of people receiving medication for depression along with mental health treatment (probably a large number of the people in our sample), whether it's the talking intervention or the med-ication that causes the improvement in depression? Tough questions force the researcher to be particularly creative and to be knowledgeable about quantitative methods.

While the benefit of the positivist paradigm is objectivity, in the real world it is virtually impossible to control for every chance occurrence or goof up in a research project. Things go wrong and those wrong things might drastically alter our findings. Does that mean that we shouldn't try to be as objective as possible? Not at all. It does suggest, however, that posi-tivist research studies are fraught with methodological problems, and that most positivist research in the social sciences can be faulted if one looks very carefully at the research methodology.

As you read reports in the newspaper about medical discoveries or some finding related to the reduction or increase in crime, you'll begin to see that large methodological issues are at play that could render the results of research using positivism fairly meaningless and contradictory. Should this make us cynical about research using a positivist approach? I hope not, but it should make us determined to learn as much as possible about re-search designs, methodologies, and statistics so that we can judge for our-selves whether the research is well done and whether there is something to be learned from a study.

These methodological difficulties create a great deal of confusion for consumers. Since 1994, crime rates in America have declined dramati-cally (U.S. Department of Justice, 2001). At the same time, interviews with perpetrators of crime indicate little change in the actual amount of crime committed. Only one in ten criminal offenses results in the con-viction of a perpetrator (Surgeon Generals Report, 2001). Fear of crime has increased steadily since 1969 and is now over 120 percent higher than it was originally in 1969 (Milton S. Eisenhower Foundation, 2001). If crime rates are down, why is fear of crime higher than it has ever been? The answer might be that these three contradictory studies, were intended to offer different information. Fear of crime, the amount of reported crime, and offender behavior are three discrete pieces of information. While they may be contradictory, it doesn't make the information incorrect. It does, however, make it confusing.

This is one of the complaints against positivism. Data are collected and analyzed, findings are reported, and the consumer, reading contradictory information, doesn't know what to believe. Rather than believe that crime is down, the consumer responds emotionally to stories of random violence and reacts with fear. For the consumer, it doesn't matter if the data indicate that crime is down, because the perception of a highly violent society precipitates a sense of danger and an unwillingness to believe the objective information reported by law enforcement.

Some researchers believe that positivism, as shown in the reporting of crime data, is a paradigm that does not work well in the social sciences because it fails to answer important social questions. While it provides data that we assume are collected in a controlled and orderly way, it often leaves the consumer more confused than ever.

In responding to the idea that positivist research is too limiting and that applied social science fields such as social work would do better using less empirical approaches, Grinnell et al. (1994) note that one form of research (quantitative, with its very strict approach to research, and qualitative, with its more lenient approach to research) is not superior to the other, and that all social research "must work toward the generation of unbiased knowledge that can be shared, withstand scrutiny and provide effective service and future investigations . . ." (1994, p. 470). A very wise statement, I think.

The Critical Theory Paradigm

In the critical theory paradigm, the researcher admits to a bias about the research study and hopes the findings will support that bias. The research itself must be as objective as possible, and the researcher must scrupulously conduct the research so that his or her bias doesn't affect the findings. However, rather than saying that the researcher has no point of view about the outcome, in the critical theory paradigm, not only do we note our bias, but we also have a firm idea about how the findings will benefit a political, social, or philosophical position we hold. Feminist research is often thought of as research using a critical theory paradigm because it tries to show the impact of gender bias on the lives of women and has, as its emphasis, social, political, and economic change.

In a sense, **post-modernism** also fits the critical theory paradigm. Post-modernism is concerned with social problems that have developed in society as a result of the belief that there are rational explanations for most issues facing mankind. Post-modernism comes from a core belief that it is this very rationality that often leads to gender bias, discrimination, inequitable distribution of wealth, war, poverty, conflict, and a range of problems confronting us as a people. In many ways, post-modernism is a reaction against a world that still cannot control its more primitive instincts and stems from the disillusionment of many people after the Vietnam War. Post-modernism believes that many current explanations of human behavior are incorrect, and that the goal of all intellectual inquiry is to seek alternative explanations of the world without the methodological limitations placed on us by positivism. Those alternative explanations might include the importance of spirituality, the significance of intuition, the relevance of non-western approaches to health, and any number of alternative views of the universe. For the post-modernist researcher, the purpose of research is to explore the world in a way that permits maximum flexibility in the use of research methodologies. In a sense, post-modern researchers are atheoretical. They value the free adaptation of research methodologies to seek alternative ways of viewing the world. They reject positivism because it limits more creative and intuitive approaches and because it discounts the common experiences, observations, and insights we all have that may not be supported by data or objective evaluations, but are valuable, nonetheless.

I'm including post-modernism under the heading of critical theory, but I suspect that most of your instructors would point out that research is a rational process and that post-modernism requires a fairly sophisticated understanding of research. In many ways, feminist research is a postmodernist approach to research because it objects to positivism and believes that research issues should be studied in ways that are more flexible and creative than positivism. If you are interested in feminist approaches to research, you have a very strong case for a critical theory piece of research. You should, however, find out much more about feminism and feminist research. References on feminist research are included in many of the chapters of this book. Consulting these and other sources will be helpful in understanding and using this approach.

Let's continue with an example of critical theory in practice. Consider the researcher who studies the impact of child molestation. Using the critical theory paradigm, the researcher would tell us in advance that child molestation is a horrendous thing and that it does terrible damage to people. If the purpose of the study is to determine the impact of molestation on the social and emotional development of children, it would be perfectly feasible and correct for the researcher to note that the findings will be used to strengthen prosecution against child molesters, help in the argument to provide free therapy for any child who has been molested, and any number of related activities to help victims. Rather than acting as if information generated by a research study is neutral, the critical theory paradigm promises that findings will be used for social change. If the data suggesting that child abuse is declining in America are correct (U.S. Department of Health and Human Services, 2001), it may well be the result of a number of researchers using the critical theory paradigm to create social change.

Can a researcher be unbiased when it comes to actually doing research? Does bias affect objectivity, and are small and large mistakes made in the belief that a positive finding will prompt needed social change? We have numerous examples of the use of critical theory affecting the outcomes of research. One of the most startling examples in the social sciences concerns the incidence of sexual molestation of women. Russell and Bolen (2000) report that a woman stands a 33 percent chance of being raped or sexually molested during her lifetime. However, estimates by the Justice Department (Nueman, 1995; *LA Times*, 1994) using census data put the number at 18 percent, almost one half that of the data suggested by Russell and Bolen. More recent data using actual reports to police, social agencies, hospitals, and rape crisis centers place the number of women raped or molested in their lifetime at 8 percent (*LA Times*, 1994), while studies using medical reports from hospitals suggest that the number is closer to 2 percent (*LA Times*, 1994).

This significant difference in molestation rates can't be explained away easily. Someone's bias must be showing. If you use a liberal legal definition of rape (unwanted sexual behavior by a man), I'd venture a guess that the numbers are astronomical. The Kinsey Reports (1948, 1953) said that one-half of the women in Alfred Kinsey's famous studies experienced date rape. In my classes, I often ask women about sexual harassment and the unwanted sexual behavior of men. Just about every woman has a story to tell suggesting experiences with men where sex was aggressively pursued well beyond a point where the woman said and meant, "No!" Two percent or 33 percent—which set of data should we believe? I'm not sure. I think sexual molestation of women is rampant, but I'm not sure whose data I should trust. Figures from the Justice Department have consistently underreported rape and sexual molestation of women. It is in the interest of government to make society appear safe and to provide data suggesting that violence to women is decreasing. Low figures for rape and molestation should have a calming effect and should make people feel safer.

Using police or medical data to project accurate rape and molestation figures isn't really an effective approach, either. Only one-third of all women who have been raped seek medical care, and a significantly lower number never even report the rape (National Center for Injury Prevention and Control, 2001). My guess is that Russell and Bolen are correct, but that their estimates of rape and molestation of women are on the low side. What do you think?

You can see, however, that the problem of molestation of women is so emotional that it begs for an objective appraisal. Critical theory may be the wrong research paradigm to use. On the other hand, it may be necessary to use critical theory or the data we generate may be completely unrelated to the reality of the problem. Someone has to care deeply about the problem or the methodology can become so sterile and unfeeling that the results of the study have no practical use.

Critical theory doesn't limit the use of other paradigms or methodologies. One can use a critical theory paradigm and positivism at the same time. Knowing that a researcher is using critical theory alerts us to the social change position of the researchers. It also forces us to look carefully at the methodology used in the study to make certain that it wasn't compromised only to reinforce the researcher's political point of view. Because many researchers looking at politically charged issues are under a certain amount of pressure to ensure findings that conform to accepted points of view, many of us fail to look carefully at the methodology of the study and accept leaps of logic or weak or non-existent relationships because the findings support our own belief systems.

Some years ago, the well-known author Norman Cousins was hospitalized with what seemed to be a type of severe arthritis. In a famous article in the *New England Journal of Medicine* (1976), Cousins analyzed his hospital experiences noting that hospitals are often bad for our health. Cousins suggested that hospital environments are often unsupportive, that treatments tend to be uncreative, and that a focus on illness rather than wellness often discourages patients from getting better. Recognizing these concerns while he was hospitalized, and failing to physically improve over a course of many days, Cousins convinced his doctor to release him to a hotel room where friends, many of whom were comedians, entertained him. While in the hotel room, Cousins watched funny movies, believing that laughter increases oxygen flow. Gourmet meals were brought in on the assumption that good food improves the body's ability to heal itself. To be sure that he wasn't in danger of a health crisis, his doctor continued to see him. Large doses of aspirin, the common treatment for arthritis when he wrote the article, were discontinued, and mega doses of vitamin C were used in their place. Cousins argued that vitamin C, which was thought to be a curative by such well-known advocates as Nobel Prize winning physicist Linus Pauling, would aide in his recovery.

As a result of these alternative treatments to hospitalization, Cousins reported that his medical condition improved significantly. Over 3,000 supportive letters flowed into the *New England Journal of Medicine* (Cousins, 1976) from doctors, all testifying that hospitals were terrible places and that if you were ill, you should avoid them like the plague. I'm exaggerating, of course, but you get the picture. No one asked, until later on, whether Cousins would have gone into spontaneous remission (become better in the course of time) had he stayed in the hospital. Further, no one looked at his past behavior (Cousins had a prior medical problem that made him deeply cynical about the medical establishment). Finally, no one considered the validity of mega vitamin C therapy (it has since been rejected and people now worry that large doses of vitamin C may cause kidney damage). The bias against doctors, hospitals, and the treatment of illness is so strong in American society, even among many doctors, that personal convictions caused many Americans to accept Cousins' findings without adequate supportive data. To be sure, good came from the article because many people in the medical professions began to realize that hospitals needed to become more humane. Changes were made in food service, visiting hours were relaxed and consideration of the patient's wishes regarding treatment improved, but as a piece of research, it was meant to appeal to our emotions and cannot be considered scientific.

This is the real problem with critical theory. You can tell the consumer about your bias. You can even show how you've controlled for it to the extent possible, but if the consumer shares your bias, bad research sometimes affects social policy with some negative and unwanted consequences. If social policy is to be changed, it should flow from research believed to be accurate, well controlled for, and objective. When social policy is affected by bad research because the findings appeal to emotions, it sometimes gets translated into xenophobic political positions and laws. Japan bashing, now just a distant memory, is an example of how badly done research, predicting the massive control of America by Japan, played into prevailing biases of the time and resulted in attitudes, laws, and political positions that were—there's no other way to say it—just plain discriminatory. The same can be said, with great sadness, about the internment of American citizens of Japanese descent during World War II.

Critical theory is an exciting paradigm to use, but it requires a high degree of objectivity and honesty and significant control of the research methodology. If you are willing to go to great lengths to explain the controls you've maintained in your study and to defend yourself against potential criticism of bias or manipulation of data to support your political agenda, then critical theory is a paradigm that offers you an opportunity to provide socially relevant data that could make a difference.

The Post-Positivist Paradigm

If positivist research is difficult to do because controlling complex social and psychological variables is nearly impossible, then might there be another option? Yes, there is. Many people call this option *post-positivism* because it relies on the positivist approach as a benchmark of what good research should be but understands the difficulty and impracticality of positivism for many forms of social research. In post-positivism, the researcher admits that many variables can't be controlled for but believes that research is possible, even necessary, for us to begin gathering information about the events that affect the social and emotional lives of people. In post-positivism, the researcher is often unable to show a cause-effect relationship among variables, and applications to other people, situations, and places are unlikely. However, a post-positivist study might indicate trends, implied relationships, and weak associations among variables that, if done enough times by enough researchers, might give us compelling information.

An example of post-positivist research is single subject research, a type of research that considers only one subject at a time (see Chapter 9 for a more complete discussion of single subject designs). Using the example of clients with anxiety problems, rather than comparing an experimental group receiving treatment for anxiety to a control group, each client is evaluated individually using goals of improvement designed specifically for that individual client. In single subject research, the researcher might be trying to find treatment strategies for use with a particular kind of problem. He or she isn't saying that the approach or strategy will work for everyone but, rather, that it may work for a single client with a particular kind of problem. After repeating the single treatment and evaluation with a number of similarly anxious clients, the researcher might then be able to explain and describe what was done in treatment and its level of effectiveness. The researcher might also encourage others to try the approaches/strategies that he or she found successful in order to determine if they might work for other clinicians treating similarly anxious clients. If others find the approaches/strategies equally effective, then we have the beginning of a helpful way of using research to positively affect treatment. Chapter 9 on qualitative methods gives three examples of goal attainment scaling, a method for determining the effectiveness of single subject treatment using behavioral goals and levels of improvement achieved over the course of treatment.

Because post-positivism is a much freer paradigm, it allows for the development of alternative research strategies that might be able to find information in the most unlikely and creative ways. One example of a post-positivist design is the use of observation. Consider the researcher who wants to find out if kidney dialysis causes depression in clients, and if that depression might, in turn, lead to non-compliance with medical advice. Rather than devising an instrument to measure depression and the level of patient non-compliance with medical advice, the researcher might observe the client during dialysis and record verbal and non-verbal indications of depressed behavior. Or the researcher might talk to the client over many weeks or months to discover changes in emotional affect and behavior. To be certain of correctly collected relevant information, the researcher would take careful notes and would try mightily to keep the research as objective as possible. However, the researcher isn't sampling the population nor is he or she using a valid and reliable instrument to measure depression. What the researcher is doing is recording patient behavior (affect, language, non-verbal behavior, crying, laughter, suicidal ideations) over a period of time, and then seeing if that behavior affects medical compliance. The researcher isn't saying that all dialysis patients act the same way or that the findings can be generalized to other dialysis patients. What the researcher is saying is that in this single experience, using a methodology that consumers of the study might accept or reject, if a certain level of depression sets in after prolonged dialysis treatment, the depression *might* lead to non-compliance with medical regimens that *might* lead to further deterioration in the client's medical condition.

The researcher might, in the prolonged observations of the patients, discover that there are a number of other factors contributing to depression in dialysis patients. Those factors might have to do with marriage, work, family life, sexual functioning, and a host of variables that may or may not relate to the dialysis. Such findings can be very helpful to treatment staff in dialysis centers by permitting them to be proactive in establishing programs for dialysis patients that anticipate and respond to potential problems related to prolonged medical treatment.

Post-positivism is an ideal paradigm for small pieces of research of the kind many of you will be doing in your undergraduate and graduate careers. Post-positivism provides the researcher with freedom to use more subjective methods of gathering information. Sample size might be small. Instruments to measure behavior might be created by the researcher, or the researcher might use checklists or consensus statements. The variety of approaches for collecting data available to the researcher using post-positivism is virtually limitless. As with all research, however, post-positivism demands that the researcher explain the research process completely and that an "audit trail" exists (Yaffe, 1999) for other researchers to follow so that each methodological decision made along the way can be understood and, if necessary, replicated by another researcher.

Are there problems with post-positivist research? Lots of them. Post-positivism encourages the consumer to believe in the honesty of the researcher. Unless there is an audit trail that explains the procedures and processes used in a study, post-positivism can be subjective to the point of being useless. All researchers need to explain and defend their research methodologies, and all researchers must provide adequate information so that a study can be replicated. Certainly, all researchers must protect the research process from the biases of the researcher. Post-positivism is particularly prone to error, and if done incorrectly, can produce incorrect information.

Yet, if it is done correctly, post-positivist research offers social scientists the ability to do small-scale studies using very creative methodologies with, admittedly, limited ambitions. Remember that the goal of post-positivist research isn't necessarily to show relationships among variables. It is meant to show trends and weak associations among variables so that other social scientists will be encouraged to look at a problem using more complex methodologies with more ambitious intentions.

Some researchers feel so strongly in favor of post-positivism that they have taken positions against positivism that may be very difficult to defend. Even though I've noted the difficulty of doing a positivist piece of research, most of us would not go so far as to support Tyson (1992) who believes that a significant occurrence in the applied social sciences is the "shift away from an outdated, unwarranted and overly restrictive approach to scientific social research which has long been unsatisfying to practitioners" (1992, p. 541). In place of positivism, Tyson supports post-positivism which she believes provides applied social scientists with the ability to seek truth without the constrictions imposed by positivism. She also notes that by reducing the limitations demanded by positivism, more applied social scientists will involve themselves in small, vital, important, and relevant pieces of research that will move the applied social sciences in a more purposeful and socially relevant direction. This is, I think, a valid position but one which should not negate the importance of the type of empirical research suggested in the positivist paradigm.

The Constructivist Paradigm

We usually think of our research subjects as passive players in the research process. We create a questionnaire and our research subjects fill it out. We choose the various methodologies used without any involvement on the part of the subjects. But why not include the subjects in every step of the process? Why not have them help develop the problem to be studied? Why not let them help develop the instrument and then, once it's developed, why not have them fill it out? This is the essence of the constructivist paradigm: Research subjects should be our partners in the research process.

When you think about it, constructivism is a radical departure from positivism with its tight control over the research mythology. It is also radical philosophically, because constructivism provides the research subject with the authority to influence the research process and gives the subject equal power to develop the research questions, conduct the study, and analyze the data.

How might constructivism be applied in a research study? An often-used research method called the **Delphi Approach** gives us a good example. Let's assume that we're interested in finding out why women abused by their husbands stay with their husbands even though the abuse continues. We might locate a group of abused women, perhaps through a shelter or through the court records of men undergoing mandatory treatment for abuse in a diversion project. We might meet with the women as a group and share with them what we're interested in finding out. The group would possibly discuss whether the original question we posed about women staying with abusive spouses is a good one, or it might consider whether there are better questions to ask that are more fundamental to the relationship between men and women in abusive relationships. Once the women in the group complete these initials discussions and agree on the questions to be asked, the group might begin to discuss the best way to approach methodological questions posed by the study. For example, might they know other women who might be involved? Is there a way to get abused women to complete questionnaires in a truthful way?

Let's further assume that at the initial meeting, our group agrees that the question we originally posed is a good one and agrees to help us develop a questionnaire. Once the questionnaire is developed by the group in draft form, we might ask the respondents (our group of abused women and others they may want us to add) to give us feedback about the questionnaire. Is it a good questionnaire? Are the questions clear? Do they convey what the women in our group originally said at our earlier meeting? Or we might just meet again as a group instead of sending out the questionnaire, allowing new people to join the group in the process. It's entirely up to the group.

We would continue going through the process of refining the questionnaire until the questions met with the approval of the group. Once the questionnaire was approved, we would ask the women in the group to respond to the questionnaire. From the responses, we might develop consensus statements based on what the majority of respondents indicated on the questionnaire. We would then provide the consensus statements to our group for review and approval, including minority views, until we had considerable agreement among the group (perhaps better than 90 percent agreement).

As you can see, the constructivist approach is interested in a democratic relationship between the researcher and the subject. It believes that research is enhanced when subjects are involved. It also believes that findings are likely to be more accurate when subjects are very involved in the process. Are there problems with the constructivist approach? Sure. If you've ever worked with people, you know that they often don't stay with an assignment. You're likely to get fewer and fewer people involved in the research process over time so that the few people who ultimately complete the questionnaire may be so small that their perceptions are biased and fail to give a true reading of what the larger group believes. Strong-willed people may dominate the process, and the study may go in directions that don't provide us with usable information. This approach is also slow and very time consuming. A Delphi study may take many months. If you use the mail to send information back and forth, it can also be very expensive.

But the idea of an equal relationship between participants and researchers is certainly worth considering, particularly if you believe that one of the by-products of research is to empower people. Empowerment can be an elegant by-product of constructivist research. Once involved in the research process, people may begin to take control over the issues being studied. The women in our Delphi study of abusive relationships may begin to gain insight into their relationships with their abusive partners. That insight might prompt changes in the way they approach their abusive mates. If the experience has been very impacting, the abuse might stop or women may leave the abusive relationship and seek healthier non-abusive relationships.

Which Paradigm Should You Choose for Your Research Project?

The paradigm you choose depends on the problem you intend to study, the amount of time you have to complete your work, your level of sophistication with various research methods and procedures, and your level of interest in the problem you intend to study. Positivist research is very time-consuming but is also an excellent learning experience. Post-positivist approaches are the most commonly used by students, but they are often weak methodologically and the learning process may be reduced. Constructivist research may be difficult to do given the limited time you may have to complete your project. Critical theory projects are always interesting, and because they are not methodologically specific, they offer the student an opportunity to do research that is emotionally stimulating but that requires great objectivity and self-control.

My experience is that it may take up to a year to complete a research study. In that year, it often takes four to six months to develop a problem formulation and do a first-rate literature review. It may take several months to gain approval for use of copyrighted instruments and for human subjects review. Additionally, it may take four months or longer to collect and analyze data and certainly a month or more to complete the research report. This assumes that your proposal is strong and that you don't run into problems receiving human subjects approval. It may be helpful to develop a schedule for data collection. Keep in mind that research subjects operate at their own speed, not yours. What may have been considered a four-month process may take much longer, particularly when subjects fail to respond to questionnaires or data are confusing and need more time to be analyzed (as might be the case when using interviews or open-ended questions). But choosing a research paradigm is a good initial step for new researchers. Paradigms help direct new studies and provide a philosophical position that new researchers often find very helpful.

Summary

Research paradigms are ways of viewing the research process and help to develop a researcher's frame of reference. Four primary paradigms were discussed in this chapter: positivism, post-positivism, constructivism, and critical theory. There are other paradigms that may interest the new researcher including post-modernism. Examples of the methodologies often associated with each paradigm were provided.

REVIEW QUESTIONS

1. What are the positives and negatives of each of the four paradigms discussed in this chapter?

2. If you were to study a politically sensitive subject such as voter reactions to the proposition passed in California to limit bilingual education, which of the four paradigms would you use, and why?

3. Do we place too much emphasis on science in this country at the expense of common wisdom, shared experiences, and opinion? Is there something distancing about always looking to the scientific method to answer questions, something that takes away from the dialogue needed in a democracy to resolve issues?

4. In reading a piece of research, what steps would you go through to determine whether the researcher had been true to the paradigm chosen?

5. Post-modernism argues against rationality. Do you believe a society is better off if it views and resolves social issues in a highly personalized and emotional way, or through rational but sometimes very impersonal and distancing approaches to problem solving?

REFERENCES

Alasuutari, P. (1995). *Researching culture: Qualitative method and cultural studies.* Thousand Oaks, CA: Sage.

Bayley, J. E. (1991). The concept of victimhood. In D. Sank & D. I. Caplan (Eds.), *To be a victim* (pp. 53–62). New York: Plenum.

Bezruchka, S. (2001, Feb. 26). Is our society making you sick? *Newsweek, 14.*

Brewer, J., & Hunter, A. (1989). *Multimethod research.* Newbury Park, CA: Sage.

Brislin, R. W., Lonner, W. J., & Thorndike, R.M. (1973). *Cross-cultural research methods.* New York: John Wiley & Sons.

Cook, T. D., & Campbell, D.T. (1979). *Quasi-experimentation: Design and analysis issues for field settings.* Chicago: Rand McNally.

Corbin, J., & Strauss, A. (1990). Grounded theory research: Procedures, canons, and evaluative criteria. *Qualitative Sociology, 13(1),* 3–21.

Cousins, N. (1976, Dec. 23). Anatomy of an Illness. *New England Journal of Medicine. 295,* 1458–1463.

Dating Violence and Acquaintance Assault. (1996). Nebraska Cooperative Extension NF 95-244.

Davis, L. V. (1986, Spring). A feminist approach to social work research. *Affilia*, 32–47.

Eisenhower Foundation. (2001). *To establish justice, to insure domestic tranquility: A thirty year update of the National Commission on the Causes and Prevention of Violence.* Retrieved December 21, 2001 on the World Wide Web: http:// www.eisenhowerfoundation. org/aboutus/fr_publications.html.

Frinter, M., & Rubinson, L. (1993). Acquaintance rape: The influence of alcohol, fraternity membership and sports teams. *Journal of Sex Education and Therapy, 19,* 272–284.

Glaser, B., & Strauss, A. (1967). *The discovery of grounded theory.* Chicago: Adeline.

Grinnell, R. M., Jr., Austin, C. D., Blythe, B. T., et al. (1994, July). Social work researchers' quest for responsibility. *Social Work, 39(4),* 469–470.

Guba, E. (1990). *The paradigm dialogue.* Newbury Park, CA: Sage.

Hudson, W., & Nurius, P. S. (1994). *Controversial issues in social work research.* Boston: Allyn & Bacon.

Kinsey, A., et al. (1948). *Sexual behavior in the human male.* Bloomington, Il: University Press.

Kinsey, A., et al. (1953). *Sexual behavior in the human female.* Bloomington, Il: University Press.

Koss, M. P., & Dinero, T. E. (1988). A discriminate analysis of risk factors among a national sample of college women. *Journal of Consulting and Clinical Psychology, 57,* 133–147.

McShane, M. D., & Wiliams III, F. P. (1992). Radical victimology: A critique of the concept of victim in traditional victimology. *Crime and Delinquency, 38,* 258–264.

Milton S. Eisenhower Foundation. (2001). *National Commission on the Causes and Prevention of Violence.* [Online]. Retrieved September 19, 2001 from the World Wide Web: http://www.aypf.org/forumbriefs/2000/fb102700.htm.

National Center for Injury Prevention and Control. *Rape fact sheet: Prevalence and incidence.* [Online] Retrieved December 21, 2001 from the World Wide Web: http:// www.cdc.gov/ncipc/factsheets/rape.htm.

Nueman, E. (1995, Winter). Trouble with domestic violence. *Media Critic, 2(1),* 67–73.

Parsonage, W. H. (1979). The victim as a focus of criminological interest. In W. H. Parsonage (Ed.), *Perspectives on victimology* (pp. 7–20). Newbury Park, CA: Sage.

Peterson, S. R. (1991). Victimology and blaming the victim: The case of rape. In D. Sank & D. I. Caplan (Eds.), *To be a victim* (pp. 171–177). New York: Plenum.

Rappoport, R. N. (ed.). (1985). *Children, youth, and families: The action-research relationship.* Cambridge: Cambridge University Press.

Roberts, A. R. (1990). *Helping crime victims.* Newbury Park, CA: Sage.

Roberts, H. (Ed.). (1990). *Doing feminist research.* London: Ridledge.

Russell, D., & Bolen, R. (2000). *The epidemic of rape and child sexual abuse in the United States.* Thousand Oaks, CA: Sage.

Sank, D. (1991). What hope for victims? The need for new approaches and new priorities. In D. Sank & D. I. Caplan (Eds.), *To be a victim* (pp. 425–437). New York: Plenum.

Tyson, Katherine B. (1992, November). A new approach to relevant scientific research for practitioners: The heuristic paradigm. *Social Work, 37(6),* 541–556.

U.S. Department of Health and Human Services. (2001). *HHS reports new child abuse and neglect statistics.* [Online] Retrieved December 21, 2001 from the World Wide Web: http:// www.hhs.gov/news/press/2001pres/20010402.html.

U.S. Department of Justice. *Sourcebook of criminal justice statistics.* (1992). NCJ-139563.

U.S. Department of Justice. *Uniform crime reports.* (1992).

U.S. Department of Justice Bureau of Justice Statistics. (2000). *Urban, suburban, and rural victimization, 1993–1998.* [Online]. Retrieved October 19, 2001 from the World Wide Web: http://www.ojp.usdoj.gov/bjs/pub/pdf/usrv98.pdf.

U.S. Department of Justice Bureau of Justice Statistics. (2001). *Violent crime rates have declined since 1994, reaching the lowest level ever recorded in 2000.* [Online]. Retrieved December 21, 2001 from the World Wide Web: http://www.ojp.usdoj.gov/ bjs/glance/viort.htm.

Williams, T. (1987). *Post-traumatic stress disorders: A handbook for clinicians.* Cincinnati, OH: Disabled American Veterans.

Yaffe, J. (1999). Lecture notes presented at the University of Utah.

ADDITIONAL READINGS

Agger, B. (1991). Critical theory, poststructuralism, postmodernism: Their sociological relevance. *Annual Review of Sociology, 17,* 105–131.

Bauman, Z. (1992). *Intimations of postmodernity.* London: Routledge.

Bell, D. (1973). The coming of post-industrial society. London: Heinemann.

Gage, N. (1989). The paradigm wars and their aftermath: A "historical" sketch of research and teaching since 1989. *Educational Research, 18,* 4–10.

Gartell, D. C., & Gartell, J. W. (1996). Positivism in sociological practice, 1967–1990. *Canadian Review of Sociology and Anthropology, 33,* 143–159.

Hall, S. (1996). The meaning of "New Times". In D. Morley & K. H. Chen (Eds.), *Stuart Hall: Critical dialogues in cultural studies.* London: Routledge.

Hoover, K., & Donovan, T. (1995). *The elements of social scientific thinking.* New York: St. Martin's Press.

Kincheloe, J. L., & McLaren, P. L. (1994). Rethinking critical theory and qualitative research. In N. Denzin & Y. Lincoln (Eds.), *Handbook of qualitative research* (pp. 138–157). Thousand Oaks, CA: Sage.

Kumar, K. (1997). The post-modern condition. In A. H. Halsey, H. Lauder, P. Brown and A. S. Wells (Eds.), *Education: Culture, economy, and society.* Oxford: Oxford University Press.

Layder, D. (1994). *Understanding social theory.* London: Sage.

Leonard, P. (1997). *Postmodern welfare: Reconstructing an emancipatory project.* London: Sage.

Little, D. (1991). *Varieties of social explanation: An introduction to the philosophy of science.* Boulder, CO: Westview.

Rosenau, P. M. (1992). *Postmodernism and the social sciences.* Princeton, NJ: Princeton University Press.

Schwandt, T. A. (1994). Constructivist, interpretivist approaches to human inquiry. In N. Denzin & Y. Lincoln (Eds.), *Handbook of qualitative research* (pp. 118–137). Thousand Oaks, CA: Sage.

RECOMMENDED INTERNET SITES

Arizona State University College of Education: Research Methods
<http://www.research.ed.asu.edu/>

Bill Trochim's Center for Social Research Methods
<http://trochim.human.cornell.edu/>

Bureau of Justice Statistics, U.S. Department of Justice
<http://www.ojp.usdoj.gov/bjs/>

National Network of Violence Prevention Practitioners
<http://www2.edc.org/nnvpp>

Sociological Research Online
<http://www.socresonline.org.uk/>

3

What's the Beef?
A Look at Problem
Formulations

Introduction

A **problem formulation** sets the tone for the study you intend to do. It explains why the issue you plan to study is important, and it describes the aspect of that issue you are particularly interested in studying. The problem formulation comes at the beginning of the research proposal. It includes supporting information and data to justify the need for the study. While it should be reasonably brief (two to three pages in your proposal and three to five pages in your final report), the problem formulation helps the reader understand why an issue needs to be studied and what the emphasis of your study will be. It also briefly states the research questions you plan to answer, gives the research paradigm you plan to use, and provides your justification for using that paradigm. It also briefly explains the methodology you intend to use and why that methodology will help answer the research questions you propose to study. A much more in-depth opportunity to explain the paradigm, the research question or hypothesis, and the approach you will use to gather data appears in the methodology section of the proposal. For practical reasons (to give the reader a sense of how you plan to approach the problem), a brief explanation of your methodology is also included in the problem formulation.

Rubin (1989) indicates that the problem formulation should answer the following questions: "What exactly do you want to study? Why is it worth studying? Does the proposed study have practical significance? Does it contribute to our general understanding of things?" (p. 72). Grinnell (1990) suggests that the following issues influence the selection of a research problem: "The problem must attract the researcher and must not be too difficult to solve. The problem must be important to others, and the problem should take into account current values" (p. 50).

Perhaps it might be helpful to see a problem formulation I wrote. This is a tongue-in-cheek problem formulation using feminist theory to justify the need to study the reasons so few men are enrolled in graduate schools of social work. I might add that what's tongue-in-cheek about this problem formulation is that women have used the argument that the lack of women in certain professions dominated by men (medicine, law, engineering, math, the hard sciences) is a clear example of sexism and the institutional preference for men. Can't one use the same argument in a profession such as social work where the predominant population is female and where men are a distinct minority? And can't one then show that the exclusion of men in social work has dire results for very troubled male clients whose social and emotional problems require a male worker? Let's give it a try.

An Example of a Problem Formulation

Title: A Qualitative Study of the Reasons for Low Male Participation Rates in MSW Programs

Introduction: Lennon (2001), writing for the Council on Social Work Education, reports that MSW programs in the United States have a male composition of less than 10 percent. This is troubling news for the many men in America who require the specialized help of a male social worker.

At present, men constitute only five percent of the active participants in any form of voluntary out-patient therapy but represent fully three times the numbers of incarcerated mental health patients, five times the number of incarcerated or residentially treated patients with addictions, and 90 percent of the incarcerated population in American jails and prisons (Soprano, 1999). One could argue that a reason for the high rates of male dysfunction leading to hospitalization or to prison is that specialized services for men offered by specially trained male workers are not available because of the small cohort of men in social work, the primary helping profession in the United States. Many of the institutionalized men might have remained in the community had they been provided needed social services by male workers. Most of the very troubled men who require the services of male workers come from very traditional backgrounds and reject help of a highly personal nature from women. The men who require male workers and often reject help from women include: New immigrants to the United States who may not know our domestic violence or child abuse laws, ethnic gang members, older men, men with hostility toward women because they have been abused by a woman, men who are in relationships with abusive women, and men who, for religious and ethnic reasons, believe that it would be inappropriate to share highly personal information with a woman.

There is considerable evidence that men receiving help from a male social worker seek help more often, remain in treatment longer, and have success rates that generally lead to less incarceration and hospitalization. Ricci (1996) notes that in a large mental health clinic in New York, when men were offered a male therapist, 78 percent of the men who were seen at intake continued on in therapy an average of thirteen sessions. In the same setting, however, when women were used as therapists with men, only 36 percent of the men continued on in treatment for an average of only three sessions. Johnson (1997) found that on a satisfaction survey following treatment, men were satisfied with male therapists 89 percent of the time but were satisfied with female therapists only 42 percent of the time. Johnson (1997) also found that higher satisfaction with a therapist translated into better social functioning. According to Johnson (1997), sixty-eight percent of the men with male therapists were judged significantly better by co-workers and spouses, while only 22 percent of the men were judged significantly better when the therapist was a female.

Small, Brutish, and Surly (1996) found that men who were seen by male therapists in perpetrator groups for domestic violence were far less likely to go to jail for additional abuse than when they were seen by female workers in the same clinics using the same treatment plan and approach. The researchers note that:

> In our findings, 6% of the men seen by male therapists were remanded to jail for violation of their court ordered diversion treatment while 28% of the men seen by female therapists in the same clinic using the same treatment approach were remanded to jail. All therapists held MSW's with an average of 10 years of post-MSW experience and were considered to be very competent by their peers. (1996, p. 56)

Tilde (1995) notes that when young male Hispanic gang members were seen in treatment while serving prison time in youth treatment facilities, recidivism rates were cut fully in half when the social worker was male and were cut by an additional 25 percent when the social worker was male, Hispanic, and bilingual. In situations where the therapist was female, the recidivism rate was nearly twice as high as the rate for male therapists.

Goe and Gently (1998) found that when a large HMO provided male patients with a male worker for mental health problems, men were 10 times more likely to go for treatment than when the worker provided was a female. There were no differences among the workers regarding level of education, professional credentials, or years of experience. Men, according to the authors, ". . . feel more comfortable with male therapists and are much more likely to follow through on treatment when the worker is male" (p. 74).

Having established that men do better in treatment with male therapists and that an absence of men exists in social work, it is interesting to note that not a single MSW program in the United States gives preference to men for admission to MSW programs. There are few scholarships specifically designated for male students offered through schools of social work, and not one document from the Council on Social Work Education (CSWE) addresses the lack of men in social work or the need to recruit and train more men. This is in stark contrast to the many documents CSWE has developed over the years that encourage the role of women in social work and mandate schools of social work to view women as impacted minorities when, clearly, they represent the majority of social work students.

Even the scholarly literature in social work shows a female bias. In a review of five social work journals over a twenty-seven year span (*Child Welfare, Health and Social Work, Social Casework, Social Service Review, and Social Work*), Grief and Baily (1990) found that "Fathers have long been a neglected area of research and concern." Reviewing the five cited journals from 1961 through 1987, the authors found only twenty-one articles, or less than one article a year on fathers, far less than the more frequently cited articles on mothers. The general tone of the articles was to paint a fairly negative picture of men, often characterizing them as perpetrators and abusers. Little in the literature search painted a sympathetic picture of men or attempted to study reasons for changing patterns of fatherhood.

Longres and Baily (1979), in a review of five social work journals from 1972 through 1976 (*Journal of Social Work Education, Social Casework, Social Policy, Social Service Review, and Social Work*), found that only 14 of 176 articles sampled contained key words such as *male, masculine, boy, son, father,* or *husband* (p. 26). The authors note that ". . . issues concerning men alone have been articulated to a minimal extent in the literature appearing in journals" (p. 26). Barrett and Robinson (1982) reported similar findings related to the literature on teenage fathers.

Significantly, as Grief and Bailey (1990) note, this absence of literature on men in general and fathers in particular occurs when the number of married couples with children under 18 actually declined from 25,823,000 in 1970 to 24,921,000 in 1990, even though the number of households increased by almost one-third (U.S. Bureau of the Census, 1994).

In contrast, it's interesting to note the explanations female social workers use for low numbers of men in social work. Farfenugan (1998) believes that the current economy encourages men and minorities to seek higher-paying careers in business and industry. What she doesn't explain is why the marketplace doesn't similarly affect Caucasian women, the primary group attending social work programs. Monroe (1999) argues that men are less aware of the social context of family life and that women are more sensitive to social interactions. This is unsupported by any data and is based entirely on her personal impressions of the way male and female therapists function. Not surprisingly, she tells us that the idea for her paper came in the midst of a frustrating treatment session she attended in which her therapist was male. Rose (1997) notes that female social workers in social agencies tend to be more productive, have better attendance records, work for less money, and tend to stay at an agency longer than their male counterparts. She compares 100 male and female workers in one agency, but commingles men without the MSW with men who have the MSW resulting in a biased sample. And ironically enough, she notes this sampling problem by admitting that she couldn't find enough male MSW's to have equal numbers of men and women with the degree. Finally, Macho and Mann (1999) argue that a profession like social work *should* be female dominated because it provides an environment that encourages female students to focus on female problems, something not likely to happen when programs have higher numbers of male students. This admission completely negates the possibility that social work even cares about male clients and further reinforces the notion that social work is dominated by a female agenda.

It seems clear that while men are needed to help a large population of very troubled male clients, schools of social work are doing little to increase the numbers of men admitted to MSW programs. This conflict between need and availability leads us to suggest the following hypotheses:

Hypothesis Guiding the Research Study
1. Men have limited enrollment in MSW programs because of a pervasive lack of concern for their inclusion in social work education.

2. Schools of Social Work are dominated by females who define social work as a female profession.

3. Men are discouraged from attending MSW programs because they are seldom recruited or offered the special incentives that define most under-represented groups.

4. The lack of men in social work is an example of gender bias.

Methodology

Twelve randomly chosen schools of social work with MSW programs in the United States will be visited from a total population of 150 MSW programs. Faculty members, current MSW students, agency personnel and administrators, and admissions and recruitment coordinators in each school will be interviewed in focus groups using pre-determined questions (a research protocol) to help discover why men are not being admitted to MSW programs in greater numbers, and to determine what can be done to increase the number of men in graduate social work programs. Four researchers will independently analyze the information provided in the focus groups. All focus groups will be video taped so that content can be evaluated in the most objective way permissible. A protocol to guide both the questions asked and the method of evaluating the data will be developed by male and female social work educators meeting at a national social work conference. All participants in that meeting will be skilled social researchers with a range of political beliefs. Care will be taken to include researchers with feminist frames of reference.

Paradigm

Because the sample size is small and the use of focus groups is qualitative in nature, the paradigm used for this study will be post-positivist. However, to provide objectivity, there will be three researchers involved in all of the interviews who will be collecting and analyzing data independently of one another. Consensus statements will be used in the focus groups to further ensure objectivity. All questions asked will have first been developed by a group of male and female social work educators meeting at a national conference who have volunteered to spend a day during the conference developing the questions and discussing the research design. In this sense, there is a constructivist element to the study. Since a major part of the study relates to what can be done to increase the number of men in MSW programs and since the findings will be used to encourage greater numbers of men to apply and to be admitted to MSW programs, there is an element in the study of the critical theory paradigm, as well.

Implications

This study of the shortage of men in social work could help increase male admissions to MSW programs by publishing the results of the study in prominent social work journals. Findings will also be shared with the public and provide funding sources who fund schools of social work to provide greater numbers of trained personnel. If the other helping professions are suffering from shortages of men (psychiatry, clinical psychology, counseling psychology, and counseling), and there is early evidence to suggest that this is the case, the study may have implications for the other helping professions. Part of the purpose of the study is to develop ways of attracting more men into MSW programs. These strategies could influence the other helping professions and could lead to the availability of more men in the helping professions who could provide services to a growing number of angry, sometimes violent and disenfranchised men in America who often do great harm to women and children and to other men.

A Feminist Response to the Problem Formulation

Fair is fair. Because I proposed a problem formulation using a feminist argument, I gave the proposal to one of my ex-best female friends who had the following to say:

> Glicken, you sexist pig, you. You've made it seem as if women are the reason for the low male attendance rates in social work but, once again, you've got it wrong, wrong, wrong. First of all, in the 1960s, at a time when men where overwhelmingly the deans and directors of social work programs and when most faculties of schools of social work were male, enrollments of men were declining. You didn't decide to include that little ditty, huh? In fact, by the late 1970s, with men fully in charge of social work education, the level of men in MSW programs dropped below 10 percent, a level even lower than it is now. And where do you get off telling us that women dominate social work? You were dean of a school of social work, weren't you? Did you do any better? I doubt it. [I'm gulping.] And furthermore, this hogwash about men doing better with male therapists is complete horse pucky. Soprano (1999) found that men preferred female therapists to male therapists because they thought women were more positive in their feedback and more responsible when it came to being on time and giving the client their full hour of therapy.

Munchkin (1998) said that the gender of the therapist is never the primary issue regarding a patient's improvement; it's the warmth and unconditional acceptance of the client by the therapist. He also said that men seem to be more judgmental than women and that they aren't as positively reinforcing as women [double gulp]. You also neglected to tell us that many schools of social work have found that male applicants have lower GPA's, less work experience, and poorer references than the women who apply for graduate social work degrees.

Social work has always attracted more women than men. The founders of the social work profession were women. It doesn't take much common sense (but more than you have) to know that a profession developed mainly by women (much like nursing) will very likely appeal to other women. And finally, you moron, where do you get off using feminist theory, anyway? You know nothing about feminist theory, women, or, for that matter, anything. Go back to your room, don't come out for a year, and don't ever, do you hear me?, don't ever say anything bad about women you bald, overweight, idiotic, condescending, ambidextrous, rotten tennis-playing male lackey of the ruling class.

The Moral of the Story

Ouch! Where did I go wrong? Well, to be truthful, all over the place. For one thing, I did what is called creating a "straw man." I purposely supported my argument with data that made it appear I had a valid problem formulation, when a close look at the data readily available to me showed that I failed to include other sources that weaken my argument. You just cannot do that when developing a problem formulation. You need to add data, opinions, and research evidence that may be contrary to your position. If you fail to do this, anyone with even a little experience in research will be able to shoot holes in your problem formulation. I should have added contradictory information. It would have strengthened my problem formulation because the reader would have felt that I was being fair to both sides of the argument. And I should have done a much better job of including research data related to other applied professions (counseling, psychology, psychiatry) that may also have shown significant declines in the numbers of men enrolled in those allied programs. As such, my problem formulation is vulnerable, and anyone with even the most basic knowledge of research could tear it apart! And if you haven't recognized it by now with names like Small, Brutish and Surly, I created many of the citations just to give myself supportive arguments. In the real world of research, you can't do that, of course. Not only is it unethical, but it's also terribly misleading. Please don't even think of trying. With the Internet, instructors can check references from their office computer by contacting a school's on-line library system. In the reference section of this chapter, you will readily distinguish the actual from the bogus sources.

By the way, a thorough review of the literature on gender and fit with clients shows little convincing data to suggest that male therapists are more effective with male clients. My therapists have almost uniformly been female. Why? Because I think women are warmer and gentler in their feedback. I also think their view of the world is sometimes different than mine and that an opposing view helps me change and grow. But one can think of a number of reasons why female therapists working with female clients would be preferable (as in the case of rape and child molestation, for example). From a scientific point of view, the argument that men work best with male therapists may be emotionally satisfying if you are a man, but it is not based on any objective data. There is a lesson to be learned here. When developing a problem to study, the more data you include to support your hypothesis, the stronger your problem formulation will be.

Choosing a Research Problem

There are a number of different ways to choose a research problem. Perhaps the following discussion will help you move from the larger issues, which may be difficult to study given the limited time you may have to complete your research project, to something more manageable.

Special Meaning

The problem should have special meaning to you but should not cause you to become so emotional that it could affect your objectivity. If you are going through a divorce, for example, it may not be a good idea to do research on divorce. If, however, you've gone through a divorce and have successfully resolved the issues, then it may make sense to do your project on divorce. Remember that all research should be objective. If you can't approach a problem without getting overly emotional about it, I'd suggest that you move on to something less troubling.

The problem of emotionality versus objectivity is a tough one. Feminist researchers correctly suggest that to do effective feminist research, one has to feel strongly about the way women have fared in our society. This deep concern for women provides a way of viewing both the content of the research and the motivating reason for doing it. It's difficult to be dispassionate about issues in the social sciences because they include racism, sexism, violent treatment of women and children, and other issues that beg for solutions. I think one can learn from the psychotherapists and social service providers who work with suffering people who are in intense emotional pain. These helping professionals are compassionate and caring yet are able to maintain objectivity and sufficient control over their emotions to help others without experiencing job-related stress, depression, and burnout.

Availability of Research

The problem you choose to study should have a considerable amount of available literature on which to base your hypotheses, research questions, or research objectives. If you have very limited literature to draw from, even after an extensive literature review, you may want to think twice about studying the problem you've chosen. Limited literature results in a very short literature review section, a limited problem formulation, and the inability to ask research questions or state hypotheses that come directly from the available literature. The reader will want to know why your literature review is so limited. There are usually two ways to determine the availability of literature based on research studies. You can do your own literature review (time-consuming, frustrating, a month without dating), or you can look for seminal (outstanding) articles or books on the subject you hope to study and see what those authors have to say. If the experts in the field say the literature is limited, that's a good sign you'll have a very small pool of research studies to draw from for your literature review. I have much more to say about literature reviews in Chapter 5, but for the sake of a successful research project, a proposal with limited literature does not bode well for the new researcher. How does he or she choose a methodology without knowing what other people have done? And more importantly, why *isn't* there more literature on the subject? Perhaps it's because other researchers have seen methodological quicksand and want nothing to do with a study that may lead nowhere.

Time Constraints

You should be able to complete your study in the amount of time available to you. Problems requiring difficult research methodologies should be avoided. Constructivist studies are notoriously time-consuming. Time series studies are also very time-consuming. Mailed surveys can take forever. Choose your research methodology wisely or the study can go many months past the report due date. You may want to discuss this with your instructor because most students new to research often choose research problems that take a good deal longer to complete than they originally thought. It may be helpful to consider Glicken's third law of driving the back roads of Michigan: On a map, it looks like a quick ride, but once you've committed yourself, it takes forever to get there. In the meantime, everyone else has graduated, beat you to that great job you were counting on, and have Beamers in their garages while you sit in the library coding your data. Onward to Mt. Pleasant, but be sure and avoid the back roads!

Human Subjects Review

The problem you've chosen should be able to pass human subjects review. This is the review of all research projects required of anyone affiliated with a specific organization. Children, incarcerated people, politically sensitive issues, designs that may be intrusive: These all may be seen as red flags by the human subjects review committee and may slow down acceptance of your proposal. A student proposal I once supervised took months to be approved because it dealt with abuse of elderly family members by caretakers. The committee worried that the researchers would have to report abuse to the authorities if they saw it. Rather than graduating on time, the extra time taken to deal with changes required by the human subjects committee delayed the student's graduation by four months. As I note in later chapters, this piece of research was a first-rate student project, but the price the student paid was high. Sometimes a study is worth taking additional time to complete because the implications are so important. Human subjects review boards can be very picky. If you've chosen a subject that red flags the committee's attention, expect the process of approving your study to be time-consuming and potentially contentious. You may need your instructor to advocate for you with the committee. That's perfectly understandable and appropriate if you make certain, in advance, that your instructor is inclined to help you out.

Relevant Problem

The problem should be relevant to the social sciences and should include research issues that are current. You should also consider the political ramification of studying certain problems. A Caucasian researcher studying African American issues is not always felt to have sufficient objectivity to do an unbiased piece of research, and the consumer might consider the findings questionable. Even when the researcher is of the same race, ethnicity, or gender as those being studied, findings that deviate from those normally held by most people may cause strong negative reactions from the professional community, as well as from other researchers. In a recent example, several researchers (Oates, et al., 1994) reviewed a number of studies on therapy with children who had been sexually abused. It is commonly felt that early intervention in sexual abuse is vital to the child's recovery. However, the authors discovered that early intervention often does more harm than good, and that, in fact, children who had emotionally supportive families who handled the child's abuse in a dignified, accepting, and non-stigmatizing way were reported to have done better than children who immediately entered therapy as a result of the abuse. This finding is very relevant to anyone who worries that the quality of therapy in this country is often ineffective, and that it may actually do harm. However, the outcry from the therapeutic community was so fierce that the journal editors were forced (or gave in to pressure) to issue a retraction citing methodological weaknesses in the article. Science is not without its political side, and taking on politically sensitive issues may result in ill will.

I'm telling you this as a cautionary tale but, actually, I think that political correctness has no place in social research and that no topic, if done ethically and with good intentions, should be prohibited. Social and political *sensitivity* is a requisite attribute for all of us in a free society. Political *correctness,* however, is a form of censorship. It has no place in the researcher's world where curiosity and the quest for knowing should form our research agenda.

Your Level of Expertise in Research

The problem you intend to study should suggest research designs and sampling procedures that are realistic given your current level of expertise. If this is your first attempt at doing a research study, don't be too hard on yourself. Choose methodologies that are "doable" and aren't so difficult that you may end up with a large amount of data that, in the final analysis, you won't understand. Surveys, interviews, the use of standard instruments to measure common emotional states, and then comparing demographic characteristics (gender, age, educational level, ethnicity) with scores on an instrument, might all be good ways to go if this is your first attempt at a research study. Clichés are sometimes wise, and "keep it simple" is one of the wiser clichés when it comes to doing an initial research project.

A New Way of Seeing the Problem

The problem you choose should be something that hasn't been done before or has a unique twist. However, you may replicate (re-do) someone else's research, although this may limit your creativity and may result in findings that don't warrant the effort. Often studies that are replicated lead nowhere. The sample may be somewhat different than the one used in the original study or the instrument may not be as appropriate for your sample as the one developed by the original researchers.

As an example of replicating a study using a somewhat different sample, one of my former students in California did a study on how African American men view marriage. She used an instrument developed by a researcher who used the instrument on a sample of African American men in Alabama. My student's results were significantly different from that of the original researcher. Why? Alabama and California are very different places for African American men. In California, inter-racial dating and marriage are quite common, but in Alabama, there is still a strong social stigma attached to inter-racial relationships. Consequently, my student found that half of the men she surveyed in California thought that their ideal mate could be of another race or ethnicity while in the original study, only a handful of African American men felt that way. To be faithful to the original study, the study should have been replicated in Alabama where a sample, similar to that in the original study, could be drawn.

Walking You through the Problem Formulation Process

One of my excellent students is developing a problem formulation for her research project. She knows that she wants to do something concerning male batterers, and she thinks she wants to see if there is a connection between attachment problems (a lack of early childhood bonding between a child and a parent) and becoming an abuser when the child reaches adulthood. Abusive adults have often been childhood victims of abuse and neglect. This often leads to attachment problems with their parents that can increase the likelihood that the child will become abusive once he or she reaches adulthood. Actually, it's a little more complicated than that. However, I'm helping her develop her ideas, and I've suggested that she write her ideas in short sentences that might help her see the logical progression of ideas that represent a problem formulation. I hope the following statements will help her in developing her problem formulation more fully. Before she does a problem formulation, I've encouraged her to do a literature review because, in reality, she needs to be able to provide citations from the literature for each of her sentences. The following are sentences I might use to help develop a problem formulation on her subject.

1. Adult men who batter women and children have often witnessed family violence as children or have themselves been the victims of family violence. (This statement comes from an overwhelming number of studies of batterers and I feel justified in saying it. I would want my student to provide sources from the literature to support this and every other statement she makes.)
2. When family violence occurs, it often creates problems in bonding between the child and the parent(s)/caretaker(s). (Again, this is a statement that comes from numerous sources in the literature.)
3. The lack of a secure attachment to parents has been linked to abusive behavior in adults. (This statement comes from the literature, but there is some confusion about the term *attachment* that the student is trying to resolve by using a valid and reliable attachment instrument developed by a well-regarded researcher.)

4. This study will determine whether adult male batterers had attachment problems with their parent(s)/caretaker(s). [It's difficult to know exactly how adults will remember their relationships with parents at crucial stages in life, particularly if the family violence occurred very early in a child's life. Nonetheless, she can only try to find out whether the men in her sample will: a) Cooperate with the study; b) give her accurate information; and c) provide any evidence or examples of a lack of bonding with their parent(s) or caretaker(s).]

5. The study will also seek to find if any links, connections, or associations exist between perceptions of attachment problems with parents by the male subjects and their current history of battering.

This progression of ideas might make it easier for my student to write a problem formulation. However, looking at what I've written, let me tell you what I might tell the student if she comes back with a similar progression of ideas. First, I would tell her, "Well done. Good job. You've written some logical statements and they all make sense. My problem is that the concept of an "attachment problem" is fuzzy. Many people have attachment problems with their parents because of physical separation or other issues in the parent-child relationship and are not considered abusive. They don't become abusive adults. How do you know for certain that a relationship exists between childhood attachment problems and adult battering?"

If she's as good as I think she is, she'll go to the literature and find hard evidence suggesting a connection between attachment problems and abuse. Then I would probably say, "Is it the attachment problem that causes the adult to abuse, or is it having been abused as a child?" In other words, is the adult abusive behavior an emotional reaction to their childhood abuse, or is it from a weak bond between parent and child? And again, because she's such a good student, she'll probably respond by saying, "In addition to the attachment disorder instrument, I'm going to use an instrument that measures prior child abuse. I'm going to run statistics between the two instruments and see whether there is any connection between very poor attachment to parents and abusive adult behavior. Furthermore, I'm going to find non-abusive adults with poor attachments to parents and see if the abusive adults have significantly poorer attachment to parents than the non-abusive adults. If that is the case, then perhaps I can say that child abuse seems to lead to attachment disorders. I can't say for certain that attachment disorders cause adult abusive behavior, but I think I can say that there is a connection between the two, and that's good enough for me because I'm only a student with a life to lead and stop pushing me so hard, Dr. Glicken, because you're giving me a headache."

This was not a fictitious example. My student actually did tell me I was giving her a headache—and perhaps I did. But this is the way one of my students developed a research idea into a proposal. A number of my students have used the simple sentence approach I've just described to very good advantage. Perhaps it will help you, as well. Good luck!

Have You Chosen the Correct Problem?

Someone once said that it isn't the answers to issues that are important, it's the questions you ask about the issues. It was probably my mother who said that, bless her memory. The point is that many students ask the wrong questions when they develop a problem formulation. Let's take my earlier research problem regarding men and social work as an example. In it I try to place the onus of so few men in social work on female social work educators. Something fishy is going on in schools of social work, according to my problem formulation. Are men intentionally being kept out of social work? Women legitimately asked a similar question of medical and law schools, and it turned out that, yes, in two overwhelmingly male professions women were being kept out because of anti-female sentiments. But can I use the same argument with social work? Maybe I can, but a better question might be, why do men seem so disinclined to go into *any* of the helping professions, including social work? Is there something about the helping process that makes men feel feminized? I think so. I'm inclined to believe that only a very small number of men find social work attractive, although certainly they are a brave, strong, and brilliant lot . . . pat, pat. So an even better question to ask might be, why don't men go into social work and the other helping professions? Instead of seeking the answer from schools of social work, why not ask men about their feelings toward the helping process and whether they view the work as something men should be doing? There are, in fact, fields that are largely considered female fields by men. Nursing and elementary education immediately come to mind. Is social work one of those fields that men believe is primarily for women and, if so, does that perception limit male interest in the helping professions?

All too often, researchers think in superficial ways when developing a research question. Their biases are apparent and they look for interactions among variables that may appear correct on the surface, but really are not correct. Why, for example, is medical care so expensive? The first thought many people have is that doctors are just too greedy and that medical care is expensive because of the high salaries doctors make by gouging patients. Consequently, a problem formulation coming from this point of view might look at doctors' salaries, comparing them to those in other professions. Or we might look at hospital costs and point out that these costs are absurd. Have you ever seen what a hospital charges for an aspirin? Perhaps $2.00? But when you really look at the reasons why medical care is so expensive, a few things become clear. Many people have no medical coverage and must use emergency rooms for simple problems that are more easily and more cheaply handled in a doctor's office. As an example, a friend of mine has an elderly mother who fell outside of her home and broke her wrist. Neighbors called an ambulance and she was taken to the emergency room of a local hospital. Total cost? $11,000. The same problem, treated in a doctor's office, would have cost less than $500. Another reason for high medical costs is that Americans use far too many drugs (CalPERS, 2001). Many medications are either not necessary or have cheaper equivalents that do the job just as well. And finally, Americans are being over-prescribed psychotropic (mood changing) medications that fail to alleviate many psychosomatic illnesses and that create a pattern of overuse of medical services. Counseling would be a much better substitute. Any of these issues would be a better starting point for a study of medical costs than the assumption that doctors are over-paid, although certainly, some of them are, and we'd all be happier if they were paid the same salaries as social workers, or provided medical care out of the goodness of their hearts. Physician, heal thyself!

So, what's the point? The point is that before you pose a research problem to study, you need to know a great deal about the subject. Furthermore, you need to ask a number of questions along the way to narrow your research question down to one of manageable size. By completing these two activities, your research problem will gradually take shape and with some help and some rational thought, your research proposal will become doable and you will go on to fame, fortune, and the BMW that will get you to Mt. Pleasant, Michigan, the center of intelligent thought in the United States and the home of really first rate apples. I rest my case.

Summary

All research begins with a problem formulation. The problem formulation should have relevance to both the researcher and to the social sciences. It should be doable in the time available to complete the study, and should be manageable given one's level of expertise. The problem formulation is a logically argued statement of what you plan to do, why it's important to do the study, the methodology you intend to use, and the hypotheses or research statements that define what the study intends to accomplish.

REVIEW QUESTIONS

1. Consider the example of the problem formulation provided in this chapter. Rewrite the problem formulation to make it more objective.

2. Using a research issue that you would like to study, write five or six logical statements that might lend themselves to further development of a problem formulation.

3. Consider an issue in your life that makes you very emotional. If you were asked to do a research study of that issue, how might you control your feelings sufficiently to write a very logical problem formulation?

4. A research study of drinking among Caucasian male college students suggests a high level of binge drinking. Write a paragraph that would suggest why binge drinking might lead to other serious social, psychological, and physical problems.

5. The problem formulation should present a case for the importance of doing a study. How might you frame a problem formulation that is only interested in abstract or theoretical rather than applied information?

REFERENCES

Barrett, R. L., & Robinson, B. E. (1982, November). Teenaged fathers: neglected too long. *Social Work, 27,* 44–48.

CalPERS, California Public Employees' Retirement System (PERS). *Health care: A closer look at the issues.* PERS Newsletter, winter 2001.

Farfenugan, V. W. (1998). I never understood the ad but it had to do with VWs and what you felt like doing once you drove one: You felt, farfenugan. Hopefully, that's something good, but who knows?

Goe and Gently. (1998). A way of viewing life: Go gently.

Grief, G. L., & Bailey, C. (1990, February). Where are the fathers in social work literature? *Families in Society, 71(2),* 88–92.

Grinnell, R. M. (1990). *Research in social work: A primer.* Itasca, IL: F. E. Peacock.

Herzberg, F. (1966). Work and the nature of man. Cleveland, OH: World Publishing.

Johnson, O. (1997). The name of my next door neighbor in Grand Forks, North Dakota: Ollie Johnson, who could make burping noises in class that drove my 5th grade teacher crazy and who used to point at me whenever he'd make the noise and the teacher would look our way. Tuskada ha, Ollie.

Lennon, T. M. (2001). *Statistics on social work educations: 1999.* Alexandria, VA: Council of Social Work Education.

Longres, J. F., & Bailey, R. H. (1979, January). Men's issues and sexism: A journal review. *Social Work, 24(1),* 26–32.

Macho, L., & Mann, A. (1999). Taken from the infamous disco song from the worst musical era of modern time, "Macho, macho man, I wanna be a macho man," but, surely, being disco music fans, you already knew this. And don't call me Shirley.

Monroe, M. (1999). My first girlfriend.

Munchkin, L. T. L. (1998). Refers to small-minded people in social research who make something so fun, so dreary. Also refers to small bites of Mt. Pleasant apples as in, "I just took a munch, Ken."

Oates, K. R., et al. (1994, September). Stability and change in outcomes for sexually abused children. *Journal of the American Academy of Child & Adolescent Psychiatry, 33,* 945–953.

Ricci, I. M. (1996). This comes from the Ritchie Valens song, *La Bamba,* when he says, off mike to the record producer, "My name is Ritchie, I'm Ritchie." The guy doing the label didn't hear accurately and when he wrote the name on the label, it came out, I. M. Ricci. That's what some guy in LA told me, anyway.

Rose, I. M. A. (1997). Someone who uses flowery language.

Rubin, A. (1989). *Research methods for social work.* Belmont, CA: Wadsworth.

Small, T. M., Brutish, F. P., & Surly, Q. E. D. (1996). The name of my first singing group and what it says of my first reference letter: Morley Glicken is Small, Brutish, & Surly.

Soprano, T. (1999). Refers to someone who sings. In the case of Tony Soprano, he sings to a psychiatrist, gets Prozac for his troubles, and has to go to sensitivity training every weekend as a condition of continuing on in his corporate America job designation: Chair of Human Subjects Enforcement, Northern New Jersey District.

Tilde. (1995). You all know that a tilde is the squiggly line over the letter "N" in the Spanish language. 1995 was an excellent year for Tildes in America.

U. S. Bureau of the Census. (1994). *Household and family characteristics: March 1994.* [Online]. Retrieved September 24, 2001 from the World Wide Web: http://www.census. gov/prod/1/pop/p20–483.pdf.

ADDITIONAL READINGS

Gottlieb, N., & Bombyk, M. (1987). Strategies for strengthening rural feminist research. *Affilia (Summer),* 22–35.

Mies, M. (1983). Toward a methodology for feminist research. In G. Bowles and R. Duelli-Klein (Eds.), *Theories of women's studies* (pp. 117–139). London: Routledge & Kegan Paul.

Miller, C., & Treitel, C. (1991). *Feminist research methods: An annotated bibliography.* New York: Greenwood.

Nielsen, J., & Bernstein, I. H. (1994). *Psychometric theory (3rd ed.).* New York: McGraw-Hill.

RECOMMENDED INTERNET SITES

The New Social Worker
    <http://www.socialworker.com>

Sociological Research Online
    <http://www.soc.surrey.ac.uk/socresonline/>

Human Subjects in Research Sites
    <www.psych.Bangor.ac.uk/deptpsych/ethics/humanresearch.html>

Social Science Information Gateway (SOSIG)
    <http://sosig.esrc.bris.ac.uk>

Web Resources for Educational Research and Evaluation
    <http://www.Stanford.edu/~davidf/webresources.html>

4 The Research Proposal

The Purpose of the Proposal

The purpose of a research proposal is to develop a plan that describes the way you intend to do an actual research study. You often need to prepare a research proposal for approval by your instructor before your study can begin. Much of what you write in a proposal can be used in the final report of your study, so it is not a wasted effort. In this chapter, we will consider how to construct a proposal that meets the requirements of your setting. That setting might be a class, a funding agency, an organization, an agency you plan to study, people you intend to evaluate, or any setting that first requires you to describe what you plan to do in your research study. Before anyone can approve a study for a classroom assignment or in any organization, they will want to see the proposal. The following content areas should be included in all research proposals.

The Content of the Proposal

The Problem

What problem or issue do you intend to study? Has your problem been studied before? If it has, why are you proposing to study it again? If it hasn't been studied before, what are your reasons for wanting to cover new ground? Can your study do justice to a new problem? Many times, previous studies have been done but not with a particular gender or ethnic group. One of my students wanted to study whether people receiving kidney dialysis actually followed medical advice. He wondered if they stayed on diets, refrained from alcohol use, and discontinued using harmful over-the-counter drugs and, in some cases, folk remedies. He found so many studies on this issue that it hardly seemed necessary to do a similar study again. But when my student, who is Mexican American, discovered that almost nothing on medical compliance and kidney dialysis had been done with Hispanic clients, and because he lived in a state with a very large Hispanic population, he now had excellent reasons for doing the study.

The Importance of the Problem

Why is it important that your study be done? You need to show that your study has relevance. In my graduate social work research classes, all proposals must pass this test. If they aren't relevant to some aspect of social work practice, the project isn't approved. Why is it important to know the compliance rates of Hispanics receiving kidney dialysis? For one thing, kidney dialysis is uncomfortable and expensive. If someone is consuming alcohol or not following their diet while on dialysis, their chances of maintaining a healthy life until they can get a kidney transplant may be poor. Bad habits before a kidney transplant suggest bad habits after the transplant. Why should a medical facility approve a costly and invasive procedure for someone who has ruined his or her own kidneys because of bad health habits and then is likely to ruin their new transplanted kidney? But what if poor compliance with medical directions is caused by a lack of good translators, or by confusing medical terms, or by any communication problem that, once resolved, might result in better medical compliance? If that's the case, lives can be saved. That's social relevance. Plus it's boring to do a study that isn't important to you or to someone else. As long as you're putting in the time and effort to do a study, you might as well do it on a subject that has social relevance.

Prior Research

What have other researchers done in the past that directly relates to the problem you intend to study? This is a key section of the proposal. It requires you to do an extensive review of the prior research on the subject you've chosen. By extensive I mean thorough, time-consuming, and complete. A weak literature review suggests a high likelihood that a study will be poorly done. If you lack the time or desire to investigate prior studies on your subject, will you put much energy into actually doing the study? Probably not. I've heard every excuse imaginable about why more information isn't provided in a literature review. None of the excuses are acceptable. With the Internet and with computerized literature searches, you just can't get away with a weak literature review. And remember, if you're testing a hypothesis (an educated and supportable prediction about the outcome of your study), the hypothesis has to be based on prior research studies available in the literature. One student told me that he couldn't find a single reference related to elder abuse. I went to the Internet and after five minutes found hundreds of references. The student smiled sheepishly and said he didn't know much about using the Internet. Well, duh! Find out, kiddo.

Your Methodology

How do you plan on doing the study? This is called your *methodology.* It includes sample size, research design, the instrument you plan to use, your paradigm, and your hypotheses. If the methodology for your study is weak, or if you fail to explain the reasons for the apparent weaknesses, you'll have trouble getting the proposal approved. Most student research projects have fairly limited and simple methodologies because of time constraints or because of difficulty in finding research subjects. You need to explain these difficulties in your methodology section and anticipate that the reader will want to know how these weaknesses might affect the results. Be honest. Don't try to manipulate people. They'll see right through it.

A student of mine doing a study on disclosure of AIDS by gay or bisexual Latino men to family members predicted a small sample size because he assumed that most Latino men with AIDS would be unwilling to discuss their illness with a researcher. He reasoned that most gay or bisexual men from traditional cultures have ambivalent feelings about their sexuality and believe that AIDS is a disease that might have been prevented had the victim not engaged in gay or bisexual sexual practices. He was correct. Using the entire AIDS network in Southern California and giving each subject $20 to do the interview, he ended up with only 20 subjects. This forced my student to take an extra six months to complete the project. It's difficult to argue with low sample size when subjects are unwilling to take part in a study.

The same is true of another former student who wanted to learn some specifics about male childhood sexual molestation. Because male abuse is significantly under-reported in the literature, she tried to get approval from three social agencies to do guided interviews with male victims and was turned down flat by all three due to confidentiality concerns. As an alternative approach, she was allowed to read files with names omitted at a local child welfare agency. She developed a protocol to guide her research and collected data from the files on the impact of sexual abuse on male clients. This is a secondary way of getting data and her study suffered because of it. The lack of permission on the part of the agencies, however, gave her no other choice. She had to report this in the methodology section of her proposal as a reason for not being able to do a more direct study using actual subjects.

What Is the Study About?

What do you think the outcome of your study will be? This is called a **hypothesis.** A hypothesis is an educated prediction of what the study will find. It is based on what similar studies have found. If you can't state a hypothesis because clear data are lacking in the research literature, you can always ask a **research question** or you can note the **research objectives** of the study. Let's consider how each of these three options might look using the AIDS issue and family disclosure as an example. Note that you can state a hypothesis in a neutral direction (also called a *null hypothesis*), or in a positive or a negative direction. Most serious researchers state a hypothesis in a neutral way to convey objectivity, and to tell the reader that they are making no predictions about the outcome of the study, because they are completely open to whatever the study finds. Examples of the kinds of hypotheses are:

1. **Null Hypothesis:** The disclosure rates of AIDS to family members by gay or bisexual Hispanic men will be no different than that for other ethnic or racial groups.
2. **Alternative Hypothesis (positive prediction):** The disclosure rates of AIDS to family members by gay or bisexual Hispanic men with AIDS will be lower than that of other ethnic or racial groups. (This may also be called a **one-tailed hypothesis.**)
3. **Alternative Hypothesis (negative prediction):** The disclosure rates of AIDS to family members by gay or bisexual Hispanic men will be higher than that of other ethnic or racial groups. (This may also be called a **one-tailed hypothesis.**)
4. **Alternative Hypothesis (a relationship but no direction):** The disclosure rates of AIDS to family members by gay or bisexual Hispanic men will be significant. (This is also called a **two-tailed hypothesis** because the researcher predicts a relationship but doesn't indicate if it will be positive or negative.)
5. **Research Question:** What is the disclosure rate of AIDS to family members among gay or bisexual Hispanic men?
6. **Research Objective:** The purpose of this study is to determine the disclosure rates of AIDS to family members by gay or bisexual Hispanic men.

Type-One and Type-Two Errors: When testing a hypothesis, we may incorrectly predict the outcome of the study and whether it will prove or disprove our hypothesis. A **Type-One Error** is said to occur when we reject the null hypothesis and conclude that there will be a relationship between variables when there won't be. A **Type-Two Error** occurs when we fail to reject the null hypothesis and predict that no relationship will exist when, in fact, one will exist.

The Relevance of the Study

What is the usefulness of the findings of the study? Another way of putting this is, so what? If you can't answer that question, you probably have a weak idea for your study. All findings have potentially important implications for social research. Often, the problem is that the researcher fails to see it. If Hispanic men with AIDS fail to tell their families about their illness, doesn't it say something about the way gay and bisexual men feel about their sexual orientation? And might it also assume a certain homophobia

on the part of families? Doesn't this suggest that we should work with Hispanic families by educating them about AIDS and by working toward re-
unification?

It's painful to think of people dying alone without their families because of a bias that may be related to a lack of knowledge. Shouldn't such
studies offer suggestions regarding the way a problem might be remedied?
I think so. Frequently, studies are done, data is analyzed and evaluated, and
the researcher completely misses the point about what the findings suggest.
Perhaps it's because the data aren't obvious, or maybe the researcher is
looking for other outcomes. This is an area in which seasoned social researchers might help you look carefully at your data and suggest alternative
outcomes that you may have missed.

Choosing a Topic for Your Research Proposal

Your first task in choosing a topic is to talk to people with expertise in
the subject area you intend to study. Also, look through recent back issues of journals in your general area of interest. Recently published articles often provide an overview of past research on a specific topic and
may suggest gaps in information. And for certain, surf the Internet to find
ideas that interest you. The Internet contains a vast array of information,
opinions, and generalized discussion on just about every topic you can
imagine. Most libraries today have an Internet connection that permits
very sophisticated searches for articles on such servers as EpscoHost and
PsycINFO. With a little work, you can access your university's Internet
system. Plus, there are Internet chat rooms on just about every topic
under the sun. People online in chat rooms can often be helpful in suggesting a variation on a topic you may want to study. Some servers provide forums to leave messages for anyone with knowledge about the
subject(s) you are interested in studying. The Internet is also a valuable
place to look for information available through public or governmental
sources. The public documents section in most libraries can also be very
helpful and includes reports commissioned through competitive grants by
city, county, state, and federal agencies. Also, consider looking at dissertation and thesis abstracts done by students to complete their Master and
Doctoral degree requirements.

One concern in selecting a topic is the availability of supportive data,
prior studies, and scholarly articles. If you have special access to an understudied population, you might also consider designing a study with that
population, keeping in mind that you may be breaking new ground and
that prior research is limited. One way to add to your literature review

when you honestly can't find prior research is to look for studies that are closely related to your subject but don't directly cover the same material. For example, students looking at the treatment of elderly Arab Americans by relatives in the home were unable to find many published sources. They were able, however, to find a small body of information on the same subject but it related to other ethnic groups. That material proved invaluable as they constructed their methodology and developed their working hypotheses.

Here are some additional ideas to help you select a research topic:

The Problem Touches You Personally

The problem might be something that touches you personally because of an experience you've had in your life. You might be familiar with abuse or domestic violence, for example, because of your professional work or because it has affected you directly. The primary constraint on choosing a topic that touches you personally is your ability to maintain objectivity. If the personal experience you've had makes you so angry or upset that you'd do anything to make certain that the outcome goes your way, you've lost the ability to be objective. Objectivity is a vital part of the scientific process. Without it, no one can possibly accept your findings.

The Problem Relates to an Agency Need

The problem you choose might relate to a need that an organization, church, or social agency has for a piece of research to give that organization a better understanding of a specific problem. The major drawback to this approach is that you may not find the topic interesting and you just may approach it with very limited enthusiasm. Given that you will be working on the proposal and the actual project for a while, you have to ask yourself if the topic will hold your attention. One of my students did a small piece of research on a shelter for women who had been abused by spouses or boyfriends. She used a depression inventory to determine if women entering the shelter had high levels of depression that were lowered after the women completed their time-limited stay in the shelter (six months). She found that levels of depression went down considerably after the shelter experience ended and tended to stay down when testing was repeated months after the subjects left the shelter. The shelter used my student's research to help obtain increased grant monies from funding sources. The added funding allowed the shelter to add additional workers so that more women and their children could leave abusive homes and live in safe and constructive environments. That's a good example of research done for an organization; one that had an exceptional outcome.

You Are Going on for a Doctorate

If you plan to go on for a doctorate, or if you're really interested in research and plan to work as a researcher after you graduate, you may want to consider a quantitative piece of research just to experience the process. Quantitative research is the most common form of research done for doctoral dissertations. Having the experience of using quantitative methodologies would be very helpful to you in your future studies. The topic you choose should probably be something very current that attracts people's attention. Violence in the workplace, school violence, and alcohol consumption among university students (hopefully that doesn't include you) are examples of very relevant research topics that might interest a doctoral admissions committee. Some graduate schools specialize in qualitative research or in specialized areas of inquiry such as addiction or violence. You should know this when you're considering which graduate school to attend and keep it in mind when you choose a research topic for your project.

Ethnic, Racial, or Gender Interests

If you have a strong ethnic, racial, or gender interest and have come upon a topic that begs to be studied but is really not a specific interest of yours, you may be motivated to do the study because the social change implications are great. This is, in fact, a very good example of why researchers would decide to use the critical theory paradigm. Two students of mine, not particularly interested in the residential treatment of female substance abusers, did a study on the length of stay in treatment of men versus women. They found that women stayed half as long in treatment as men did because of serious child care problems that forced women to leave treatment before they were ready. The student researchers noted that a simple change in the agency's philosophy, to allow children to be with their mothers while the mothers underwent residential care, strengthened treatment. However, they used the residential setting of substance abuse treatment as a way of showing how women are often unable to get needed help for serious problems because no one seems to remember that mothers have large child-rearing responsibilities, often with no one to help out in times of crisis.

The Methodology Outweighs the Problem

The actual topic or problem you choose to study may be secondary to gaining experience in using a certain type of methodology. Perhaps you would really like to develop competence using the constructivist paradigm but the topic to be studied isn't necessarily one that excites you. This may happen when a classmate has an idea for a study and wants you to be a partner in the study. It may also happen if your instructor, or someone doing a piece of research, asks you to help out and is willing to offer academic or scholarly publication credit.

Replicating Another Study

You may find a study that has already been done and because the findings are interesting, but need to be expanded, you may want to replicate the study. This underscores the need to do an in-depth literature review. By reading other pieces of research, you may find a subject, methodology, or design that lends itself to replication. The author of the original study may even help you replicate the study by giving you additional data or by letting you use copyrighted research instruments, free of charge. The added benefit of replicating a study is that much of the work has already been done. The problem formulation, much of the literature review, and the methodology have already been developed by the original researcher. The downside of replicating a study is that if the initial researcher proves to be uncooperative (this often happens when students are trying to replicate a study), the study may have unsolvable methodological problems that you aren't aware of, and your study may run into numerous difficulties that make completion of the study impossible.

Other Ideas

There are many other ways to pick topics including brain storming with your instructor, friends, other instructors, classmates, and co-workers. E-mailing developers of instruments to ask if they have ideas about how their instrument might be used with special subjects or topics might also be a good way to choose a research topic. Reading abstracts of prior studies in an area of interest might also be useful.

Issues to Consider When Choosing a Topic

Difficult Populations

Try not to design studies for difficult to reach populations unless you can first be certain of obtaining a sample. An example of a difficult population are the victims of child abuse or rape. It's very difficult to get people to discuss traumas they've experienced to strangers who may or may not respect confidentiality and who may respond in ways that are particularly insensitive to victims. I'm not saying that it's impossible. I am saying that it poses a number of practical problems that may be difficult to overcome.

Surveys

You need a very large population to do surveys. You may not have the resources to send out letters and develop questionnaires in large enough numbers to produce meaningful results. Surveys are also very time-consuming and expensive, and the number of respondents may be so low that nothing statistically meaningful can be obtained from the data.

Studies in Public Agencies

Be careful when designing studies that require approval of a public organization, particularly if research subjects are to be individually studied and politically sensitive subject matter is to be assessed. Public organizations often stonewall students by telling them that the proposal hasn't been approved because of the slowness of the bureaucratic process. The proposal, they may tell you, is stuck at the state level, or the committee to determine whether the study is acceptable hasn't met because of the illness of the chair. It's bunk. The local administrator of any public agency usually has the power to allow relevant research studies. The reason studies are often not allowed is the paranoia public officials have that researchers may discover something negative about the agency. None-the-less, delays of 6 to 8 months in receiving approval to do a research study in a public agency are not unusual in my experience. On the other hand, a simple phone call from someone who knows the administrator (your instructor, perhaps) might result in immediate approval. Such is the wonderful world of politics, favoritism, and personal agendas.

Overly Long Instruments

It's not wise to design instruments that require more than 10 minutes to complete. Subjects simply won't answer the questions, and you'll be left with incomplete data. Keep the instrument short, relevant (no fishing expeditions), and easy to understand. Don't use words like "attachment," "bonding," or "enmeshment." Real people in the real world think that these words convey something inappropriate and they'll refuse to complete the instrument. If you plan to do a study using a mailed instrument, expect very small response rates, perhaps less than 20 percent, and beware that many of the instruments might only be partially completed when returned.

Political Correctness

Be aware of the political implications of the proposed research as you design the study. It should go without saying that we live in a very politically charged society. Studies of women done by men are suspect. Studies of certain ethnic groups done by someone not of that ethnic group are often felt to be overly subjective or biased. I'm not telling you not to do politically sensitive studies, but I am saying that in the social sciences, there is a certain amount of legitimate criticism about the objectivity of such studies.

Human Subjects Problems

Use of certain groups (i.e., children, incarcerated felons, the mentally ill) may create human subjects problems. Think about these issues early in the development of your proposal, and make certain that you can get agency approval to conduct the research. Researchers can sometimes contact populations often thought to be inaccessible with some careful and logical planning. Don't go through the entire process of designing a study without considering ways of obtaining subjects who may pose human subjects concerns. One way to do this is to have agency approval to contact a certain population before you write the proposal. I encourage students to do this so that they do not spend needed energy writing a proposal that will never be approved because the population one hopes to study is unavailable or inaccessible.

Time Limitations

If you are under time constraints, be realistic about how much time it may take to complete a study. All proposals should have a schedule included with the dates on which certain aspects of the study are to be completed. Your instructor will probably give you feedback about how realistic your schedule is, but the best time for feedback is when you're developing the proposal and deciding on your methodology. Always factor in Glicken's Second Law of Time and Space Travel: "It always takes a heck of a lot more time to get there than you ever imagined."

An Adequate Literature Review

The idea for your research study may come from your personal experiences, prior work, and/or observations of social phenomena. These prior experiences should help direct your literature review, and they may be helpful in designing your study. Most researchers know that they will encounter problems similar to those experienced by other researchers. The best way to understand the problems you might encounter in a particular type of study is to look carefully at the literature.

In reviewing the literature, focus on a general issue such as abusive behavior, or narrow the focus of your search to a specific type of abuse, such as elder or child abuse. Look for interactions among the many variables that contribute to abusive behavior. For example, it might be relevant to study the relationship between elder abuse and child abuse to determine if adult children of child abusers are likely to abuse their own elderly parents. Once the problem has been narrowed down, consider an expanded literature review of research issues pertaining to your specific area of interest. This could include methodological concerns shared by other researchers, prior instruments used, human subjects problems, or discussions about the most appropriate way to gather information. Most journal articles discuss difficulties encountered during a study. You should read this as a cautionary note to guide your decision to study an issue that has caused other researchers problems. Here's a good behavioral thought to remember: The best predictor of future behavior is past behavior. If another researcher has encountered serious problems while studying a subject, it's very likely that you will too.

When reading the literature, you have to be very focused, which is to say that you need to know what you are looking for. Selecting articles at random with titles that sound promising will often require that you review literally hundreds of articles. That can be a time-consuming and frustrating experience. A better way to select articles is to look at titles and abstracts, those little summaries that usually come before the article begins. Abstracts can help you narrow your literature search. Try and search for literature that is relevant for each stage of the proposal. If your problem focus is on elder abuse, the first step may be to find out the amount of elder abuse in the United States and the ways in which elder abuse is defined and determined by adult protective service agencies. Step two might be to find out the socio-demographic characteristics of children who abuse their elderly parents. Step three could be to look for articles that show relationships between elder abuse and any aspect of the child-parent relationship that might explain why the elderly parent is being abused. Step four might be to search for appropriate ways of constructing useful methodologies. By dividing your literature search into stages, you can narrow the focus of each search and save time and energy.

Assuming that you will find one article that answers all of your questions is probably wishful thinking, although it happens from time to time. There may be books on elder abuse that answer many of your questions. The problem with using a book or two is that most books use reference material from other authors. When your instructor reads your literature review and finds out that you've only read one or two books, and that the authors you've quoted are those authors used by the author of yet another book, your instructor may be a bit concerned. It's permissible to use another person's interpretation of what an author says, but remember that in doing so, you will be getting and giving second-hand information. The information may also be incorrect. It's usually best to go to the original source and quote the author of that source rather than use a second- or third-hand source.

A Suggested Outline for the Proposal

Each person uses a proposal outline that works for him or her. This outline is one I like to use, but your instructor may suggest a different outline.

A. Title

The title indicates the nature of the study and should be brief, descriptive, and accurate. Many students use very long titles. This is not a good idea because the essence of the subject you're studying may get lost and, additionally, they can be boring. Here are two titles that I think qualify as good examples. "Job Satisfaction among Child Protective Service Workers," and "Parent Abuse among Adult Victims of Child Abuse."

B. Abstract

The abstract should be one paragraph of 100 to 150 words. It should be stated in the future tense because at this point you're still planning to do the study. The content should provide the problem statement, the research methodology, how the data will be analyzed, and the implications of the study for the social sciences. The following abstract containing 94 words is an example of an abstract with elder abuse as the topic:

> This study will evaluate the relationship between the abuse of elderly parents by their adult children and whether those children were abused by their own parents. The study will review the files of 500 abused elderly clients with open cases in an adult protective service agency. A research protocol originally designed by the researchers will be used to collect data. Frequencies, *chi*-squares and correlations will determine the relationship between elder abuse and child abuse. If the data show a significant relationship, extreme care should be made in placing elderly parents with adult children they have abused.

C. Text

1. Problem Statement (three to four pages)

The problem statement contains a specific description of the problem being studied, the need for the study, and the purpose(s) of the study. You should present brief background information about the problem and its significance for the social sciences. You should provide the paradigm you plan to use and the reasons you've chosen to use that specific paradigm. You should also include the hypotheses, research questions, or objectives guiding your study. Finally, you need to explain how the results of the study will have relevance for the social sciences. Using the elder abuse example, one important result of the study for the social sciences might be the recommendation not to place abusive parents with their adult victims.

2. Literature Review (ten to twelve pages)

The literature review is a summary of the literature directly related to your problem formulation and your proposed methodology. It should contain the number of sources consulted, the number of sources used, and the various ways you went about finding sources (Internet search, search of relevant abstracts, etc.). If I were preparing a concise summary of the literature on elder abuse, I would include enough evidence to indicate why elder abuse is a serious problem. Data are always a better way to prove this than testimony. For example, if I were to say that the rate of elder abuse in America is the highest in the world (I'm using this as an example, not as fact) and that the amount of elder abuse in the United States is fully four times that of the country with the next highest rate of elder abuse, I think you would be much more influenced by the data than if I were to quote a reliable source.

Continuing with my example of a literature review on elder abuse, I would include research evidence regarding the cause and impact of elder abuse as well as the major methodologies researchers have used to obtain this data. I would also include literature related to treatment programs designed to reduce abuse among caregivers. The literature section of the proposal should end with a summary statement that briefly reports your major findings and provides added support for the need to do the study and for the hypotheses, objectives or research questions used to guide the study.

3. Methodology Section (six to eight pages)

A. Purpose and Design of the Study

In this section of the proposal, you explain the purpose of your proposed study as well as the research paradigm, the reason for using the paradigm you've chosen, and the design of your study. You do this in more detail than in the problem formulation section. You also state your research question(s) and objectives and/or hypothesis(es). Using the elder abuse example again, I would choose a post-positivist paradigm utilizing an interview protocol with the caretakers and the elders who have been abused by their caretakers. My hypothesis would be: "The primary reason for elder abuse is the abuse by elderly parents of their adult caretakers when the adult caretakers were children." The material presented in the literature review should support your hypotheses.

B. Sampling

In this section, you describe the population you intend to sample (abused elderly and their caregivers) and the approach you plan to use to survey the sample. You also indicate the number of people in your sample and explain why that number is enough to prove or disprove your hypotheses. If there are limitations that impact the sampling process, note those limitations. For example:

> Forty abusive caretakers and forty abused elders will be interviewed in their homes thereby providing a 10 percent sample of the number of active cases in adult protective services of elder abuse in Isabella County, Michigan. The clients and their caretakers must take part in the sampling process as part of a court ordered arrangement providing caretakers with alternative punishments for their abusive behaviors. It isn't certain that elders will talk to the researchers out of concern that what they say may negatively affect their relationships with caretakers. We expect a good response rate from caretakers but a less positive response rate from the elderly clients, although caseworkers from Protective Services will be working with clients to encourage their participation.

C. Data Collection and Instruments

In this section, you describe your plan to collect data. If you are using an existing instrument, you present information regarding the validity, reliability, and cultural sensitivity of the instrument and identify the strengths and weaknesses of your data collection method and the instruments you plan to use. Go on to explain how you will address any weaknesses in the data collection process. If you have created your own instrument, explain why and how you created the instrument and your plans for pre-testing the instrument. Identify the strengths and limitations of your instrument. Describe how the data are to be gathered. Describe how long data collection will take, and explain who will be collecting the data. Suggest a possible schedule to guide your study using a realistic time frame. *If you are using someone else's instrument, remember that you must have the written permission of the developers of the instrument before using it. That written permission should be included in the appendix of the proposal.*

Here is an example of the discussion regarding the use of a research instrument:

> Forty abusive caretakers and forty abused elderly will be chosen at random from a list of 400 active cases of elder abuse with the Isabella County Adult Protective Services providing a 10 percent sample with a margin of error of plus or minus 4.5 percent. The Goldfarb Survey of Elder Abuse, an instrument used to understand the reason for elder abuse by caretakers, will be adminis-

tered. The Goldfarb has very high validity and reliability (provide that data). The abused elders living in their homes will also be interviewed using the CES-D instrument to measure depression. A critical incident interview protocol developed by the University of North Dakota Department of Human Development will also be used. Both instruments have high reliability and validity (give that data). The data from these instruments plus sociodemographic information about the subjects will be correlated to establish a profile of the characteristics of the abusers and the abused, and the possible causation of elder abuse.

D. Protection of Human Subjects

In Chapter 13, we will discuss the human subjects review process. Your proposal must describe how the confidentiality and anonymity of participants will be protected. All proposals that study people must include informed consent and debriefing statements. If an agency site is to be used, you must have the written consent of that agency included in your human subjects application. If you are using a copyrighted instrument, you must include the author's permission to use the instrument. If in doubt about the human subjects review application form and the way it should be completed, contact your instructor or the university human subjects review board chair before you submit the material. (A discussion of human subjects reviews and the typical forms required are provided in Chapter 13 in much more detail.)

Here is an example of what you might say regarding human subjects protection (but in more detail in your proposal:

> Application has been made to the university Institutional Review Board for human subjects approval. The application includes a completed form signed by my research instructor, an informed consent and debriefing statement, a copy of all instruments used with the approval of the authors to use them, and a summary of the design and sampling procedures used along with an approval form from Isabella County Adult Protective Services to conduct the research using a sample of clients with open cases of abuse in that agency.

E. Data Analysis

In this section, explain the way you intend to analyze the data. Include the statistical package you intend to use to run your statistics (SPSS for Windows, as an example), the statistics you intend to use, and why you intend to use them. You also need to explain how you intend to analyze open-ended questions and how you will deal with subjective information including information from focus groups. (See Chapter 6 for more details on open-ended questions and Chapters 11 and 12 for information related to statistics.)

The following is an example of how to write this section:

> SPSS for Windows will be used to analyze the data. Measures of central tendency, *chi*-squares, T-Tests, regressions analysis, and the ANOVA test for variance will be used to analyze the data. Open-ended questions will be evaluated using the content analysis techniques described by Glicken (2003).

F. References

References should follow the American Psychological Association (APA) format or the format required by your instructor. Normally, references come at the end of the proposal and before the appendices. They are listed in alphabetical order. Most researcher instructors expect a fair number of references showing breath and depth of the literature review. (See the discussion in Chapter 5 for more detail about the literature review and issues of breath and depth of scholarship.)

G. Appendix

Here you include instrument(s), debriefing and informed consent statements, any questions or scales you have created, and approval letters to conduct the research.

Constructivist Proposals

A constructivist study requires you to include some additional information in the proposal. You need to identify the initial group of people to be included in your study explaining how you will allow new members to join the group and how you will decide when the group has enough members (usually when new information is not being given). You also need to indicate the answers to the following questions:

1. What open-ended questions will be asked to develop major themes of the study?
2. How will the information gathered through open-ended questions be evaluated?
3. How will you report back to the initial group any major themes that evolve from your initial discussion?
4. What process for collecting data will emerge that will maintain the content of the initial round of discussions?
5. How will you report back to the group the procedures used in collecting data?
6. How will you control for the size of your sample, data collection, and conclusions that truly represent what your group has reported?
7. How will you make sure that you have correctly reported the stages of your study so that the reader has an audit trail to follow?

Critical Theory Studies

Because the critical theory paradigm does not have its own unique methodology, you can follow the outline that is most appropriate for your study. However, you must include a discussion of your philosophical and political views and how they relate to the study. You also need to explain how the findings will be used to further, or support, your political and philosophical views. Your literature review should include sources that further articulate your philosophical position and explain how they relate to the study. It's very important in critical theory proposals that you assure the reader of objectivity. One way to do this is to provide an independent review of your procedures, particularly your data collection approach and the analysis of your data. Another way to maintain objectivity in your discussion is to strive not to politicize the reason for doing the study and to use objective language in your proposal. You have an opportunity to use more emotional language when you discuss the implications of the study.

An Evaluation Protocol for Research Proposals

The following is an example of the way I evaluate the quality of a research proposal. I'm sure your instructor has his or her way of doing the same thing, but this may help you recognize the salient points instructors are looking for when evaluating a proposal.

I. Abstract and Title (5 points):   The title is clear, relevant, and appropriate. The abstract clearly indicates what you intend to do in the study and is consistent with the material presented in the following sections.

II. Problem Formulation (25 points):   A well-done problem formulation makes a strong case about why an existing problem needs to be studied. It presents prior research and data to support the need to study an existing problem. It clearly describes that aspect of the problem the researcher wishes to study and some good reasons why this is so. And finally, it briefly explains how the researcher hopes to approach the problem, methodologically, and describes the paradigm without going into the detail one would expect in the methodology section.

III. Literature Review (40 points):   A good literature review has covered some primary issues related to the study. It should include data on the severity of the problem in more detail than the problem formulation. It should present a number of prior studies of the problem and their methodologies and conclusions. There should be a sufficient number of references to let us believe that the issues related to the study have been covered in detail. About twenty-five or more references would be indicative of a well-done literature review at this point. When we finish reading the literature review, we should know a great deal about the problem to be studied.

IV. Methodology (30 points): A good methodology section includes clearly written research questions, hypotheses, or statements of purpose for doing the study that are consistent with the problem formulation. It should tell us about sampling, instrumentation, and the paradigm you intend to use in clear and concise language. The methodology section should suggest any problems you may encounter and how those problems or limitations may affect your study. And finally, it should also indicate the importance of the study and what the data might suggest regarding the social sciences and the social change process.

Summary

This chapter discusses the way to approach a research proposal and includes the format, outline, and areas of content to include in a proposal. Examples are given of the way to approach positivist and post-positivist proposals as well as alternative proposals including critical theory and constructivist proposals.

REVIEW QUESTIONS

1. The idea that a social researcher can be absolutely objective seems very unlikely. How would you be able to control your impulse to see that a study turns out the way you want it to when you are emotionally tied to the results?

2. The null hypothesis seems fine in medical or physical research, but in social research, shouldn't you have a pretty good idea of what the results will be from your literature review?

3. Isn't it a little tedious to suggest that a study must have tight controls and audit trails when the natural inclination of science is to permit great leaps of thought that suggest a less structured approach to inquiry?

4. Consider the problem formulation and how it guides your literature review and your methodology. Isn't it incorrect to think that the problem formulation is static and remains the same when, as you begin collecting and evaluating data, you discover that you've asked the wrong questions for the wrong reasons?

REFERENCES

Becker, H. S. (1998). *Tricks of the trade: How to think about research while you're doing it.* Chicago: University of Chicago Press.

Cook, J. A., & Fonow, M. M. (1990). Knowledge and women's interest: Issues of epistemology and methodology in feminist sociological research. In J. McCarl Nielsen (Ed.), *Feminist research methods* (pp. 69–93). Boulder, CO: Westview.

Duelli-Klein, R. (1983). How to do what we want to do: Thoughts about feminist methodology. In G. Bowles and R. Duelli-Klein (Eds.), *Theories in women's studies,* (pp. 88–104). London: Routledge & Kegan Paul.

Eichler, M. (1988). *Nonsexist research methods.* Boston: Allen & Unwin.

Glicken, M. (2003). *A simple guide to social research.* Boston: Allyn & Bacon.

Gorelick, S. (1991). Contradictions of feminist methodology. *Gender and Society, 5,* 459–477.

Keller, E. F. (1990). Gender and science. In J. McCarl Nielsen (Ed.), *Feminist research methods* (pp. 41–57). Boulder, CO: Westview.

Krathwohl, D. R. (1965). *How to prepare a research proposal.* Syracuse, NY: Syracuse University Press.

Moss, K. E. (1988). Writing research proposals. In J. R. Grinnell, Jr., (Ed.), *Social work research and evaluation* (pp. 429–445). Itasca, IL: Peacock.

Reinharz, S. (1992). *Feminist methods in social research.* New York: Oxford University Press.

Sandelowski, M., Holditch-Davis, D. H., & Harris, B. G. (1989). Artful design: Writing the proposal for research in the naturalistic paradigm. *Research in Nursing and Health, 12,* 77–84.

RECOMMENDED INTERNET SITES

PsycINFO
<http://www.apa.org/psycinfo>

Beginner's Guide to the Research Proposal
<http://www.ucalgary.ca/md/CAH/research/res_prop.htm>

Proposal Writer's Guide, University of Michigan
<http://www.research.umich.edu/research/proposals/proposal_dev/pwg/pwgpage.html>

The Literature Review: A Few Tips on Conducting It
<http://www.utoronto.ca/writing/litrev.html>

Resources for Proposal Writers, University of Wisconsin, Madison
<http://www.wisc.edu/writing/Handbook/handbook.html>

5 The Literature Review

Introduction

The literature review is the key section of any research project. It is also one of the most poorly done. Students often feel that a cursory review of the literature is all that is needed and that there is a limited number of studies available related to their research topic. Both assumptions are wrong. A limited review of the literature will probably tell you nothing about the subject, while a well-done literature review will answer the following questions: Is the study worth doing or has it been done so many times before that it's pointless to do it again? Is the research topic important or does the literature suggest that the problem chosen is no longer relevant because of the overwhelming weight of prior research findings? What methodologies do other researchers favor who have studied the problem? Is there sufficient literature to state a hypothesis or will you be left without the ability to predict the outcome of your study? Will your instructor be awed by the number of sources you've looked at and assimilated, or will he or she be bored, depressed, offended, amused, or just plain unmoved by your level of work? Bad literature reviews (too few sources reviewed and cited) often suggest a bad research report. But hey, you can always try to get away with a poorly done review, or you can consider this discussion I had with one of my research students:

Me: Five sources on the effectiveness of psychotherapy with child victims of sexual abuse? That seems pretty light.

Student: Dr. Glicken, I swear on the grave of The Viking God Thor that I looked at everything I could find and this is all there is.

Me: Did you look at . . . ? (Then I listed five independent sources the student would need to find before I would consider her literature review acceptable.)

Student: Well, I just don't have time to do that much work. I mean, after all, the course is only worth two credits.

Me: It won't take that much time, and don't you have a desire to do an in-depth review? I mean it *is* a pretty important subject, after all.

Student: No.

Me: Then get your lazy behind outta here and start acting like a serious student!

Well, that's not exactly what I said, but you get the idea. Someone who isn't willing to do an adequate literature search is also unlikely to put much effort into the research study. You can try to fool us old folks who are probably in the midst of academic senility and who never read anything you submit, or you can hunker down and work.

The Steps in Doing a Serious Literature Review

Let's assume that you have a topic for your study. You're trying to get as much information about the topic as possible to help develop your problem formulation and to expand the literature review section of your proposal. The suggestions that follow may help you do an excellent literature review.

Know Your Library

Go to the library at your school and find out what sources are available for a literature review. Don't be afraid to ask questions that show you don't know much about libraries. Librarians are accustomed to unfamiliarity with the library and are usually happy to explain the many ways that you can find information about your topic. But I have to also say that some library-phobic people have had scary experiences with librarians who don't want you in their library messing around with those neat stacks of books. Like the librarian back in North Dakota who used to glare at me for taking out books that she was secretly saving to give to her bully son who lived down the block so he could do well in school and ace me out of a scholarship to the North Dakota School for Alien Research, Brewery Sciences, and Junk Food Consumption. But that's another story.

Libraries often have tours or give classes to help people find source material. I recommend that you attend these classes and take the tours. In my research classes, we spend many hours in the library learning about on-line academic Internet servers to locate material. It is well worth the time spent as there are a large number of academic servers available on line. Some servers even provide full-length articles that you can download. I would guess that one could spend an entire day, or more, learning about all of the services available in our library. That may sound like a lot of time, but you could spend that much time walking around the stacks just spinning your wheels and looking at all the neat people who hang out in libraries. Ever notice how many really attractive people hang out in libraries? Well, you should. Going to a library beats going to a party any day because you meet so many really interesting, attractive, and intelligent people. People just like you, in fact. If I'm wrong about that, at least the magazines are pretty terrific.

Free Online Servers for Literature Searches

Almost all universities and colleges provide a free online service that, with a minimal amount of work, can be accessed from your home. The online servers such as EbscoHost and PscyINFO are free as long as you are a registered student. These services permit you to do many things. They allow you to do a search for a general subject or for a more specific subject. For example, let's assume that you're interested in finding out more about male abusive behavior, but that you are mainly concerned about abusive behavior among a younger population (ages 15 to 18 years). You can narrow your search to those age parameters. On some servers, you can eliminate non-academic sources such as newspaper or magazine articles. You can also see if the full text of an article is available in your library. If it isn't, you may be able to order the article through inter-library loan via an e-mail message. If the full article is available, you will be able to access the full text of the article (sometimes without tables or pictures), and you will also be able to e-mail the article back to your home computer so that you can download it there. Using a university online service saves a great deal of money because you don't have to spend time duplicating articles at the library and dealing with broken machines and coins that get lost in the great abyss of the duplicating wars. You can also find out if the article is available in full-text form in your own library and, you can learn where it is in the stacks. Walking through the stacks is good for your health, and you never know if, by chance, you'll meet some really great person with whom you will form a loving, tender, and emotionally satisfying bond, all of which you owe to me for making this suggestion in the first place. See, isn't research great?

The library at my former university, a university with fairly modest means for a state institution, had over 30 sub-servers on Ebscohost alone. To access library Internet servers from your home computer requires a fair amount of RAM (perhaps 32 megs) and a processor speed of at least 300 megahertz. And, of course, you need an Internet service provider (ISP) such as AOL, Earthlink, MSN, or any of the other national servers available. They normally charge about $20 a month for unlimited service. I recommend paying the extra few dollars and installing a high-speed cable connection through the same folks who bring you television cable and 150 channels of pure nothingness. Most national Internet companies also provide cable service. The cost for cable service is about $40 a month, or the approximate cost of a weekend shopping spree and dinner for two at The Brass Café in Mt. Pleasant, Michigan. Cable companies claim that their service is fifty times faster than non-cable Internet service accessed through your telephone line. If you have a non-cable connection now and try to access the Internet during peak hours, the process can be painfully slow, and many people complain about regularly being cut-off (bumped) from service. Whether you use normal service or cable, you need a good home computer. Make certain that you have a fast modem on your computer because it will allow you to use the Internet at enhanced speeds, even without cable.

If you're shopping for a computer, my advice is to take someone along who knows a lot about computers. The software that comes with the computer can also be very important. You need a good word processing program. A computer that comes with a statistical package to run data can save you many hours at the computer center. The three important technical terms to remember when purchasing a computer are *RAM, megahertz,* and *memory.* More RAM runs the computer more quickly. A higher number of *megahertzs* generally suggests how many programs the computer can handle in a fairly efficient way. *Memory* refers to the amount of information you can store on the hard drive. Most new computers come with CD burners that allow you to place the equivalent of many hundreds of floppy discs on one CD. If you're like me and you have unlabeled discs all over the place, you can spend hours searching for information. Sophisticated computers are very inexpensive these days. My advice is to buy a new computer and not a used one. Newer computers are infinitely faster to operate and have advanced features you will come to value.

Accessing Non-Library Servers from Home

Without going to the library server, you can use the services available on your home Internet server for certain types of literature searches. The same search engines you use to access computer dating services or to buy airline tickets online can provide good information that can help in your literature search. As with any Internet search, you have to experiment with keywords and you may need to search more than one company (Yahoo!, Netscape, Lycos, Infoseek, Google, etc.) to get the needed information. Much of what is provided by these searches is non-academic, fairly unreliable, and subjective. For those reasons, using general search engines can be somewhat unproductive for academic purposes, although even your home computer service permits you to access government agencies and departments, as well as some academic libraries. You may also discover very rich sources of data through websites that charge a nominal fee (perhaps $5 to $15 a month) for data searches on specific topics (mental health, criminal justice, demographic data, etc.). Not all fee-for-service data search websites are reliable, and you should find out about their reliability by asking people in your department. Remember to by-pass those websites that promise to write your research report for you. It's unethical, it constitutes plagiarism, and it can result in your getting dismissed from a university or college.

Good and Bad Sources

In an academic search, sources have an order of quality. They are presented below in highest to lowest quality.

Refereed Academic Journals

Information that comes from refereed scholarly journals publishing primarily empirical research are of the highest order. A refereed scholarly journal indicates that other professional readers and an editorial board consisting of scholars have reviewed and approved the article before publication. The review process often involves asking the author to do extensive revisions of the article and to include more detail regarding the methodology used. The average length of time between submitting a refereed article to a scholarly social science journal and having it published can be as long as two years. Many social scientists worry that by the time an article is published in a scholarly referred journal, the information is already dated. Academic journals are often published by universities. They might also be the flagship journal for professional organizations such as the American Sociological Association or the American Psychological Association.

Some examples of refereed academic journals are: *American Economic Review, Social Service Review,* and *The Journal of the American Medical Association.* Refereed scholarly journals usually present data and use language that is disciplined and includes the technical terms used in a specific field of study. You often have to understand the technical language of that field to read and understand the articles.

Academics have been taught to use a writing style that is often very abstract and heavily technical. One of the reasons I wrote this book was that many of my students could not understand the texts I had assigned—texts I consider to be superior, accurate, and comprehensive. There is a kind of orthodoxy among academics that empirically-based articles should use a language that is often undecipherable to the layperson or student. I think it's a harmful orthodoxy that only those very well versed in a field are able to read and understand the material. Social research should be comprehensible to everyone interested in the research. I'm gratified to see that in social work, an attempt has been made to write about serious issues in language that is very easily understandable to almost all readers. Alter and Adkins (2001), noting the decline in writing skills among graduate social work students, write, "Using a global writing assessment, the authors found that one-third of entering MSW students had inadequate writing skills, and only 57 percent of these took advantage of the writing assistance offered" (p. 493). This finding scares the dickens out of me, but it is written very clearly; no one can miss the fact that there are many graduate social work students who can't write well, or that the finding should cause concern among social work academics. Something really needs to be done to improve the writing skills of social workers. Consider the important reports social workers are expected to write: abuse and neglect reports that affect parental rights; reports on involuntary institutionalization; and custody reports favoring one parent over the other in a custody dispute. These are critical issues, and bad writing might lead to incorrect decisions by the courts that end up hurting people.

Let's compare the well-written work of Alter and Adkins (2001) with that of Goldfarb, Himmell, and Gadzooks (2001) who note, when covering the same material on writing:

> The Lambda Chi Alpha Omega test for hypersensitivity to tactile influences suggests an inability to conform to expected levels of modified use of vocabulary in a sample of 234 graduate social work students attending evening classes at the Jack Daniels Center for Exceptional Verbiage. Unfortunately, the subjects don't seek stimulation from the verbiage centers and the aggregate group members are lazy swine who should be forced into picking potatoes every fall to motivate better writing. (pp. 20, 657)

Well, okay, but you see what I mean. Academics are under the same pressures as students to write well. The purpose of research is to share information. If you, the reader, can't make sense out of the language in an article, trust me, the author is either hiding something, the review panel is overly impressed with abstract language, or the material really is too technical for you to fully understand and, perhaps, you should ask for help in deciphering it. Don't feel badly. Asking for help is essential to the research learning process.

Professional Journals

These journals may also be refereed and usually have an editorial board. The difference between them and refereed academic journals is that the articles are often somewhat less empirical (less statistical and experimental in nature) and may also include theoretical articles without any supporting data. The articles published in professional journals may also be summaries of other published articles. Professional journals are often published by a professional organization such as The National Association of Social Workers. They are usually more practitioner-oriented (written for people in the field who are non-academics and non-researchers) with emphasis less on scholarship and more on easy access to important information. As with most academic journals, the review process can prolong the publication process as much as two years. These journals can be very helpful, but are sometimes thought to be of a second level or tier in quality.

Journals Published by Commercial Publishers

Journals published by for-profit publishers are often viewed as third tier journals. They attract primarily practitioner readers and are often, but not always, more theoretical and less empirical. They are often on specific subjects such as domestic violence or child abuse and are usually published quarterly. They may also have a limited publication lifetime cycle of eight to ten editions, or less. Sometimes they may devote an entire edition to only one subject. Publisher journals also have a review process and an editorial board; it often takes up to two years after submitting the article for it to be published.

Books Published by Academic Presses

As with journals, not all books are equal in quality, but books published by university presses such as the University of Indiana Press often confine themselves to issues of an arcane (obscure) nature that might not attract a commercial for-profit publisher. Scholarly presses usually publish a limited number of books that undergo an extensive review process. This is not to say that books published by university presses are higher in quality than those published by for-profit publishers. It *is* to say that academic publishers often consider it their mission to publish books for a very limited readership interested in highly academic and scholarly information.

Books Published by For-Profit Publishing Companies

These books are usually contracted to authors by the editors of a publishing house after the editors do a review of a lengthy book proposal and some sample chapters. In addition, other academics are normally asked to review the book proposals and the sample chapters. Most editors base their willingness to offer a contract to the author on the recommendations in the reviews. Once the author completes writing the book, the entire book may be reviewed again by several different academics in the field who may suggest revisions or who may give the book such a negative review that the publisher decides not to publish it. This is a risk all writers face, and it can be very discouraging to spend a year or two, under contract, writing a book that is ultimately turned down by the publisher. The reason a book is turned down for publication can have little to do with its quality: Editors leave and new editors might not be interested in the book; and publishing houses merge or are sold and the new owners change the subject areas in which they publish. Many books published by commercial publishers may be somewhat (but not always) less scholarly if the publisher has mass-market sales in mind. This book on research and most textbooks are good examples of books published by for-profit publishers.

Magazines or Newspapers That Are Highly Regarded

Highly thought of newspapers and magazines include the *New York Times,* the *Christian Science Monitor,* the *New Yorker,* or *The Economist.* Although these newspapers and magazines are very good and generally have excellent news articles that interpret daily world events, they are sometimes less stringent in their reporting and articles can tend to be fairly short and superficial. Articles about drugs or new research on disease are sometimes misleading. It may be acceptable to use these sources, but generally, you should go to original sources for the information. Government documents, for example, are considered excellent sources for data. Newspaper and magazine reporters are not trained social scientists and may misinterpret data even in the best newspapers and magazines. This is not to say that academics don't do the same thing; they sometimes do. But the chances of that happening are less in a refereed scholarly journal than in highly regarded newspapers and journals because of the review process used in scholarly journals.

The Mainstream Popular Press

Most newspapers are poor sources for information. When researchers see them quoted a good deal, it's often a sign that the student has done a limited job of researching the issue. Additionally, the press tends to sensationalize many subjects of great importance, worrying less about accuracy and more about attracting readers. Newspapers get much more mileage out of sensationalizing news than calmly reporting it. For that reason, you need to go to the original source of information. Research demands that you be as objective as possible. Over-using local newspapers as source material suggests that you're less than serious about the issues you're reporting on. Why use them, anyway? It's just as easy to access hard statistical data through Internet searches.

The Sensational Press

This is your conscience speaking. It is not OK to use information about space aliens or two-headed monsters roaming through Central Park found in newspaper articles from papers with names like *The Tattler* or *The National Examiner*. While these publications may have juicy information about an actor's private taste for things that go bump in the night, serious researchers exclude these sources of information because they lack credibility. My guess is that if you use a story from one of the sensational newspapers, your instructor will be unimpressed, to say the least. So, unless the story is about space aliens landing in Grand Forks, North Dakota, on a foggy winter night in January when it was 40° below zero, which really happened (I was there and saw it), I'd suggest you stick to reliable academic sources.

Are Scholars So Smart? Do They Know Everything?

I'm inclined to say "yes" because I'm an academic and think of myself as a scholar, but the fact of the matter is that most data in the social sciences is generated by academics. And while the information may not always be sterling, you do have to credit the tough and tender academics who publish in journals that may not only pay them nothing, but often treat authors like dirt, sending rejection letters that make us want to tear our hearts out. Academic research is also usually reliable. Not always, but mostly. It can also be very sophisticated. So the answer to the original question is: Academics are like everyone else. We don't have a corner on intelligence or on information. Yet I would rather use an academic source because my sense is that it will be an honest and thoughtful effort. Always? No, of course not. Usually? Yes.

How to Judge a Well-Done Literature Review

We usually think of a well-done literature review as having both high quality and breadth. That is to say that your literature review must consider a large number (breadth) of high-quality sources from which you can draw information. The sources you include in your review should be current (within the last five years), although some older sources are always acceptable, particularly when they are considered classics or if they report data that are unique or have not been reported by other researchers. Be equitable in your literature review by including studies that are in disagreement with your hypothesis if they come from respectable sources. It is always considered good science to include information that challenges or contradicts your hypothesis. Using sources from other disciplines, if the study is related to your area, is also considered good science. Some professions are considered more empirical than others. Medicine, for example, is often thought to be more empirical in its approach to reporting on mental health issues. Social work research tends to be post-positivist or quasi-experimental. This is not to say that one profession has better research than another. It does suggest, however, that to provide breadth to your literature review, you should include sources from professions other than your own. Furthermore, most researchers tend to accept well-done, empirically-based studies as having a higher level of quality than non-empirical studies. Similarly, studies with large samples are thought to be of a somewhat higher caliber than those with smaller samples. You can certainly see that making a great deal out of a study with a sample size of five people may leave the consumer a little reluctant to accept the findings as either reliable or valid.

Unfortunately, this has frequently been done in the applied social sciences, particularly when a researcher is trying to understand an emotionally perplexing condition. Anorexia, for example, is a very challenging eating disorder. No one seems to have a good explanation for people (usually women) starving themselves to death. Several therapists running groups with five to ten anorexic patients who, in the course of group therapy, began to suspect sexual molestation as the culprit are not a good source of information. The numbers of clients treated are far too small for us to accept as generalizable, and the bias or lack of objectivity of the researchers may provide incorrect information. Imagine the harm done to patients and their families when a link to sexual molestation is implied with no hard data to support such a finding? These small-scale studies with five or ten subjects are common in the applied sciences. Don't make the mistake of assuming that a study done with such a small sample has much relevance, even when the research literature is limited.

Plagiarism

People have a tendency to get a little lazy when it comes to not using the words of another writer. Sometimes we forget to place quotes around a block of words, and sometimes we lift whole sections of someone's writing in another source and claim that it's ours. Well, we don't necessarily claim that it's ours, but we conveniently forget to note that it isn't. **Plagiarism** is considered cheating, and in most universities it is an offense punishable by dismissal. My experience in reading thousands of student papers is that plagiarism is rampant. Students want professors to see how "wise" they are, and it can become a real temptation for them not to substitute the wisdom and writing of a published author for their own clumsy and sometimes convoluted efforts.

There is another threat: Internet companies that sell papers on academic subjects or tailor papers for a specific use. It's a terrible temptation and one you must, in the words of Mrs. Ronald Reagan, "Just say no" to. Why? Because it's cheating and because the point of education is your learning how to do your own research. Now I'm talking as a therapist. If you cheat at school, you'll cheat on the job, and getting fired for cheating at work is something that will dog you forever. Trust me on this.

So here are the rules.

- Do your own writing. If you write badly, use the writing centers most universities provide to help students with writing problems. Have them look at your work and let them help you write better.
- Give people credit for what they've done. If you're taking a paragraph or even a sentence or two, from someone's published work, place the material in quotes and provide a citation that includes the name of the author, the title of the article, the publication it is in, the date of publication, and the page number.
- Follow the rules of whichever writing style you are using. Most social science teachers use APA style, so buy a stylebook from the bookstore, for heavens sake, and consult it whenever you're in doubt.
- Don't use the Internet term paper mills that some of you may be considering. Professors know the difference between student work and professional work. If you've gotten away with it once, then lucky for you. The next time you may not be so lucky.

The head librarian at my former university told me that a librarian checking the holdings on graduate research projects was curious about the title of a project because it seemed similar to one he had recently seen. It turned out that the research project was a verbatim copy of a professional monograph and the student had used it, title and all, in place of his own original work. Let's forget that the professor who approved it must have been asleep at the wheel. The librarian notified the dean of students who consulted the school attorney and the degree granted to the student was rescinded and the record was changed to show that the student was expelled for cheating. This meant that the student would be unable to apply for state licensure, and that if the dismissed student lied about the episode on any government job application and was hired, immediate termination would result upon discovery of the truth. Plagiarism has major consequences. If you think professors are always going to miss plagiarism, or that they only scan your paper or count the number of pages (I used to think that. As an undergraduate I'd write jokes in the middle of a paper until a professor called me in and told me how unfunny he thought it was), some instructor with strong feelings about plagiarism is going to walk into your life and rock your world. One of the things she'll do is request a review of past papers or drafts of the papers you've just submitted in which plagiarism is suspected. Checking the Internet for term paper mills is simple and finding your specific paper will be a breeze. She'll accuse you of plagiarism and you know what? She'll win. Instead of the school you're attending now, you'll be attending Territorial University in the Canadian Northwest Territories where in spring it's 20° below zero and in summer it's 200° above. And let's not forget the hungry polar bears and the wolves. Best of luck. Enjoy your stay.

Rather than considering plagiarism, you should consult with your instructor or people on your campus who can help you develop your research paper, and who understand the rules of literature searches, and can help you write well. As Susan Tschaburn, reference librarian at California State University, San Bernardino (1999) writes in her paper on plagiarism, "Many term papers available for sale on the Web are old and out-of-date."(p. 1) She goes on to add (and now I'm paraphrasing what she said and still giving her credit for the ideas) that instructors can help eliminate plagiarism by checking drafts of a student's work as it progresses. They can also ask that you bring in any portion of a published article, book, or monograph used in your paper. If your instructor isn't following a stringent set of rules that eliminates the possibility of plagiarism, it may encourage you to cheat. Don't! Now I quote a paragraph from Tschaburn taken from another source, Tom Rocklin (1996), in his article, "Downloadable Term Papers: What's a Prof to Do?" The paragraph is for professors, but it will be relevant to students as well.

> A student who hands in a plagiarized paper has not bought into the instructor's goals for a course. The plagiarist and the instructor are in an adversarial [sic] relationship. Somehow, the student has come to conclude that the goal is to "beat" the instructor, to fool the teacher . . . If we ask students to complete assignments of demonstrable value and offer to work with them as they complete their assignments, they are likely to join us in the educational enterprise we envision. (p. 1)

Locating Documents on the Web

Government Documents

- If you know the title of a document and you think it is distributed as part of a Federal Depository Library Program (FDLP), you can look at the *Catalog of U.S. Government Publications,* a monthly catalog that is on the Web and includes documents published from 1994 to the present. <www.access.gpo.gov/su_doc/locators/cgp>.
- If you believe the document you are looking for is part of the FDLP and that it might itself be on the Web, enter the FDLP website above, and search either by its title or by its subject.
- If you believe the information you are looking for is on a government agency website (e.g., The Department of Justice), but not formally sent into the FDLP, search Hotbot (<www.hotbot.com> maintained by

Lycos, Inc.). Use the advanced search option on Hotbot to limit your search by selecting the location/domain option.

- If you believe the source you're looking for is a technical report and you know the name of the government agency that sponsored the report, look at that agency's website. (For instance, The Department of Energy has an excellent report finder.) Agency websites can be located through the FDLP website above. (Thanks to Jill Vassilakos-Long, Government Documents Librarian at CSUSB, for help with the information on government documents.)

Full-Text Social Science Databases

Social Sciences

- Britannica Online
- EbscoHost
- I.D.E.A.L.
- JSTOR
- Lexis/Nexis Universe
- Project MUSE
- Wilson Web Social Science Index

Citations and Abstracts

General

- EbscoHost (selected full-text)
- Wilson OmniFile (selected full-text)
- Carl Uncover (citations)

Specialized

- Social Work Abstracts (citations and abstracts in social work)
- PsychINFO (citations and abstracts in psychology)
- Sociological Abstracts (citations and abstracts in sociology)
- Criminal Justice Abstracts (citations and abstracts in criminal justice)
- Lexis/Nexis (full-text law reviews)

Social Work

- Institute for the Advancement of Social Work Research
  The goal of this website is to enhance opportunities for social work research, including providing information on resources for funding

technical assistance and career development in social work research.

- National Association of Social Workers (NASW) <www.naswdc
  .org>
  This website includes a catalog of publications, the NASW Code of
  Ethics, accreditation information, links to job resources, and current
  issues in social work.

- Social Work and Social Service Website
  <Gwbweb.wustl.edu/websites.html>
  From the George Warren Brown School of Social Work, this site is
  broken down into 99 areas of interest.
- World Wide Web Resources for Social Workers
  <www.nyu.edu/social work/wwwrsw>
  This site organizes a huge number of links according to subject.

Summary

This chapter discussed the importance of the literature review in the research process. Suggestions were made regarding the best sources to use in
a literature review. Guidelines were offered to help students rank order the
quality of sources. The use of the Internet in literature searches was also
noted and several sites of special interest to social scientists were provided.
Rules governing plagiarism were discussed, and the reader was cautioned
to be very careful in using the verbatim responses of authors as their own
and in using the term paper mills available on the Internet. Plagiarism is a
serious problem and not a few students have found themselves to be in serious academic difficulty because the line between their work and that of
someone else has become blurred. A good literature review is essential to
any research project and will suggest to your instructor the potential level
of quality of your study.

REVIEW QUESTIONS

1. There is a suggestion that the Internet is the fastest way to access information
   necessary to your literature review. In a way, doesn't that make most of us less
   likely to use conventional libraries?

2. Isn't it possible that a literature review may be very well done but the project
   doesn't take advantage of it? How might we ensure that the material in the
   literature review is used in a wise and productive way?

3. The argument is sometimes made that not all students know or understand
   the rules of plagiarism and that they plagiarize without any intent to deceive.

How do you respond to this notion that plagiarism is not always done with malevolent intent?

4. How do we know that the information obtained on the Internet, even if it comes from a good source, is accurate? Isn't it possible that the people doing Internet summaries make substantial mistakes?

REFERENCES

Alter, C. & Adkins, C. (2001). Improving the writing skills of social work students. *Journal of Social Work Education, 37(3):* 493–505.

Bakanic, V., McPhail, C., & Simon, R. (1987). The manuscript review and decision-making process. *American Sociological Review, 52,* 631–642.

Bakanic, V., McPhail, C., & Simon, R. (1989). Mixed messages: Referees' comments on the manuscripts they review. *Sociological Quarterly, 30,* 639–654.

Beasley, D. (1988). *How to use a research library.* New York: Oxford University Press.

Goldfarb, Himmell, & Gadzooks. (2000). The firm handling the defense of kosher bagels in Mt. Pleasant, Michigan. The case involves whether it's kosher to put chocolate chips in a bagel, or, for that matter, if it is even civilized.

Rocklin, T. (1996). *Downloadable term papers: What's a prof to do?* [Online]. Retrieved December 29, 2001 from the World Wide Web: <http://www.uiowa.edu/~centeach/resources/ideas/term-paper-download.html>.

Tschabrun, S. (1999, Fall). Plagiarism: Internet style. *John M. Pfau Library Newsletter,* 1–2. [Online]. Retrieved December 31, 2001 on the World Wide Web. http://www.lib.csusb.edu.

RECOMMENDED INTERNET SITES

Academic Writing: Reviews of Literature—University of Wisconsin Madison
   <http://www.wisc.edu/writing/Handbook/ReviewofLiterature.html>

Writing a Psychology Literature Review—University of Washington
   <http://depts.washington.edu/psywc/handouts/litrev.html>

Writing a Literature Review—Columbia University
   <http://www.columbia.edu/~cbf11/lit.html>

Checklist of Sources for a Social Work Literature Review—California State University, Stanislaus
   <http://wwwlibrary.csustan.edu/lboyer/socwork/sw_checklist.htm>

Resources for Graduate Student Writers—University of Michigan
   <http://www.lsa.umich.edu/swc/grad/resources.html>

6 Using Instruments to Measure Behavior

An instrument in research is a tool, generally a questionnaire, to measure behavior, values, or opinions. You can use an instrument created by others that has good validity and reliability (as long as you have the permission of the research instrument's author, or it is available to use without permission and is said to exist in the "public domain"). You can also create your own instrument. The benefit of using a standardized instrument is that its author has already resolved validity and reliability issues. Data are available to tell us whether the test measures what it is meant to measure (**validity**) and whether, once having taken the instrument, subjects are likely to receive the same scores on the instrument if they take it repeatedly (**reliability**). However, many new researchers like the idea of developing their own research instrument because it provides a valuable experience they might not otherwise get using an established instrument. Furthermore, a newly-created instrument is tailored to the specifics of a study while an established instrument may not have been developed to test the issues you have in mind. I always encourage new researchers to create their own instruments, although they can often use their own instrument along with one that has already been created, just to be on the safe side. Let's first consider the conditions necessary for creating your own instrument.

Creating Your Own Instrument

In general, the following steps are used when creating an instrument for a research study:

Make the Questions Relevant

The questions you ask should be relevant to the issues you want to measure. No fishing expeditions (questions that are interesting but have no real relevance). You can determine which questions to ask by looking at other instruments measuring similar issues and by doing an in-depth literature review to determine the important attributes you intend to measure. For example, in the area of work satisfaction, most instruments ask questions related to satisfaction with the work itself, co-workers, the supervisor, promotional opportunities, and the salary. You may want to ask other questions related to socio-demographic issues (age, ethnicity, level of education, etc.) to find out if there are links between scores on a job-satisfaction instrument and certain socio-demographic factors. Your job satisfaction measure should ask questions consistent with what the literature considers important in the measurement of job satisfaction. This isn't necessarily an easy task, because the literature on job satisfaction is rife with disagreement about what actually constitutes job satisfaction. To navigate your way through the maze of contradictory beliefs and findings, do a **meta-analysis** of the available information. In a meta-analysis, you consult the primary literature on job satisfaction noting the areas of agreement that seem to persist through almost all of the articles and studies you read. In this way, you can be fairly confident that the questions you ask on your instrument are germane (relevant) to your study of job satisfaction.

Ask One Question at a Time

Always remember to ask only one question at a time. Some researchers make the mistake of packing three questions into one. This makes it impossible for the respondent to know exactly how to answer the question. Here's an example from a student satisfaction scale I recently saw: "My field instructor listens, provides feedback and, when necessary, acts on my concerns about my learning experience in an agency." Which of these three issues is the person responding to: listening, providing feedback, or acting on concerns? This single question is actually three questions measuring three different behaviors. I had to take these and other badly-worded questions to a university faculty senate meeting for approval. I was substituting for a colleague who couldn't make the meeting. Forty smart professors skewered me for the questionnaire that violated every rule of questionnaire construction. My response was: "I'll encourage my colleague to attend my research lectures and to read the book I am writing." Be sure you don't make the mistake my colleague did. It's maddening for the respondent. Most people stop completing an instrument if there are too many questions of this sort.

Pre-Test Your Instrument

Preview the instrument for language. This is also called conducting a **pre-test.** Using ten to fifteen people, ask them if the language is clear and whether they understand the questions you are asking. Some people use English professors or high-level professionals familiar with the problem they are trying to measure for the pre-test. They might also use a sample of people similar to those who are most likely to complete the instrument. When constructing an instrument, try to use language that is clearly understandable by the least able among us. A sixth-grade reading level is often thought to be the standard for most instruments. Anything requiring a higher level of reading may not be understandable to many subjects. If an instrument is intended for a non-English-speaking population, the instrument should be translated into the specific language and pre-tested by a sample of people speaking that language. Many instruments intended for a Latino population have already been translated into Spanish and have been tested for validity and reliability with a Spanish-speaking population. The CES-D, a measure of depression included in the next chapter, is an example. The pre-test should be used to weed out poorly worded questions and to simplify the directions for using the instrument. If the directions on the instrument are unclear, you can bet that people will either not answer all of the questions or will answer them incorrectly.

For years, a university I worked for asked references to rate candidates applying for admission to a school of social work using a five-point Likert Scale. (The scale went from one to five with one being the highest and five being the lowest rating.) Guess what? Even though the directions were clear, most people thought that the higher scores meant a higher rating. Guess how many references incorrectly rated candidates? Lots of them, even though the directions were pretty clear. We changed the rating scale to make five the highest score, and guess what? No more problems. Amazing! Your instrument must take into consideration the way people ordinarily organize information. For most of us, ratings begin with a low number and continue on to the highest number. When confusion like this exists, even though the directions are clear, take the confusion as a sign that not all people read the directions and, given that reality, will probably respond in ways that are familiar to them.

Test Your Instrument for Validity and Reliability

A serious weakness in creating and using your own instrument is that it is neither reliable (provides consistent responses over time for each test-taker) nor valid (measures what it is intended to measure). The problem this raises is that your findings might be interesting, but because the instrument is neither valid nor reliable, the instrument fails to meet the rigorous expectations of a well-developed instrument. This can call into question the usefulness of the data you've collected. However, a self-developed instrument can give you some limited but interesting findings which may help you develop a more sophisticated instrument in the future. Validity and reliability issues are important concerns even in more sophisticated instruments.

One way to determine whether your instrument is well done is to test it against other valid and reliable instruments. For example, if you create an instrument to measure job burnout, one way to determine whether it is a good instrument is to see how people do on an established instrument. By running appropriate statistical analysis, you can compare the validity of your instrument against one already in use. If the scores are similar, you have a better sense that the instrument *may* be valid. Note that you haven't as yet determined if the instrument *is* reliable. The question then becomes, "Why not use the valid and reliable instrument already in use?" And the answer is, it's a darn good question to ask. One good answer is that the instruments available for use may have validity and reliability scores that aren't terribly impressive. Another good answer is that available instruments fail to measure the unique aspects of behavior that you're interested in studying. Have you ever seen an instrument to measure the experiences of someone who claims to have had an encounter with aliens? Neither have I. I suppose you could give subjects a lie detector test, but what if they pass? When you want to study something with a sparse to non-existent literature, you may need to create your own instrument. If I were creating an alien encounter instrument, my first question would probably be: Describe the food you were given during your time on the space ship. If the answer sounded strangely like a Big Mac or a double crusted, cheese filled pizza with pepperoni and North Dakota anchovies . . . bzzzzzzz . . . no encounter with aliens of the third kind. If the answer sounds disgusting and doesn't describe any food you'd ever want to eat, then maybe the person really *did* have an encounter with aliens. Of course, they may also have eaten my mother's cooking which, according to my brother, was so bad that to this day, whenever he sees a sign over a restaurant that says "Just like mom's cooking" or "Homemade cooking," he has an anxiety attack and rushes on to another restaurant. Mom on a space ship? Yeah, it's possible.

Decide on the Construction of the Scales

Decide if you're going to use **open-ended** or **closed-ended** questions. An open-ended question permits the respondent to answer the question in their own words. A closed-ended question gives the respondent possible choices. The most common closed-ended scale is the Likert Scale, one you may be familiar with. It gives people a range of choices, usually from one to five or one to seven choices with a high-end and a low-end choice. Open-ended questions don't give the respondents an option when answering and require the respondent to think for him- or herself. Open-ended questions can sometimes be confusing for the respondent who may not know the answer, or perhaps knows the answer but doesn't want to tell you because it's embarrassing or possibly socially undesirable. Asking someone to fill out an open-ended question considering attitudes toward race, gender, or ethnicity might find people choosing the most socially desirable, but least honest response. This is called responding with a **socially**

desirable answer. Open-ended questions also require the researcher to do a content analysis and categorize answers so the data can be entered into the computer. Although open-ended questions tend to yield answers on a questionnaire that may be unanticipated, they sometimes discourage people from completing the instrument because of the time it takes to write the answer.

Likert Scales are good if you have some idea about what the potential answer to a question might be. You might be able to develop a useable Likert Scale if you first used open-ended questions with a small sample of respondents. From their responses, you could create questions for a Likert Scale. At the end of each question on a Likert Scale, you might leave space for open-ended answers to provide more subjective information. Many researchers end each question on a Likert Scale with the ubiquitous question, "Other?" as an opportunity to provide additional information.

Staying with the example of worker burnout, let's see what an open-ended and closed-ended question might each look like.

Examples of Open-Ended and Closed-Ended Questions

An open-ended question: I would describe my level of burnout at work as follows:_____
A closed-ended question using a five-point Likert Scale: The following answer best describes my level of burnout at work:

1. My level of burnout is almost non-existent.
2. My level of burnout is below average for my work setting.
3. My level of burnout is about average for my work setting.
4. My level of burnout is higher than I would like it to be.
5. My level of burnout is extremely high.

Most researchers use a five- to seven-point Likert Scale. It's best to use choices on the Likert Scale that have very precise answers. For example, we can ask someone how often they drink alcohol and the answers provided on an instrument might be:

1. Very often
2. Often
3. Sometimes
4. Hardly at all
5. Never

However, these answers tell us nothing, because everyone's definition of alcohol use (frequency) is different. A choice of "Drinking Often" on the Likert Scale might mean once a week for one person, while for another person, it might mean every day. A better way to get specific answers is to give response options that are related to a specified period of time and an amount of alcohol consumed. Heavy drinkers are often unrealistic when they report whether they're drinking too much. That's why we need to give them choices that accurately measure alcohol usage. As an example, you might ask: "During the past week, how much alcohol did you consume?" The answers you provide might be:

1. A quart or more of alcohol a day
2. A half quart a day
3. A fourth of a quart a day
4. An eighth of a quart a day
5. less than an eighth of a quart a day
6. An occasional drink during the week but far less than is indicated here
7. I didn't consume any alcohol during the week.

When using this approach, you also need to define the amount of alcohol consumed. You might want to do it this way: "In completing this questionnaire on alcohol consumption, use the following conversion scale: 1 ounce of alcohol equals 1 beer, 4 ounces of wine, or 1/2 shot of hard liquor." While this is crude, it better helps you understand the actual amount and frequency of the drinking.

On a five-point scale, the number three is a neutral response. However, some researchers prefer to use a four-point Likert scale without a neutral response. Their reasoning is that people should be forced to answer the question rather than avoid it by giving a neutral response. The argument against using a four-point scale is that people might not answer the question at all if they're forced to take a position, or if they really *do* feel neutrally about the answer.

Other Options

You are not limited in using open-ended questions or Likert Scales when creating an instrument. You can use vignettes (short descriptions of a situation) with directed questions; scenarios with any combination of questions; questions that force the respondent to make specific choices, as in yes/no questions; or any combination of creative ways of obtaining information from respondents. You can ask the respondent to create his or her own questions as is the case in Delphi Studies, or you can use facial expressions as a way to measure depression and anxiety levels. (Various models are available from The National Institute of Mental Health.) Some researchers have even developed ways of measuring bigotry levels by showing research subjects pictures of individuals from one ethnic or racial group kissing a person of another racial or ethnic group, and then comparing the subject's facial expressions to facial expressions of known bigots responding to the same pictures. There is no limit to the number of creative ways you can develop instruments. Chapter 7 includes examples of four instruments, but researchers are not limited in the way they collect information as long as validity and reliability issues are resolved.

Questions to Guide an Interview

If you use a guided interview to collect information (this is a form of instrument), remember that it's necessary to have all questions completed before you begin the interviews. If you use different questions with each respondent, it will be impossible for you to make any sense out of the information. You'll have numerous responses, to be sure, but each response will be to a different question and you will be unable to effectively categorize the data. Also remember that once having asked the question, you have the ability to go below the surface to get a more accurate or complete answer. Herzberg (1966), a writer on job satisfaction, said that before you can get an accurate answer to the question, "Are you happy at work?" you must go seven layers below the first answer. "Are you happy with your job?" he might ask a worker. "Sure," might be the response. "Are you really happy with your job?" he might ask. The next answer might be, "Well, most of the time." The process might continue on until the worker admits that he isn't happy at all, but that it's the only thing he can do given his age, level of experience, and education. In fact, in the book *Work in America* (1973), it was said that questions regarding work satisfaction were felt to elicit such unreliable and superficial responses that it was necessary to finally ask, "Is this a job you would like your children to do?" That specific question, according to the book, would probably elicit the most honest measure of job satisfaction.

One problem with personal interviews is the length of time they take. Another problem is one of accurately collecting the data. To overcome the first problem, some people use focus groups of 10 to 15 people who are interviewed in a small group using guided questions and consensus statements (statements that summarize what most respondents feel and think). The researcher might also use an audio or video machine to record the answers, or they might have an assistant to write the answers down. Several of our students videotaped focus groups who were asked guided questions. The students later analyzed the tapes for content. There are even sophisticated ways of evaluating affect (the non-verbal emotional responses of group members) in addition to determining what the group members verbally say about an issue. You may want to read any number of books about focus groups and guided interviews if you decide to use this approach. Suggested books on the use of focus groups are in the reference section at the end of this chapter.

Choosing an Instrument Developed by Others

It makes a lot of sense to seek out and use instruments that have been developed by others. Issues related to validity and reliability have probably been resolved, and the directions for using the instrument are most likely clearly stated so that pre-testing is not necessary. If you choose to use an instrument created by someone else, the following are some guidelines:

The Preference for a Valid and Reliable Instrument

Obviously, it's best to find an instrument that has already been developed and is valid (measures what it's suppose to measure) and that when taken again and again by the same person, usually results in the same answers (is said to be reliable). Some researchers believe that developing an instrument is a good skill for students to have, because it helps them understand the pitfalls and the joys of instrument construction and leads to more learning.

A primary reason for using an instrument is to determine associations or relationships between the answers on the instrument and certain socio-demographic characteristics. Obviously, the better the instrument the more accurate the associations or relationships will be between the scores on the instrument and socio-demographic variables. On a job satisfaction measure, for example, it might be very interesting to determine how women and men differ in their degree of job satisfaction. The same might be said of race/ethnicity. The workplace is very diverse. Having certain groups of people unhappy at work may lead to low productivity and organizational turmoil. The more valid and reliable the instrument, the safer it is to say that such relationships, or associations, do, in fact, exist.

Reliability and validity are very important issues to consider when selecting an instrument. A high degree of validity is achieved when the instrument measures what it is intended to measure. Validity is determined by pegging the instrument to some behavior. For example, a job satisfaction instrument, if it is valid, should correlate well high productivity, low turnover, low levels of absenteeism, and behaviors we associate with productive and satisfied workers. A job satisfaction instrument that finds very high job satisfaction in an organization with a significant degree of absenteeism, theft, turnover, and low productivity is obviously not doing the job it is intended to do and fails the validity test. A good validity score should be above .85 on a measure of the relationship between what the instrument is designed to measure and whether or not it does. A score of .85 on a scale of −1.00 to +1.00 suggests that the relationship between a score on the instrument and the actual behavior being measured (job satisfaction, perhaps) is fairly strong. While a score of +1.00 represents a perfect relationship, in the real world of social research finding a perfect relationship is as unlikely as finding a perfect relationship between people who are intimate. It would be nice to think that it might happen but, usually, there are enough problems in the study to reduce a perfect relationship to one that is very good. The same thing can probably be said about relationships of intimacy. If you have a relationship that is absolutely perfect at the + 1.00 level, write me immediately for a free bushel of Mt. Pleasant apples.

Reliability is concerned with whether the respondent chooses the same answers each time he or she retakes the instrument. Wide fluctuations in scores over a short period of time on the same instrument make us wonder if the instrument is useful. To deal with reliability issues, many instruments have reliability checks that ask the same question three or four times in slightly different ways. To establish reliability, instrument developers give the same instrument to the same population of respondents over a period of time. Reliability should remain at a .90 level or better for the instrument to "pass." In other words, people should respond to the same questions the same way almost all of the time. If you ask someone whether they're happy at work on Monday and they tell you they're very happy but by Friday they're very unhappy, you should immediately think that the instrument has poor reliability; there is something in the construction of the questions that doesn't lend itself to consistency over time.

If you provide an experimental input and the post-test score shows gain and a week later that gain is lost, it might be a reliability issue or it could be what is known in research as the **Halo Effect.** The halo effect is the tendency to respond positively to an experimental input, but only for a short period of time and until the "glow" of the experience wears off. No real change has taken place at all. Sensitivity groups, used often in the 1970s to increase organizational cohesion, are perfect examples of the halo effect. When satisfaction with a group experience was measured at the end of the experience, it was normally very high. Within a short period of time, however, people could see that little actual change had taken place at work and their level of satisfaction not only decreased but was often lower than it was before the group experience. This is one reason why you seldom hear about sensitivity groups being used to increase organizational productivity. They don't seem to be terribly effective and sometimes they actually do harm.

Obviously, it is better to use a reliable and valid instrument, if possible. Many valid and reliable instruments are free or are discounted to students, but some creators of instruments may charge a fee. If you want to use an instrument created by someone else, you must first get his or her permission to do so. If you don't, your study will not be given human subjects approval. Doing a study without human subjects approval means that if you are sued for any reason, the university or whoever has responsibility for your research won't back you up, and you could face a liability process that could be very costly and damaging. It's best to start looking for a good instrument as soon as you begin developing your problem formulation, because it can be a tedious and time-consuming process to find the right one. If you can't find a good instrument, your results may be compromised. You may want to think twice about a problem that doesn't lend itself well to an established instrument. Some students find three or four different instruments and use questions from each instrument that have good validity and reliability scores. They then paraphrase each question so that it reads somewhat differently from the original. But I caution you against doing this because it can be a violation of the copyright laws. It's best to get permission from the developers of the instrument first. The Internet is a good way to find instruments and to contact the developers. Use of *Psychological Abstracts* is another way. Most of your research instructors will be happy to contact the developers of the instrument and assure them that you are a student, if a student discount is offered.

Problems with Meaningful Relationships

If you are using an established instrument to measure something it wasn't intended to measure, you will have problems showing meaningful links, associations, or relationships among variables. Using an example from the last chapter, attachment disorder is a concept suggesting that the origin of unhappiness in some people is the lack of bonding between their parents or adult caretakers. Poor attachment to parents might be caused by abusive behavior, divorce, or any number of possible reasons. Let's assume that we find an attachment disorder instrument that was developed solely for the purpose of establishing relationships between attachment problems and eating disorders. However, you want to use the same instrument to help determine if adults who are abusive with their own children tend to have attachment problems with their parents. The questions on the original attachment disorder instrument were developed with eating disorders in mind. The validity and reliability data were determined by using a group of people with eating disorders. The questions were **normed** (developed) with eating disorders in mind. Using that specific instrument to find a relationship between poor attachment to parents and current abusive behavior as an adult might result in a relationship between the two variables, but that relationship would be erroneous (the word *spurious* is used in the literature to describe the relationship). The reason the relationship is spurious is because an instrument developed to measure one behavior for one reason is not generally applicable to another behavior or for another reason. Consequently, the findings would not be considered meaningful.

Lack of Data Generated by the Instrument

An instrument may have good validity and reliability, but it may not have been developed using a very large or diverse population of respondents. Consequently, it is difficult to use data derived from that instrument because too few people have actually used the instrument to develop a normal distribution of scores. The same problem can occur when using an instrument that has not been normed to include certain ethnic, racial, or socio-economic groups. Let's take, as an example, the use of a depression scale that has been normed for Caucasian college students but will be used with a group of ethnically and racially diverse students. On a scale of 0 to 30, depression for Caucasian students begins at 15 and goes higher until it reaches 30. A score of 30 for this group suggests severe depression requiring hospitalization. We know this because we have developed validity and reliability data for Caucasian college students. Would an African American or Asian American student receiving a score higher than 15 also be considered depressed? There is no way of knowing, because the test was developed using only Caucasian students to get normative data. Consequently, we would have no way of knowing what a meaningful depression score might be for any group other than Caucasian students. The instrument would be inappropriate for use with a diverse college population.

Validity of the Instrument

When we want to know whether an instrument we're using actually measures what it is intended to measure, we look at its validity. There are six types of validity issues related to determining the validity of an instrument. Let's briefly consider each one.

   1. **Content Validity:** This type of validity refers to whether the questions asked on your instrument provide an accurate range of questions to cover the issues you are trying to measure. Content validity means that every question you ask on your instrument is directly related to the major issue of concern. If you're trying to devise a measure of depression, then each question must be directly related to some aspect of depression. (No fishing expeditions or questions that have no real relevance to the study but are sort of interesting are allowed.) A good question on a depression scale asks whether the respondent has missed work or school because of feelings

of depression. A bad question asks whether the depression has resulted in diminished interest in baseball. The second question is irrelevant. Many people have diminished interest in baseball, but it doesn't mean that they are depressed, only wise.

2. Face Validity: Face validity asks whether a question appears, on the face of it, to be valid. Face validity has more to do with the respondent's reaction to an instrument than to another researcher's evaluation of the instrument's validity. If the respondent doesn't think a question is logical and meaningful (that it has face validity), he or she probably won't answer the question, or the answer might be untruthful.

3. Criterion Validity: This type of validity compares the questions asked on the instrument to some established normative measure. For example, in trying to measure the effectiveness of a selection process that was used to accept students into a very competitive educational program such as law or medicine, any instrument devised to predict success that is used as a screening device ultimately needs to look at the student's grade point average once the student is admitted to the program as one measure of criterion validity. Unfortunately, this example of criterion validity avoids the reality that students who do well academically do not always end up being the best doctors or lawyers, although, for the most part, we believe that there is a relationship between how well one does on entry exams, one's GPA in an academic setting, and one's ultimate success in work. A criticism of most standardized tests for admission into professional schools is that they are unrelated to the ultimate task performed by that profession. While that sounds good, in reality would you like to have surgery done by a physician who failed his human biology courses and ranked in the bottom third on his surgical residency? Not me. Although we may not know for a fact that a student who functions poorly academically will do badly in practice, we certainly have enough folk wisdom to want our doctors to be smart, highly motivated, and knowledgeable, something grades and achievement tests tend to tell us.

4. Concurrent Validity: Concurrent validity refers to how well an instrument measures current functioning. An example is a social functioning scale to determine how well people function in such areas as interaction with others, ability to form relationships, quality of life, socially responsible behavior, etc. The purpose of concurrent validity is to show whether the scores on an instrument translate into the way someone actually functions in their life. If someone is doing well in her life but receives a score on a depression scale that suggest very high risk for suicide, we immediately suspect poor concurrent validity. That is to say that the depression scale is a less accurate measure of depression than a person's current functioning. Can a person be suicidal and still function well on the job or at school? There are certainly cases where this happens, but for the most part, suicidal people normally function poorly because their depression is so overwhelming.

5. Predictive Validity: This type of validity measures a person's future functioning. In the area of work-related problems, most researchers use the term *job satisfaction* to measure current happiness on the job (concurrent validity), while *morale* is a way of measuring what their work satisfaction might be like in the future (predictive validity). Managers need to know about present and future problems in the workplace to be effective. Current problems require remedies that are swift and immediate, while future problems require remedies that are more thoughtful and planned.

A good example of predictive validity is the reliance on the SAT for entry into many universities and colleges. For many years now, the SAT has been thought to be a very good measure of how well students will do in college. However, a recent study done by the University of California and reported in the *New Yorker Magazine* (Gladwell, December 17, 2001, p. 87) suggests that the SAT is a poor predictor of university achievement. What are the better predictors? High-school grades and achievement tests. To further reinforce the poor predictive validity of tests like the SAT that supposedly measure some innate intellectual or abstract ability, researchers in England tried to compare the scores on the national test used in England to measure musical ability and the actual achievement of 256 highly-able musical students (Gladwell, 2001, p. 88). Guess what they found? That the best predictor of musical achievement was the number of hours students practiced and the encouragement and support of their parents. The national test was a poor way of predicting student success in schools of music. Surprised? You shouldn't be. The best predictor of future behavior is past behavior. Highly motivated people achieve at a higher level than less motivated people even though less motivated people might receive a higher score on tests like the SAT.

6. Construct Validity: This type of validity is interested in answering questions about whether an instrument helps us prove theories. For example, let's say that a person's mental health is made up of many important attributes such as resilience, the ability to achieve love and intimacy, close friendships, spirituality or deep personal beliefs, etc. Construct validity, in this example, is interested in knowing how many behaviors that define a healthy human being can be measured by a specific test. In the sense that we have listed several attributes of healthy human beings, we are suggesting a theory that our instrument might help us prove or disprove.

Determining Reliability of the Instrument

Reliability refers to whether the instrument is dependable or stable. Will the instrument give us similar results when we use it repeatedly? Grinnell (1997, p. 173) notes that a reliable instrument should: a) give consistent (stable) scores when the same person takes it repeatedly; b) give about the same scores for people taking another equivalent test, using either instrument; and that c) scores for reliability on the first half of the instrument should be about the same as on the second half of the instrument.

There are two approaches we might use to determine reliability. They are the test-retest and the split-half methods.

The Test-Retest Method

In this method we give the subject the same test several times and determine whether the results are similar. We usually want the reliability coefficient (the statistical measure of reliability) to be very high, perhaps better than .90. If it is significantly less than that, we would wonder if the test is stable over time. An unstable test is highly problematic because we can't trust the results.

The Split-Half Method

If we divide the questions on an instrument into two parts with each part measuring roughly the same thing, then giving each half of the instrument to different people should result in consistency in the way the questions are answered. In other words, each half of the instrument should repeatedly be responded to in the same way (Grinnell, 1997, p. 176).

Using the Instrument: Approaches to Data Collection

Interviews

A face-to-face interview is a wonderful way of collecting data. There is nothing quite like the feeling of being able to personally interact with your research subjects. But before you decide to do a face-to-face interview, let's consider some of the problems. You may have to drive a long way to interview people, so interviewing can be time-consuming and expensive. Because you have to ask the same questions in the same tone of voice and not deviate from your pre-determined format, you can't wander off into other interesting areas without it affecting the validity of the information you're collecting. Your tone of voice, dress, general demeanor, and non-verbal communication may affect the subject's response to your questions. Liking or not liking the subject, or your being attracted to or repulsed by the subject, may affect the information you receive as well as the way you interpret that information. You may overly identify with the subject and find yourself entering responses that reflect your feelings and not those of the subjects. Consider the researcher who is interviewing child abuse victims when the researcher has a lost memory of his own abuse. Will he be accurate in what he hears and records? Perhaps not. However, interviews are wonderful ways for new researchers to learn about the research process, and I highly recommend them. But do keep in mind the concerns I've just mentioned.

Telephone Interviews

Telephone interviews have become very common lately. They certainly save time and money, particularly if your sample is out of your driving area. You can also complete a study fairly quickly by using the telephone. Because of telemarketing, however, people are usually turned off to being interviewed on the phone. If a phone interview is really the best way for you to collect data, it may be a good idea to send out letters before the interview explaining the purpose of the research. Include an informed consent form and a debriefing statement asking subjects to return them before you call. Or you may just call and do the informed consent over the phone providing the subject with a coded number proving that human subjects issues have been explained. You may then want to mail them a copy of the consent and debriefing forms.

Researchers have encountered the following problems with phone interviews:

- Many people have a telephone call waiting feature that can wreck havoc with the interview because of interruptions.
- You may experience interruptions at the person's home that may distract the subject.
- People may be watching TV, or noise from their stereo may make it difficult for them, or for you, to hear.
- It may be difficult for the subject to understand the question if it is too long. Questions using Likert Scales can be confusing when they are read to subjects. It may be difficult for the subject to remember the question let alone the five to seven options provided on the Likert Scale.
- If you're thinking of taping the telephone interview for more accu-

racy, remember that it's illegal to tape an interview without the person's consent. It is also illegal to have someone else listening to the interview to record material without the subject's knowledge and consent.

Still, the telephone can be a very good way of getting material quickly. Here are some suggestions to assist you in doing telephone interviews:

1. Write a letter to the person you want to interview explaining the research study and providing them with the time and date when you will be calling. Include the human subjects forms and have them sign and return the forms to you before the interview. In the letter you send them, include the questions you will be asking and suggest that they have the questionnaire with them when you call. The questions you ask should be open-ended. It doesn't make a great deal of sense to use forced-choice questions on the phone since we've just discussed how difficult this can be for the subject.

2. Get the subject's permission on the phone to have a second person record their answers. Tell the subject it will go faster that way. Don't ask to audiotape the interview because it often troubles people to have things they say on the phone recorded.

3. Make the interview fairly brief, perhaps no longer than 15 minutes.

4. Before you begin the interview, ask if they have any questions about the study, about you, or about how the material they provide will be used.

5. Always be very polite and answer all questions truthfully. Don't tell them the research is about one thing when it's really about something very different. The subject will catch on and you'll probably experience a hang up or some very strong language . . . or both.

6. Don't call during dinnertime or too late in the evening. I take calls between 7:00 and 9:00 PM. Remember, working people get up very early in the morning and go to bed early, so the window of opportunity to call is somewhat short, unless you call on weekends.

7. Thank people for their time when you finish. Ask if they have any additional questions or comments before you say goodbye. Leave them with your name and phone number, and encourage them to call if they have additional questions or comments.

8. And never, you wild and crazy people out there, never flirt on the phone when doing an interview. Not only does it negatively affect the data you're trying to collect, but it's also just on the cuff of sexual harassment.

Critical Incident Interviews

Rather than create a long list of questions on a questionnaire, a critical incident interview simply asks the subject to think about a time when something happened to them and to discuss it. The questions you ask should be brief, probing, and relate directly to the purpose of the research. To better understand the critical incident approach, let's say that we're interviewing the adult child of an alcoholic parent. We want to know how the alcoholism of the parent affected them as a child as well as how it currently affects them. Here are some questions you might ask using the critical incident approach.

- Think of a time when your father or mother (whomever was alcoholic) did something to you that was very upsetting.
- What did he or she do?
- How old were you?
- How did you respond?
- How did the incident affect you as a child?
- How did the incident affect you as an adult?

The nice thing about the critical incident approach is that you can delve as deeply as you would like. There is no set limit to what you can ask as long as it stays within the boundaries of the questions you ask each subject. You can go into more depth, you can pursue certain statements that are vague, and you can follow up with questions meant to add information. Obviously, this is a very subjective way of gathering data. Generalizing to other subjects may be impossible. But the information you gather from a critical incident interview can be highly charged, emotional, and probably so pertinent that it may not be possible to get similar information using other data gathering approaches. Be aware that you run the risk of delving too deeply and you may touch on old wounds that cause the client considerable pain. There are powerful pros and cons for every approach you may use. The critical incident approach should be used with caution, and new researchers are generally better off not using the approach, or limiting their use of the approach by observing how an experienced researcher might use it.

The Focus Group

One of the more exciting approaches to data collection is meeting with your subjects in a group and trying to develop consensus statements (statements that represent the opinions of the majority of the people in the group). You can have both majority and minority consensus statements. The beauty of a focus group is that it allows you to talk to many people in a short period of time. The weakness of this approach is that group pressure can be very strong, and one person might dominate the group to such an extent that the information you get is biased. Because I like focus groups, a number of my students who have used focus groups in their research projects have had experiences that suggest the power and appropriateness of this approach for retrieving certain types of information. Focus groups are appropriate forums for opinions or attitudes, while gathering personal information from subjects (such as their traumatic life experiences) may be inappropriate because of confidentiality issues.

The Survey

A mailed survey is a simple but expensive way to collect data. Remember that you need to enclose a cover letter explaining the purpose of the research and include informed consent and debriefing statements. You also need to enclose the instrument and a stamped, self-addressed return envelop. This can be very expensive when you send it First Class mail. The post office tells me that if you send the survey fourth class, the least expensive way to send mail, the cost will drop dramatically, but that most people do not read or respond to fourth class mail. To reduce the expense of mailing questionnaires, one strategy is to use envelopes with printed postage numbers so that you only get charged for the questionnaires that are returned to you. If you're very lucky, you might get a 20 percent response rate with the first mailing. To get the remaining 80 percent, you will have to send out a letter or postcard reminding respondents to complete the questionnaire. More expense. What if respondents throw the questionnaire away, as they frequently do? You'll have to send them another set of questionnaires. More expense. Your total response rate may be, at best, another 20 percent.

Should you code the questionnaires to determine who has returned it? It might save you money but then again, knowing that the questionnaire is coded might limit the number of people who respond. Most people are a little conservative when it comes to completing questionnaires sent by strangers. If you're thinking you can unobtrusively code the surveys so that you know who has returned it but the subject doesn't, don't do it—it's unethical.

So what can you do if you want to have people complete a mailed instrument but have concerns about the expense and the time it takes to do a survey? You can choose settings where people work and just have the questionnaire sent to your subjects through the organization's internal mail system. It's quick, it's easy, and, best of all, it's free. Hooray! I like it already! If people don't respond, you can just send out a general memo to everyone urging them to complete the survey and letting them know that they can get new ones if, for any reason, the original surveys are not available. Many of my students have used this approach with very good results. Return rates may be as high as 80 to 90 percent, particularly when people in authority co-sign the letter asking for surveys to be returned. Another easy way to complete surveys in an organization is to hand them out at a staff meeting, and provide time during the meeting to complete the instrument. Return rates can be almost 100 percent.

You can also give out questionnaires at social, religious, or educational functions. My students are gutsy. They use church services, social gatherings, their classmates and families, or any other convenient source of data to save money and to get a good return rate. One of my Egyptian American students did a survey of Egyptian members of a church to find out if traditional forms of child rearing (strict, use of corporal punishment, rule setting) related to the level of acculturation of respondents (how unassimilated they were in American culture). It didn't show any association between acculturation and traditional child rearing approaches, by the way, but as she told me, "Where am I going to find Egyptian subjects? Where they gather, that's where." You see how wise my students are?

The beauty of a survey is that if you have access to a large number of people, you can give out numerous surveys, and within a short period of time you can have a large number returned. Student satisfaction surveys are a good example of how you can get information very quickly.

Guidelines for Surveys

1. Be Honest: Tell the research subjects what the research is about and why you're doing the study. This should be done in your informed consent and debriefing statements, but it should also be included in your letter accompanying the instrument or, if you use a focus group or telephone interview, at the beginning of the interview process. Be very candid about what you're trying to find out and why it's important.

2. Don't Overdo Rewards: If you offer a reward for completing the survey, don't overdo it. A reward is a thanks-for-the-time-spent completing an instrument. Some researchers give coffee and donuts when the survey is done in person. Other researchers might give small gift certificates. Advertisers often overdo rewards to make subjects feel obligated to answer a survey in a way that insures a positive response. I bought a car once, and the obnoxious salesman who sold me the car sent along a personal letter with a $100 bill thanking me for my business. Two days later, a satisfaction survey came from the car manufacturer asking if I was satisfied with the car salesman. I gave the money back to the salesman, and wrote a very negative evaluation of the salesman for what he had done. I also sent a letter to the manager of the car dealership describing what had happened. But you get the point. A reward should not be a bribe.

3. Be Reasonable: Don't expect people to complete a long and badly written survey. Make it short, sweet, and if possible, fun to complete. If it takes more than 10 minutes to finish an instrument, you may find people just giving up and leaving the instrument unfinished.

4. Give People Time to Return Surveys: Give people enough time to complete the survey and, if you're using a mailed survey, factor in the length of time it takes for the subject to receive, complete, and send the survey back. It irks people to be asked to complete a survey but then not be given enough time to do it. I always use three weeks from the date I place the survey in the mail as the date it's due.

Summary

This chapter discussed instrument construction and the use of instruments to collect data. We also discussed validity and reliability, issues related to ways of constructing instruments, and ways of determining if an established instrument might be useful. Terms related to instrument construction were provided that might be important for you to learn and understand sufficiently to construct your own instrument.

REVIEW QUESTIONS

1. Why are validity and reliability issues so important in the construction of any instrument?

2. If you create your own instrument, what are some important elements in the construction of your instrument to make the data collected useful?

3. Explain the process one goes through to make an instrument valid and reliable.

4. Why is it not permissible to use an instrument intended to measure a certain behavior for the purpose of measuring another behavior the instrument was never intended to measure?

5. Why is it a good idea to develop your own instrument?

REFERENCES

Aldenderfer, M. S., & Blashfield, R. K. (1984). *Cluster analysis.* Beverly Hills, CA: Sage.

Banaka, W. H. (1971). *Training in depth interviewing.* New York: Harper & Row.

Berelson, B. (1952). *Content analysis in communication research.* Glencoe, IL: Free Press.

Bolton, R. N., & Bronkhorst, T. (1996). Questionnaire pretesting: Computer assisting coding of concurrent protocols. In N. Schwarz and S. Sudman (Ed.), *Answering questions* (pp. 37–64). San Francisco: Jossey-Bass.

Brenner, M. (1985). Survey interviewing. In M. Brenner, J. Brown, and D. Canter (Eds.), *The research interview: Uses and approaches* (pp. 9–36). New York: Academic Press.

Brenner, M., Brown, J., & Canter, D. (Eds.). (1985). *The research interview: Uses and approaches.* Orlando, FL: Academic Press.

Briggs, C. L. (1986). *Learning how to ask: A sociolinguist appraisal of the role of the interview in social science research.* New York: Cambridge University Press.

Burgess, R. G. (1982). The unstructured interview as a conversation. In R. G. Burgess, *Field research* (pp. 107–110). Boston: George Allen and Unwin.

Cannell, C. F., Miller, P. V., & Oksenberg, L. (1981). Research on interviewing techniques. In S. Leinhardt, *Sociological methodology* (pp. 389–436). San Francisco: Jossey-Bass.

Carney, T. F. (1972). *Content analysis: A technique for systematic inference from communications.* Winnipeg: University of Manitoba Press.

Corcoran, K. J., & Fischer, J. (1987). Enhancing the response rate in survey research. *Social Work Research and Abstracts, 21,* 2.

Crittenden, K. S., & Hill, R. J. (1971). Coding reliability and validity of interview data. *American Sociological Review, 36,* 1037–1080.

Dean, J. P., & Whyte, W. F. (1969). How do you know if the informant is telling the truth? In G. McCall and J. L. Simmons, *Issues in participant observation* (pp. 105–115). Reading, MA: Addison-Wesley.

Dillman, D. A. (1991). The design and administration of mail surveys. *Annual Review of Sociology, 17,* 225–249.

Dillman, D. A., Singer, E., Clark, J., and Treat, J. (1996). Effects of benefits, appeals, mandatory appeals and variations in statements of confidentiality on completion rates for census questionnaires. *Public Opinion Quarterly, 60,* 376–389.

Fowler, F. J., Jr. (1992). How unclear terms can affect survey data. *Public Opinion Quarterly, 56,* 218–231.

Geer, J. G. (1988). What do open-ended questions measure? *Public Opinion Quarterly, 552,* 365–371.

Gladwell, M. (December 17, 2001). Stanley H. Caplan and the S.A.T. The *New Yorker,* 86–89.

Gorden, R. (1992). *Basic interviewing skills.* Itasca, IL: Peacock.

Goyder, J. C. (1982). Factors affecting response rates to mailed questionnaires. *American Sociological Review, 47,* 550–554.

Grinnell, R. M. (1997). *Social work research and evaluation.* Itasca, IL: Peacock.

Groves, R. M., Fultz, N. H., and Martin, E. (1992). Direct questioning about the comprehension in a survey setting. In J. Turner (Ed.), *Questions about questions: Inquiries into the cognitive bases of surveys* (pp. 49–61). New York: Russell Sage Foundation.

Groves, R. M., & Mathiowetz, N. (1984). Computer assisted telephone interviewing: Effects on interviewers and respondents. *Public Opinion Quarterly, 48,* 356–369.

Herzberg, F. (1966). *Work and the nature of man.* New York: T. Y. Crowell.

Herzog, R. A., & Bachman, J. G. (1981). Effects of questionnaire length on response quality. *Public Opinion Quarterly, 45,* 549–559.

Keeter, S. (1995). Estimating a telephone non-coverage bias with a telephone survey. *Public Opinion Quarterly, 59,* 196–217.

Krosnick, J. A., & Abelson, R. P. (1992). The case for measuring attitude strength in surveys. In J. Turner (Ed.), *Questions about questions: Inquiries into the cognitive bases of surveys* (pp. 177–203). New York: Russell Sage Foundation.

Labaw, P. (1985). *Advanced questionnaire design.* Cambridge, MA: Abt Books.

Lavrakas, P. J. (1993). *Telephone survey methods.* Thousand Oaks, CA: Sage.

National Institute of Mental Health. (1995). *Report: A national investment.* [Online]. Retrieved December 31, 2001 from the World Wide Web: http:// www.nimh.nih.gov/publicat/baschap1.cfm.

Work in America (1973). *A report by the President's Commission on work.* Cambridge, MA: MIT Press.

RECOMMENDED INTERNET SITES

FAQ: Finding Information About Psychological Tests (American Psychological Association)
<http://www.apa.org/science/faq-findtests.html>
Ericae.net Clearinghouse on Assessment and Evaluation
<http://ericae.net/>.
Social Work Databases, University of Southern California
<http://www.usc.edu/isd/locations/ssh/socialwork/sowkdatabases.html#tests>.
Resources for Test and Research Instruments, Florida Atlantic University
<http://www.library.fau.edu/depts/ref/bibl/nurs/research.htm>

RESOURCES FOR TESTING INSTRUMENTS

Academic Therapy Publications
20 Commercial Boulevard
Novato, CA 94949
(800) 422–7249
http://www.academictherapy.com

Consulting Psychologists Press, Inc.
3803 East Bayshore Road
P. O. Box 10096
Palo Alto, CA 94303
(800) 624–1765
http://www.cpp-db.com/

Educational and Industrial Testing Service
(800) 416–1666
http://www.edits.net/

Educational Testing Services
Rosedale Road
Princeton, NJ 08541
(609) 921–9000
http://www.ets.org

Institute of Personality and Ability Testing
P.O. Box 1188
Champaign, IL 61824–1188
(800) 225–IPAT
http:// www.ipat.com/

Psychological Assessment Resources
16204 N. Florida Avenue
Lutz, FL 33549
(800) 727–9329
http://www.parinc.com/

United States Department of Defense, Testing Directorate
Attn: MEPCT
Fort Sheridan, IL 60037
(312) 926–4111

United States Department of Labor
Division of Testing, Employment, and Training Administration
Washington, DC 20213
(202) 376–6270

Western Psychological Services
12031 Wilshire Blvd.
Los Angeles, CA 92126
(800) 648–8857
http://www.wpspublish.com/

7 Examples of Research Instruments

Introduction

To help you see the options available in using an existing instrument or in creating your own, I provide four instruments here for you to consider.

Instrument 1: A Vague Likert Scale

The first instrument on spirituality shows the vagueness of certain types of measurements found when using a Likert Scale format. On this type of scale, it's up to the respondent to determine what the answers on the Likert Scale mean. The probability is that the scores will cluster around the mean. Vague Likert Scales generally show the emergence of social desirability. People want to say they *have* spiritual feelings but that they aren't necessarily *strong* feelings. Your findings on these scales will very likely be meaningless, because the instrument is vague and responses are too open to socially desirable answers.

> ### The Dakota Measure of Spirituality
> **Directions:** This is a measure of the importance of spirituality in your life. There are three parts to the questionnaire. All three parts should be answered as honestly as possible. **Please do not skip any of the questions.**
>
> *Part One: Socio-Demographic Questions*
>
>   1. Age _____
>   2. Years of Education _____
>   3. Marital Status _____
>   4. Occupation (the work you do) _____
>   6. Race/Ethnicity _____
>   5. Number of Children in Your Family _____

Part Two: Spirituality Questions
Spirituality is defined as the degree to which thoughts of a higher being or of a higher meaning in life define the way you approach life issues, your value base, and the way in which you cope with life decisions.

Directions: From the following scale, please place the number that best represents your level of spirituality after each question asked: 1 = Very Low/Very Seldom; 2 = Low/Seldom; 3 = Neither Low Nor High Nor Seldom Nor Often; 4 = Somewhat High/Somewhat Often; 5 = Very High/Very Often.

1. What is the degree to which a higher being plays a role in your life?
2. How often do you attend spirituality meetings?
3. Do you feel there is carryover from your involvement in spirituality to your personal life?
4. Do you pray?
5. Do you read about spiritual subjects?
6. Do you attend study sessions on spiritual subjects?
7. Do you financially support spirituality organizations or provide services as a volunteer?
8. Do you have a joyous feeling inside when you think about your spirituality?
9. Do your friends and family support your spiritual beliefs?
10. Do you have objects in your home of a spiritual nature (paintings, poems on the wall, spiritual messages, as examples)?
11. How often do you find yourself thinking about spiritual issues?
12. Are your personal spiritual beliefs related to an organized spiritual doctrine?
13. Does your notion of spirituality come from an organized religious doctrine or affiliation?
14. Would you celebrate major events in your life (marriage, birth, death) in a religious institution?

Part Three: Questions Concerning Your Physical and Emotional Health
Please use the following scale in responding to these questions: 1 = Almost Never; 2 = Perhaps Once a Month; 3 = Twice a Month; 4 = Once a Week; 5 = Almost Everyday.

1. I generally feel discouraged about my life.
2. I feel great, physically.
3. I have moments of intense panic.
4. I see the doctor _____.

5. I feel the need for a drink _____.
6. My anxiety attacks occur _____.
7. I exercise _____.
8. I feel the love of others_____.
9. I see a therapist for emotional problems _____.
10. I feel very low self-esteem _____.

Discussion

You can readily see that this instrument is full of vagueness. The definition of spirituality is much too broad. I'm sure a better definition is available, since this one might be called an "Aunt Fanny" definition: it fits everyone in the world including our Aunt Fanny. The questions are also vague. Is this about religion or spirituality? These are, of course, two different concepts. I fail to see the tie to anything substantive in many of the questions. Consider question 8. It asks, "Do you have a joyous feeling inside when you think about your spirituality?" I mean, really! What does a "joyous feeling" mean, and how often do most of us have one? Those feelings could be confused with happy feelings or feelings of contentment. Joyous feelings are serious and connote a sense of euphoria. Would you define "joyous" that way? Perhaps not, but you can see the problem of trying to understand unclear language. This Likert Scale is much too vague. What do the words "Very Low" and "Very High" mean? What may be high for one person is very likely to be low for another person. And finally, what is this about, anyway? Is it about believing in God? Is it about believing in a moral view of life? Is it about being religious? I'm not sure, and I created the scale.

The physical and mental health questions aren't bad and having a Likert Scale tied to measurable behaviors is a good idea. After answering the questions about spirituality, however, the respondent may see the link made between high levels of spirituality and good physical and mental health. If so, knowing that the researcher is suggesting that spiritual people are also healthy people insures that the answers suggest that respondents have good emotional and physical health. It might be interesting to see if there really is a tie between spirituality and good physical and emotional health, but I'm not sure this scale can accomplish that function. Additionally, in this type of measurement, we only have the subject's word regarding their level of spirituality and their physical and emotional health. A better measure of spirituality and health would be a standardized instrument to measure spirituality, a doctor's evaluation of physical health, and a mental health worker's evaluation of emotional health. Now *that* could make for a very interesting study, because an entire movement in the health field believes that high levels of spirituality correlate with better ability to cope with physical and emotional difficulties in life. Anyone want to give it a try?

Instrument 2: A Behaviorally-Oriented Likert Scale

The second instrument is one in the public domain called the CES-D (Radloff, 1977), a measure of depression. It is very behaviorally oriented and gives the respondent a definite idea of how to answer questions. Questions are based on a one-week time frame and the number of times certain behaviors related to depression are experienced. You'll need to be the judge of which instrument is the most appealing to you and how it relates to the intent of your study.

The CES-D: A Measure of Depression

Directions: I am going to read you some statements about the ways people act and feel. On how many of the last 7 days did the following statements apply to you?

	None	1 or 2 Days	3 or 4 Days	5 or more Days
1. I was bothered by things that usually don't bother me.	0	1	2	3
2. I did not feel like eating. My appetite was poor.	0	1	2	3
3. I felt that I could not shake off the blues even with help from friends and family.	0	1	2	3
4. I felt I was just not as good as others.	0	1	2	3
5. I had trouble keeping my mind on what I was doing.	0	1	2	3
6. I felt depressed.	0	1	2	3
7. I felt that everything I did was an effort.	0	1	2	3
8. I felt hopeful about the future.	0	1	2	3
9. I thought my life was a failure.	0	1	2	3
10. I felt fearful.	0	1	2	3
11. My sleep was restless.	0	1	2	3
12. I was happy.	0	1	2	3
13. I talked less than usual.	0	1	2	3

14. I felt lonely.	0	1	2	3
15. People were unfriendly.	0	1	2	3
16. I enjoyed life.	0	1	2	3
17. I had crying spells.	0	1	2	3
18. I felt sad.	0	1	2	3
19. I felt people disliked me.	0	1	2	3
20. I could not get going.	0	1	2	3

Discussion

The CES-D is one of the simplest depression inventories available. The choices are easy to make, the language is simple, the instrument appears culturally neutral, and it is very short. In other words, it's quite a good measure of depression. But are there problems with the instrument? Yes, there are. One problem is that a person may have been depressed last week but feel hunky-dory this week. A week of depression is a very short period of time. Even the *Diagnostic and Statistical Manual*, the DSM-IV (American Psychiatric Association 1994) says that one needs to have been depressed for at least a month before the term *depression* can be used clinically or diagnostically. If you reflect back on the questions, some of them seem just a little too vague. Question 20 is an example: "I just could not get going." I can imagine some confused clients, or those unfamiliar with English, wondering where they were supposed to get going to? Also, some of the questions might confuse medical problems with depression. Question seven is a good example. It says: "I felt that everything I did was an effort." People with the flu often feel that way. Consider question 15: "People were unfriendly." People often *are* unfriendly, particularly in large cities. That doesn't mean that the respondent is depressed, does it? And so on. I like the behavioral aspect of the questions, and many of them really do look at depression. But in the light of the issues I've raised here, you should look for the small and large flaws in all instruments. Flaws usually occur because the instrument hasn't been pre-tested to the extent that it should have been. If enough qualified people read an instrument, trust me, they'll come up with problems in the instrument pretty quickly.

Instrument 3: The Use of Vignettes

The third instrument uses vignettes combined with open-ended questions. Answers are difficult to manufacture. It is an instrument with the least possible likelihood of socially desirable answers.

> ### The San Bernardino Crisis Scale
> **Directions:** A series of short vignettes describing the crisis situ-

ations in people's lives will be presented. Please write down the first thought that comes to you since this is almost certain to be the most relevant answer. We will appreciate your cooperation in writing about 150 words on each question, because we would like to know not only what you would do, but why you would do it. Don't worry about whether the answer is right or wrong. We are only interested in knowing what you might do in each stressful situation. This scale is meant to measure how people deal with crisis situations.

1. You are driving along in your car when suddenly the driver in front of you swerves off the road. You watch the car flip over several times and come to a halt. Smoke is coming from the car, and your fear is that the car might explode. What would you do next?

2. You have just been informed by a doctor that preliminary tests show that you have a serious form of cancer that could end your life in less than a year. What is the first thing you would do?

3. The person you love the most in life has just informed you that they no longer love you, and that they have found someone else to be with. What is the first thing you would do?

4. The person next to you in class is cheating on examinations. You see that she has a crib sheet with her every time she takes an examination. The course is graded on a curve and even though you're doing well in the course, that person's grade is throwing the curve off. Instead of getting the A you deserve, you're getting a B−. What would you do?

5. You go to your place of worship and are asked to help pass the donation plate around and then count the money. You're stone-broke and haven't had a meal in two days. You begin counting the money and see that the donations are higher than usual. You could probably take $10 from the donation plate without anyone missing the money. You are so hungry that your judgment is poor. What would you do?

6. Your parents throw a party for your older brother (or sister) and his girlfriend (or boyfriend). You happen to be in your bedroom getting dressed when the girlfriend/boyfriend comes into your room and tells you that he or she really isn't in love with your sibling. The person needs to be honest about it, because it's making him/her very unhappy. What would you do next?

7. Your best friend at work is using liquor on the job. He's very careful about it, but you've seen him drink on the job a number of times. His work has been going downhill lately and it's affecting your salary and opportunities for advancement because both are dependent on how well your department does. What would you do?

8. You've just been "reamed out" by your boss who used gender-specific terms with you like bitch, dyke, queer, and so on. Your boss and his boss are best friends. There really isn't anyone else on the job to whom you can complain about what's happening without it affecting your job. What would you do?

9. You know for a fact that your father is having an affair, because he's shared that information with you on the promise that it remains confidential. Your mother calls you up to talk about the problems in their marriage: She tells you that Dad just doesn't seem interested in her anymore whereas before, he was very interested in her. She's become very depressed, almost suicidal because of the change in their relationship. What would you do?

10. Your best friend, not one of the greatest students in the world but a really wonderful friend who has done lots of favors for you, asks you to take her place in a national examination. If she gets a high enough score, she'll be certain to be admitted to the school and the profession she has dreamed of for years. You know your friend would make a wonderful professional in her chosen field and she *is* your best friend. What would you do?

Discussion

This scale is an open-ended scale that is pretty difficult to fake, although not impossible. There are certainly socially desirable answers that some people might be able to think up. For the most part, however, it would be difficult to fake responses on every question, because there isn't necessarily a correct or socially desirable response. The problem with this instrument is, what is it measuring? The directions say that it's measuring the way people might act in a crisis, but the underlying theme is the respondent's value system. Could you see someone giving you this instrument at your job? I can, because within the questions are choices that not only suggest someone's ability to handle stress, but they also suggest the person's value base. This type of instrument might be used to determine whether you would cheat or steal at work. It's an instrument that appears to be about one thing but it certainly could be about something else. And yet, it's not a bad instrument, and it does demonstrate the use of short vignettes to elicit open-ended answers that would probably contain minimal levels of social desirability.

One thing to consider when using this type of instrument is the amount of time it could take a respondent to complete the instrument. Very often, people with poor writing skills just give up or they make answers so brief that they can be meaningless. Let's take Question 10. It asks if you would cheat on a test for a really good friend. The briefest answer would be "No, because it's dishonest." What you're hoping for, though, is a more detailed response, perhaps something on the order of: "I wouldn't cheat for my friend because I might get caught. I would help him study for the test and I'd probably encourage him a great deal. I'd certainly have negative things to say about cheating and I'd also point out that asking me to cheat goes way beyond what friends ask other friends to do. I'm wondering if I don't cheat for him, if it will affect our relationship." The trick in this type of open-ended instrument is to give the subject encouragement to provide more complete and informative answers. One way to do this is to provide a sample question with a possible answer. You may affect the way the subject responds to the remaining questions by doing this, but it *is* a possible way of getting respondents to give more self-disclosing answers. You might also ask the respondent to provide written answers and then, in a second part of each question, to explain the answers more fully.

Instrument 4: An Open-Ended Instrument

The fourth instrument is an open-ended instrument developed by a former student of mine in an MSW program. It tries to determine the reasons Hispanic HIV Positive/AIDS victims fail to inform their families about their health problems. The instrument also tries to note the coping mechanisms used by this population in dealing with a socially stigmatizing terminal illness.

This instrument was given verbally in Spanish, although the respondents could refer to the written questions in both English and Spanish. All of the subjects chose to speak in Spanish. The questionnaire was done verbally because many of the subjects had poor writing skills and some were too weak from AIDS to write. The researcher also felt that doing the questionnaire verbally would encourage the subjects to speak at length about each question. This did happen but it made recording the interview difficult. After several interviews, the researcher asked the respondents if he could tape the conversation. All consented, although he asked each of them to sign a release form giving him the right to record the interviews and promising to destroy the tapes after they had been analyzed for content.

Hispanic Men and the Disclosure of Their HIV\AIDS Status to Family Members

Socio-Demographic and Self-Disclosure Questions

1. What is your age?
2. Where were you born?
3. How many years have you lived in the United States?
4. What church do you attend?
5. What is the actual date of your diagnosis of HIV positive?
6. What is your HIV positive status? Asymptomatic or symptomatic?
7. Describe the type of relationship you currently have with your family.
8. How often do you see your family?
9. What does your family know medically about HIV/AIDS?
10. How would you describe your parent's view of life?
11. Describe your family's attitude toward gay men.
12. If your family knew that you were HIV positive, how do you think they would react?
13. Explain why you haven't disclosed your HIV/AIDS status to your family.
14. If you had an opportunity to disclose your HIV/AIDS status to a family member, who would that be? Why would you choose that person?
15. In explaining how you are dealing emotionally and physically with your HIV/AIDS status, what *dicho* (a proverb or wise saying commonly used in Hispanic culture to convey metaphorical meaning) best describes it?
16. In dealing with your family regarding your HIV/AIDS status, what dicho best describes it?
17. In dealing with your sexual orientation, what dicho best describes it?
18. In your heart, what has it done to you not to tell your family about your illness?

Questions Related to the Culture Subjects Identify With (An Acculturation Scale)

The following scale was added to the prior instrument because the instrument developers thought it might be important to know the extent to which traditional Hispanic values were related to the answers the respondent's gave.

One way to determine the level of a person's identification with his or her country of origin is to give what is called an *accultura-*

tion measurement. That simply means that an instrument will be used to help determine the extent to which the values, beliefs, and experiences of someone's country of origin still affect their lives today. A high score on the five following questions suggests that the respondent is primarily identifying himself as a traditional, Hispanic male and that American culture plays a limited role in his self-identity. This is relevant to the study since acculturation may affect whether men in this sample disclose their HIV/AIDS status to their families. The more strongly the level of acculturation to North American culture, the more it might be possible for men to disclose their illness to their family. At least that was the theory held by the developers of the instrument.

An Acculturation Scale
Directions: Please use one of the five answers provided to let us know about the way you view your ties to your country of origin.

1 = Not at all
2 = Very little or not very often
3 = Moderately
4 = Very often
5 = Almost always

　1. I like to identify myself as _____.(country of origin)
　　 1 2 3 4 5
　2. I speak Spanish.　　 1 2 3 4 5
　3. My thinking is done in the Spanish language. 1 2 3 4 5
　4. I write in Spanish. 1 2 3 4 5
　5. I listen to Spanish language radio/television. 1 2 3 4 5

Discussion

This instrument deals with heartbreaking issues: AIDS, homophobia, family denial and rejection, and issues of the subject's own feelings about his sexual orientation and AIDS. These are not easy subjects, and one could predict that the respondents would have a difficult time answering truthfully. That certainly was the case in this study. Many of the answers given by the men in the sample were very socially desirable even though, in the end, it became painfully clear that Hispanic men in the sample did not disclose their illness because of the shame they thought it would bring to their families and the family rejection they might experience as gay men with AIDS. These are painful issues and no instrument will get it exactly right. I like the acculturation scale and many of the questions seem right on the mark. There is an opportunity in this instrument for some very revealing answers. This, as we discovered, was the case. The thrust of the responses received indicated that Hispanic men in this sample, dying of AIDS, would prefer the anonymity of dying alone rather than the rejection of their families. And while the respondents often told mothers and sisters about their AIDS, they almost never told fathers or brothers. The thought of living with this sort of deception in the midst of the absolute misery of dying from AIDS troubled us a great deal. That's why we added questions about dichos or proverbs. We wanted to know what coping philosophies the subjects used, and we thought that asking them questions about their philosophy of life would result in very revealing responses.

What we received were a number of proverbs suggesting that the subjects were as homophobic as their families. Many of them said that they were living doomed, unnatural lives and that they would eventually pay for it. They were able to deal with AIDS because they saw it as a form of "punishment" for having chosen an "unnatural and unhealthy" lifestyle (in the subject's words). These are tragic thoughts about their lives, made at a time of supposed enlightenment toward gender issues. You can see, however, that the instrument tries to study socially upsetting issues in a gentle and unobtrusive way, if that is ever completely possible.

Making Sense out of Open-Ended Answers

Okay. We have an interesting open-ended instrument. What do we do with the material we've collected? First, we read through the answers and sort them by categories (discrete groups) of answers until we have six or seven (more or less) categories. Then, for computing purposes, we assign each subject's response a number related to the category the answer most closely resembles. Clear? Maybe not.

To help explain how we create categories from open-ended responses, let's take question number 10 in the preceding measure of client disclosure of their AIDS status to their families. That question asks, "How would you describe your parent's view of life?" Let's say respondent number one answers, "Very traditional." We create a category we call "Very Traditional" and assign it the number 1. The next respondent says, "Very Catholic." We then create a new category and assign that category, "Very Catholic," the number 2. The third respondent says, "Very traditional." We already have a category for "very traditional" so that response gets a number 1. Respondent four says, "A small town view of life." We now have another category to which we assign the number 3. (In reality, the responses usually include roughly 5 to 7 categories.) Instead of having 20 or 30 statements, we now have 5 to 7 categories. Each response is given the number corresponding to the category it most closely resembles. In effect, we have created a Likert Scale from the open-ended responses on the instrument. We can now enter open-ended answers into the computer as numbers and conduct a statistical analysis from our open-ended responses.

You might be thinking that it would be easier to create a Likert Scale to begin with and that doing so would have saved us a lot of work. Well, yes, that's probably true. But how would we know the categories for our Likert Scale without first having asked open-ended questions? Furthermore, open-ended answers sometimes provide elegant answers that can be quoted in our report and tend to add more meaning to the study. If we are using a standardized instrument, one that is valid and reliable and has been created to measure a certain kind of behavior like depression or self-esteem, our open-ended responses can sometimes completely negate the findings on the standardized instrument. The reason for this is that the answers to the closed-ended questions may be socially desirable while the answers to the open-ended questions may be painfully honest. Even the most instrument-oriented researcher knows that when dissonance (disagreement) exists between a closed-ended and an open-ended response, you should give more meaning to the open-ended response.

As an example, I did a very large job satisfaction survey of MSW Social Workers in the western part of the United States (Glicken, 1977). The instrument I used was called the Job Descriptive Index or, as it is known in its abbreviated version, the JDI (Bowling Green State University, 1997). It defines and attempts to measure job satisfaction in five primary categories: satisfaction with pay, promotional opportunities, co-workers, the work itself, and the supervision. All five categories of satisfaction, after the study was completed, showed very high levels of satisfaction with the exception of satisfaction with co-workers, which was fairly low (odd that social workers can't get along with one another, don't you think?). On the face of it, the sample looked pretty job satisfied except in the area of co-worker satisfaction. Satisfied, that is, until I read the open-ended answers to three questions asking respondents: 1) what they didn't like about their jobs; 2) their future work plans; and 3) anything they would change on the job, if they could. The responses to these three open-ended questions were so negative, and there were so many of them (80% of the 400 returned questionnaires had written responses to the open-ended questions), that I concluded the sample was very job dissatisfied even though the standardized measure (the JDI) said they were quite satisfied. Respondents provided highly negative statements such as, "I love my clients, but the agency is so punitive and so brutalizes clients that I can no longer continue working here." Another respondent wrote, "My clients are wonderful, but when I listen to colleagues calling them bums and other insulting things, I just can't see myself continuing on in social work."

I had so many negative responses and so many of them were very well written, that I created an entire section in the appendix of the final report with verbatim responses to each of the three open-ended questions. It was, according to the readers of the study, the best part of the report. Had I not included an open-ended section of the survey, you can bet that my conclusion would have been that social workers in my sample were fairly satisfied with their work. My experience, and that of many other social researchers, makes a strong argument for having enough open-ended questions in any study to check the validity of a standardized instrument. While the instrument I chose to use had validity and reliability data that were compelling, the fact is that my sample demonstrated that the instrument was not a valid measure of job satisfaction with a social work population.

But how could that be? Social workers were included in the original data norming the instrument. I wouldn't have used the instrument had I not been able to compare my data against that of the normative data on social workers found by the instrument developers. Several reasons come to mind. First of all, I think job satisfaction is a subject influenced by social desirability. It just isn't okay for most of us to tell strangers about our job unhappiness. Social workers who work in organizations that can be very meddlesome and autocratic (large public agencies, for the most part) may worry about the impact their statements have on their professional identity. Social workers, like many people in the helping professions, hate to admit that they're in life situations that cause them pain. I can imagine the respondents saying to themselves as they filled out the survey that social workers should be in control of their emotional lives. Being unhappy at work suggests poor control and, therefore, that something is wrong with the social worker. Secondly, the open-ended questions were about issues external to the social worker. I can also imagine the social workers who filled out the open-ended questions saying to themselves, "I'm a hard-working, honorable, and responsible person but that darn agency or those darn co-workers of mine—if only they'd shape up." In other words, the JDI was a measure of their satisfaction with *their* performance on the job while the open-ended questions were a measure of other people's performance on the job. Finally, it's possible that my sample of social workers differed from the sample on which the JDI was normed. I find that difficult to believe but, none-the-less, it's possible.

Isn't research interesting? Who would have thought that I would get such unusual data? This is the sort of puzzling thing that happens a good deal of the time in social research. If you like trying to solve mysteries, you'll love doing social research.

Cover Letters Used with Instruments

If you are planning on using an instrument that is mailed, or one that you might pass out at an agency or some other public setting, it's a very good idea to include a cover letter. A cover letter is probably most effective if you use the letterhead of some official organization. In the case of students, perhaps you could use the letterhead of your university department with your instructor co-signing the letter. Good cover letters explain the reason the research is being conducted. They also give a strong emotional argument about why the respondent should complete the questionnaire and return it as quickly as possible. Good cover letters can substantially increase the response rate.

In a cover letter, you need to give vital information that includes: who you are, what the study is about, why it's important for the respondent to complete the questionnaire, how the research will be disseminated, and how it might positively affect the life of the respondent, or of others. You also need to include an informed consent and debriefing statement. More on that in Chapter 13. The letter should be short, direct, and to the point. Let's give it a try.

Example of a Cover Letter

Dear Sir or Madam:

Please, please, please complete the enclosed questionnaire and mail it back to me today. If you don't, I'll fail research, my parents will go into a depression, I'll never graduate, and I will spend the rest of my life breaking rocks in the local rock quarry. That will lead to alcoholism, depression, and homelessness. Please don't let this happen to me.

Signed,

Desperate

Well, maybe not. Too emotional. Let's give it another try.

Dear Sir or Madam: January 1, 2003

The questionnaire I've enclosed is very brief. It should take no more than 10 minutes to complete. The questionnaire asks you to rate your work satisfaction. All responses are confidential. None of the questionnaires are coded and I can assure you of complete anonymity.

This national survey of teachers is an attempt to find out what is good and bad about life at work for primary and secondary teachers in America. The results will be published in most local papers and will be presented on the CBS, ABC, and NBC nightly news. You will also be sent, free of charge, a brief synopsis of the findings.

People often feel that there is nothing they can do to change how they feel at work. This is your opportunity to respond to a national survey on the work satisfaction of teachers. Your responses can have a direct and immediate impact on your workplace and your job happiness.

Please take the few minutes it will require you to complete the survey and send it in the enclosed, stamped, self-addressed envelope by January 21, 2003.

Thank you for your assistance.

(Your name and title)

Sending out the Results to Participants

If possible, send the results to everyone in the survey. A one or two page report makes people feel good about taking part in the study. The following is a short report (in Spanish) sent to a group of professionals in Chiapas, Mexico where several of my students did a depression study on the impact of the civil war in Chiapas, Mexico on women near the war zone. I wrote the report in English and it was presented at a symposium on international research at California State University, San Bernardino (Glicken & Alamsha, April 1998).

> *The Brief Report: Depression among Women in Chiapas, Mexico*
> Seventy women in rural and urban areas of Chiapas, Mexico were given a depression scale (the CES-D), translated into Spanish by the Mexican Institute of Psychiatry, to determine if the political unrest in Chiapas was having a detrimental affect on the mental health of women living in, or near, the most violent areas of unrest. Additionally, the seventy women were interviewed at length about support systems that kept them well, emotionally. Finally, eighteen professional mental health workers in Chiapas were interviewed regarding their impressions of the level of depression among Chiapas women with particular concern for the helping networks these women had developed to cope with the stressors of living in an area beset by political unrest.
>
> The research was conducted by two graduate social work students at California State University, San Bernardino under the direction of a social work faculty member and with assistance from several faculty members at a university setting in Chiapas. The Mexican Institute of Psychiatry gave additional assistance. The research was done during the last two weeks of December 1997 when forty-five dead bodies were discovered in a community not far from where the research was being conducted.

Preliminary findings of the study are as follows:

1. The women interviewed had levels of depression lower than the average of other women living in Mexico as normed by the Mexican Institute of Psychiatry.

2. Support systems for the women interviewed included extended family and church affiliation although, for the most part, church affiliation was non-Catholic and was what we in the United States would probably consider Evangelical or Fundamentalist Christian. Many of the women, however, also attended traditional Catholic mass and saw no particular inconsistency in their involvement in two dissimilar Christian denominations.

3. There was considerable distance between what the professional mental health workers thought about the way this population coped with political unrest and the way the women themselves reported their coping. One example is that professionals believed that most women in the sample used folk healers to treat depression, yet every woman interviewed (n=70) denied the use of folk healers, informing the interviewers that folk healers were primitive and unhelpful. However, the interviewers spoke to four folk healers in the geographic area of the study who estimated that their average client load was about 150 clients per day, many seeking help for problems with depression.

4. While the women in the study had very low scores on the depression instrument (the CES-D), suggesting that they were not depressed, they did admit to hiding feelings of depression. The literature refers to this as *masking* depression, and there is some anecdotal evidence collected by the interviewers that the women may have been more depressed than noted by the depression instrument. It's possible, of course, that social desirability played a strong role in lowering depression scores on the instrument.

5. The researchers used a technique that compares pictures of people who are depressed to the facial expressions of actual clients. The National Institute of Mental Health in the United States developed this technique. Using this method of testing, more than one half of the women in the sample looked depressed. This subjective approach was tested against the clinical impression of the two researchers, one of whom is originally from Chiapas. Both researchers felt that almost 90 percent of the sample, through verbal and non-verbal communications, indicated levels of depression that would sug-

gest the need for treatment (counseling or medication). The differences in these three measures suggest that scores on the CES-D depression instrument were influenced by social desirability.

6. The women were far more sophisticated about depression than the researchers expected. Many had heard of anti-depressant drugs familiar in the United States (such as Prozac), and most knew something about counseling and psychotherapy. However, most of the subjects denied that they had ever been in therapy or that they had ever used anti-depressants. Many of the rural women interviewed admitted that they used alcohol in excess, but explained that it was almost always used in conjunction with social events, holidays, and celebrations where heavy drinking was socially condoned.

7. While the women interviewed were quite aware of the political situation in Chiapas and the personal risks involved in being critical of the government, the researchers found them to be surprisingly open in their opinions about the various problems facing the people in Chiapas and the role played by the opposing political factions in contributing to or resolving these problems.

8. There were very few women who refused to be interviewed, but the interviewers felt that the women, while honest in their responses, were also very guarded. This may have been a function of the fact that none of the women in the study had ever been interviewed by a researcher. It may also have been possible that the subjects were uncomfortable with what they felt was an obtrusive process (homes were chosen at random and the interview protocol, even though it was pre-tested at length before the study began, turned out to take over an hour to complete). Politeness is an important aspect of Mexican behavior and the women, rather than being guarded, may have felt some degree of hostility.

Summary

In this chapter, we considered four common types of instruments. Each instrument was evaluated for its potential use as a way of collecting data. The chapter considered ways of writing cover letters and the brief report that might be sent to the respondents in a study as a way of informing them about the findings in the study and thanking them for their help with the study.

REVIEW QUESTIONS

1. When would a Likert Scale be most useful to the researcher?

2. When might open-ended questions be most useful in a research study?

3. Why should you abide by the 10-minute rule in instrument construction?

4. Questions that are interesting but not really relevant are called "fishing expedition" questions. What are the pluses and minuses of these sorts of questions?

5. When might it be appropriate to create and use our own instrument?

REFERENCES

American Psychiatric Association. (1994). *DSM-IV questions and answers.* [Online]. Retrieved January 2, 2002 from the World Wide Web: <http://www.psych.org/clin_res/q_a.cfm>

Bowling Green State University. (1997). *Job descriptive index.* [Online]. Retrieved January 2, 2002 from the World Wide Web: http://www.bgsu.edu/departments/psych/JDI/

Camilli, G., & Shepard, L. A. (1994). *Methods for identifying biased test items.* Thousand Oaks, CA: Sage.

Dean, J. P., & Whyte, W. F. (1969). How do you know if the informant is telling the truth? In G. McCall and J. L. Simmons (Eds.), *Issues in participant observation* (pp. 105–115). Reading, MA: Addison-Wesley.

Fink, A., & Kosecoff, J. (1985). *How to conduct surveys.* Thousand Oaks, CA: Sage.

Geer, J. G. (1988). What do open-ended questions measure? *Public Opinion Quarterly, 552,* 365–371.

Glicken, M. (1977). *The job satisfaction of social workers in the southwest.* Unpublished doctoral dissertation, University of Utah.

Glicken, M., & Alamsha, K. (1998, April). Levels of depression in women of Chiapas, Mexico. *Symposium of International Scholarship,* California State University, San Bernadino.

Herzog, R. A., & Bachman, J. G. (1981). Effects of questionnaire length on response quality. *Public Opinion Quarterly, 45,* 549–559.

Mooney, L., & Gramling, R. B. (1991). Asking threatening questions and situational framing: The effects of decomposing survey items. *Sociological Quarterly, 32,* 227–288.

Ostrom, T. M., & Gannon, K. M. (1996). Exemplar generation: Assessing how respondents give meaning to rating scales. In N. Schwarz and S. Sudman (Eds.), *Answering questions* (pp. 293–318). San Francisco: Jossey-Bass.

Pearson, M. R., & Dawes, R. M. (1992). Personal recall and the limits of retrospective questions in surveys. In J. Turner (Ed.), *Questions about questions: Inquiries into the cognitive bases of surveys* (pp. 65–94). New York: Russell Sage Foundation.

Radloff, L. S. (1977). The CES-D scale: A self-report depression scale for research in the general population. *Applied Psychological Measurements, 1,* 385–407.

Schaefer, D., & Dillman, D. A. (1998). Development of a standard email methodology. *Public Opinion Quarterly, 62,* 378–397.

Schumann, H., & Presser, S. (1979). The open and closed question. *American Sociological Review, 44,* 692–712.

Schumann, H., & Presser, S. (1981). *Questions and answers in attitude surveys: Experiments on question form, wording and content.* New York: Academic Press.

Schwarz, N., Knauper, B., Hippler, H. J., Noelle-Neumann, E., & Clark, L. (1991). Rating scales: Numeric values may change the meaning of scale labels. *Public Opinion Quarterly, 55,* 570–582.

Schwarz, N., & Hippler, H. J. (1995). Subsequent questions may influence answers to preceding questions in mail surveys. *Public Opinion Quarterly, 59,* 93–97.

Smith, T. W. (1995). Trends in non-response rates. *International Journal of Public Opinion Research, 7,* 156–171.

Wiens, A. N., & Matarazzo, J. D. (1983). Diagnostic interviewing. In M. Hersen, A. E. Kazdin, & A. S. Bellack (Eds.), *The clinical psychology handbook* (pp. 309–328). New York: Pergamon.

Zook, A., Jr., & Sipps, G. J. (1985). Cross-validation of a short form of the Marlowe-Crowne social desirability scale. *Journal of Clinical Psychology, 41,* 236–238.

RECOMMENDED INTERNET SITES

APA Testing Information Clearinghouse
<http://www.apa.org/science/testclearinghs.html>
Code of Fair Testing in Education
<http://www.apa.org/science/fairtestcode.html>
Statement on the Disclosure of Test Data
<http://www.apa.org/science/disclosu.html>
Statement on the Use of Secure Psychological Tests in the Education of Graduate and Undergraduate Psychology Students
<http://www.apa.org/science/securetests.html>
Rights and Responsibilities of Test Takers
<http://www.apa.org/science/ttrr.html>

8 Quantitative Designs

Introduction

The benchmarks of good research are those designs we call quantitative. They are also known as ***experimental designs.*** The two terms are sometimes used interchangeably. Quantitative designs use statistical analysis to show findings. They follow a stringent set of rules to make them as objective as possible. Issues related to sampling, instrumentation, control and experimental groups, and internal and external validity are controlled for so that the designs and methodologies used in the social sciences approximate those used in the hard sciences.

In social research, however, it is often difficult to use quantitative methods as easily as in the hard sciences. We can't, for example, deny services to clients just to determine whether a control group might fare as well as the experimental (treatment) group. We can't deprive people of needed financial services just to find out what will happen if we eliminate certain welfare programs. Realistically, we can't place people in a laboratory and have them smoke huge numbers of cigarettes to discover what the impact of smoking will be on their health. These are quantitative controls that do not work in the real world where people take researchers to court for unethical and harmful behavior.

As you will see from the following characteristics of the ideal quantitative design, the standards called for by Grinnell (1994) raise the level to a very high point. Those characteristics that define a methodology as quantitative, according to Grinnell, are as follows.

The Independent Variable Must Come before the Dependent Variable

This simply means that if we want to show that something causes something else to happen, the causing factor has to come before the outcome. If we believe that smoking causes cancer, then smoking must come before the cancer. This may be easy to show in medical research but it's much more difficult in the social sciences. We can't say, for example, that a certain type of emotional problem will be the outcome of a specific type of occurrence. We know that many children who have been abused develop a variety of emotional problems. We can't say with certainty what type of emotional problem they'll develop and, for certain, we can't say that everyone who has been abused as a child will develop emotional problems. We suspect that a relationship exists but we're uncertain whether one actually does. Many abused children grow up to be well-functioning adults.

You Must Be Able to Vary the Independent Variable

Using the smoking example, the number of cigarettes smoked would need to be manipulated for us to have any idea about the extent of the relationship between smoking and lung cancer. Theoretically, the fewer cigarettes smoked over a lifetime, the less the impact should be on the development of cancer. However, since cancer is a complex disease, perhaps diet, weight, and external environment (smog, dust, smoke, dirty rain, etc.) might exacerbate the impact of even minimal amounts of smoking on the development of cancer. The point is that to determine the true culprit in the relationship between smoking and cancer, we would have to be able to make radical changes in the experimental input (the independent variable) to determine the actual relationship between smoking and cancer. Often these radical changes are difficult in medical research (how can we control for dirty rain?) but impossible in social research. This is one of the limitations of social research. Some changes in a design may be unethical, impractical, or impossible.

In social research, changing the independent variable may lead to a number of incorrect conclusions. Are there degrees of physical abuse? Is abuse at an early age more damaging than abuse at a later age? Is verbal abuse more harmful than physical abuse? You can see that these are questions for which we may have opinions but to truly know the answers would require manipulation of the independent variable. This manipulation is nearly impossible for us to do. Asking children after they've been abused, or asking the adult victims of child abuse about the experience and how damaging it was, does not live up to the requirement that we need to be able to vary the independent variable. The only way we could do that would be to observe children being abused and follow their emotional and social growth from childhood through adulthood. How could we possibly permit ourselves to do that, even in the name of science? We just couldn't.

You Must Base a Hypothesis on Something Already Proven

Before you can state a hypothesis suggesting the existence or the lack of existence of a cause-effect relationship, that relationship must first be shown to exist in the research literature. A hypothesis must come from somewhere. It usually comes from prior research. Hypothesis testing, even when it is null (neutral and predicts that nothing will happen), must be based on something other than your intuition or your belief that, in a perfect world, research will always come out the way you expect it to. News Flash: In social research, outcomes are almost never predictable. Even with the best literature review, you may be surprised at how off the mark your results are when it comes to hypothesis testing.

This is a good time to discuss the difference between a theory and a hypothesis. A **theory,** according to Tripodi, Fellin, and Meyer, is a set of hypotheses that are logically related and seek to explain relationships. A **hypothesis,** on the other hand, is a beginning idea about relationships that does not as yet have the power of a theory. It lacks a substantial body of knowledge and while it has some research evidence to support it, a hypothesis is seen as a beginning way of viewing relationships between variables.

You Must Control for Other Explanations of Your Hypothesis

The research design must make certain that it controls for other possible reasons for relationships among variables. In our smoking example, two other factors causing cancer might be a very isolated and lonely personal life or food that is highly carcinogenic. To show a relationship between smoking and cancer, all other possible reasons people develop cancer must be controlled for. Is it ever possible to control for the complex and infinite number of reasons that something happens? Some researchers doubt it. In the applied social sciences, there is a belief that early childhood trauma usually causes severe problems that affect people both in childhood and as adults. If trauma alone causes poor social functioning, why are there so many well-functioning people who have been traumatized in childhood? A possible reason is that while trauma is certainly a terribly aversive event in a child's life, there may have been a host of positive influences (parental support, therapy, a healthy ability to cope with aversive experiences) that neutralize the impact of trauma. These variables must be considered when trying to show a relationship between childhood trauma and poor social functioning throughout a person's life span.

In all research using the quantitative approach, the researcher must always suggest other reasons why something may have occurred. And to be even fairer, the researcher must indicate how these reasons were controlled for in the study. This requires an inordinate amount of knowledge about the subject being studied. It also requires a sense of objectivity, fairness, and humility suggesting that while every effort has been made to control for every possible alternative reason that something may have occurred, as a fallible human being, things happen in a study that may be completely out of our control to prevent. And even if we show a cause and effect relationship, be honest about it. There are an infinite number of reasons why the findings may be erroneous. We owe it to our consumers to suggest alternative explanations for the outcome of our study. If we're pretty sure that we have good evidence regarding the validity of your findings, we should say so, but don't deny the consumer the alternative reasons why something may have happened. It's just good practice to let people know that a study isn't perfect so that they don't make more of the findings than are warranted. It should not be "consumer beware" in social research. Rather, it should "consumer be informed."

All Quantitative Studies Require a Control Group

A control group is essential for any quantitative study. You cannot be certain of relationships between variables without an adequate comparison group. A control group allows us to compare findings between groups receiving a treatment and others who have not received the treatment. It isn't always easy to protect the control group from contamination, but we try. The more completely the control group actually goes without the treatment we are providing to the experimental group, the more likely we are to have findings that really do provide meaning. Later in this chapter we'll discuss alternatives to using control groups in situations where people might be harmed if denied treatment. But for now, consider the use of an absolutely similar control group as essential in determining what happens to people who are not given the treatment received by the experimental group.

I encourage you to take a look at the information provided by drug manufacturers regarding the effectiveness of any medication you may be using. I just happen to have an inhaler handy for use with asthma attacks. The insert inside the box containing my inhaler tells me that, "in controlled trials involving adults with asthma, the onset of improvement in pulmonary functioning (the ability to breathe) was within 15 minutes" (Medeva Pharmaceuticals, rev. 2000). Excuse me, but coffee does the same thing for many asthmatics. Where is the control group? Why is there no mention of a control group composed of asthmatics that might be using an inhaler with no medication in it? What about the folks who get better by relaxation therapy, medication, or drinking caffeine? There is nothing about these alternative treatments. How serious are the attacks? Did everyone studied have the same level of breathing problems? This is basic information we all should know before we can judge the effectiveness of this medication.

Now I know about the medication. It works really well, and God bless the folks at Medeva Pharmaceuticals for making it. But tough research people that we are, we want to know how the control groups did with alternative treatments. Oh my, I'm reading some of this stuff in the insert now. Do you want to know what this medication did to mice over an 18-month period? Nope, neither do I.

Random Sampling and Assignment Are Essential

Random sampling and assignment are hallmarks of quantitative studies. We must select and assign subjects to both the experimental and the control group randomly or there will be a bias too great to permit the findings to be acceptable. It is always a problem when researchers know that certain people might be helped in treatment by the independent variable. So, says the researcher, why not put them in the experimental group to make certain that they receive the help they need? Because by doing this, the researcher may nudge the findings in a more positive direction. Furthermore, the findings won't be accurate and the study will be of no real value to anyone. This tendency to want to help people so badly that certain people are placed in treatment groups without the benefit of random assignment sometimes happens in the midst of a study when members of the control group begin to deteriorate and need help. You can understand the impulse to provide the needed help while understanding that to move someone from the control group to the experimental group may compromise the study. Even if the subjects moved from the control group to the experimental group improve dramatically, the knowledge that the rules of random assignment were violated will make others leery of accepting the findings and, then, the reasons for doing the research in the first place will be completely negated.

Some of you may have seen the movie about a scientist who discovers a cure for cancer in the Brazilian jungle. With only one dose of serum left made from that cure, the scientist must choose between saving the life of a child and keeping the serum for science. This being a Hollywood movie, the child is saved and science is forgotten. That's fine for a Hollywood film. Just remember that research can be a very serious enterprise. If you accept the challenge, then you have to stick to the rules.

With that in mind, let's look at some simple quantitative designs.

Comparisons between an Experimental and a Control Group

This is the most basic quantitative design. Both the control and the experimental groups are chosen by random selection. The experimental group is given some form of treatment input and the control group, theoretically, goes without treatment. We perform pre-tests to determine the baseline (before treatment) measures for both groups. If our selection process is done correctly, the pre-test scores should be the same for both groups. If the pre-test scores aren't the same, there may be a problem in the sampling procedures. Once the study begins, after a certain amount of time, both groups are given a post-test to determine what, if any, improvement the experimental group has made over the control group. If the control group does better than the experimental group, it may tell us the treatment is unhelpful. If the opposite is true, it may tell us that the treatment is helpful. But how helpful? That's where statistical analysis comes in.

Statistical analysis helps us understand the role that chance plays in our findings. If chance occurs more than five times out of 100 in a research outcome, it negates the findings. Chance may enter into the study when something unforeseen happens. An example of chance would be a client with anxiety problems who has come for therapy but is placed in the control group who then receives anxiety-reducing medications from their physician (something we don't know about nor can we prevent from happening) while those in the experimental group receive no medication. We may not be aware of this when the findings are evaluated. Other chance occurrences might be that the control group gets non-professional help, or that members of the control group get therapy from another professional without telling us. Correlational statistics help us determine if the strength of the relationship between our treatment and people getting better is a function of the treatment itself or of some intervening and, consequently, unexpected reason. Let's consider an example of the way in which an unexpected reason confuses our findings.

Let's assume that in the post-test, only 20 percent of the control group sample in our research achieved a score on an Anxiety Inventory suggesting normal amounts of anxiety when, at the pre-test, all members of the control group and experimental group had anxiety measures in the highly anxious range. The experimental group, after treatment, achieved a 50 percent level of normalcy. Running appropriate statistics could help us know whether the improvement in the experimental group was related to the treatment itself or whether there might be something else at play that explains the improvement rate.

This is where the relationship between two variables becomes important. Even though the experimental group may have achieved greater control over their anxiety, the reasons may have little to do with the treatment.

A very low correlation (say, .10 to .20) would suggest that while there is some relationship between the reduction of anxiety and the treatment, the real reasons for the improvement rates are unknown. Low correlation scores between variables would also suggest that there are other reasons for improvement that may not have been considered in the research. While the experimental group may have done better than the control group in lowering levels of anxiety, the reasons could be a **spurious** or **chance** occurrence which might not happen again if the study were to be repeated (replicated).

These spurious or chance occurrences plague social science research. The environment we work in, the real world, often makes it impossible to control for events that may upset our study. Working in a research lab where we control virtually every factor in our study might make for a different story. But when we do quantitative studies outside of the lab, many things that affect our findings can, and do, go wrong. The relationships we get in social science research are often weak, making the researcher wonder if the important reasons for any change in the experimental group have to do with other variables not even thought of. Perhaps many variables, each contributing a small amount to the relationship, explain why our experimental group did better than the control group. Chance occurrences, which we haven't or cannot control for, increase almost geometrically in complex social science research because, in real life, everything that can go wrong, does. Murphy said that a long time ago. He must have come to that conclusion while he was trying to do a quantitative research study. Does that mean we don't do even simple quantitative studies? No, of course not. It only means that beginning researchers, like you, who hope for excellent and meaningful results should be prepared for outcomes in quantitative research that are not terribly meaningful. Meaningful relations in research may come with experience when we learn to control those nasty little **intervening** (unpredictable) **variables.**

Solomon Four-Group Designs

As you will note in the discussion of threats to internal and external validity later in this chapter, one of the major concerns researchers have in using quantitative designs is the impact of the pre-test on the post-test. That is to say, does the use of any instrument make the subject "test-wise" for future use of the same instrument? In the Solomon Four-Group Design, we use four groups instead of two (two experimental and two control groups). One control group and one experimental group are given the pre-test and post-test, while the other two groups are given only the post-test. In this way, problems related to subjects being test-wise might be avoided.

Test-wise subjects are always a concern in research. Most of us know that certain questions on a psychological test are measures of poor mental health or some degree of dysfunction. Questions regarding attitudes toward certain ethnic groups are fraught with political correctness. To a healthy person, it is obvious that some questions on the Minnesota Multiphasic Personality Inventory (MMPI), a personality test used to determine emotional problems, have obvious questions that to a healthy person would suggest a certain answer. "Are people following you at night? Do you have thoughts of violence? Are you afraid to go to sleep for fear that something will happen in the night?" All of these questions would be answered in the negative by discerning test takers even if the opposite were true. But for unsophisticated test takers, once having taken a test and having answered the questions honestly, the more times the test is given, the more aware the subject is that the answer should not suggest a dysfunctional response. "Am I afraid to go to sleep because something might happen to me at night? Yes, I am," says the test taker, "but I'm not going to admit it to you or you'll think I'm crazy." Should we change tests when we do a post-test? We could do that but then we wouldn't be able to compare the results between the pre-test and the post-test. Perhaps, as an alternative, we could use a non-paper-and-pencil measure such as heart rate, blood pressure, muscle tension, sweating, and brain wave patterns. In essence, we could give subjects a lie detector test to measure their physiological state and its relationship to their emotional state of well-being. A good idea perhaps, since it is used as a basis for treatments using bio-feedback procedures.

Because of the concerns about subjects being test wise, a number of researchers believe that the only way to measure change is to evaluate actual changes in behavior. In the next chapter on qualitative designs, we consider goal attainment scaling which is a way of measuring changes in behavior independent of any psychological instrument. Briefly, this approach believes that if you have a client with depression and you have symptoms consistent with depression such as sleep problems, eating problems, and decreased social contact, the only way to truly determine a change in depression is to check the behaviors symptomatic of depression and decide whether they have improved as a result of treatment.

Time Series Studies

One of the intriguing questions in the counseling field is the average length of time that it takes for someone to improve in treatment. Some clinicians believe that the longer therapy continues, the more the client improves (Seligman, 1995). One way to determine this is to utilize time series studies that vary the length of time of treatment and then compare the results. Randomly selected multiple control and experimental groups each receive, or do not receive, counseling for a fixed period of time. Let's make those fixed periods of time three months, six months, nine months, twelve months, fifteen months, and eighteen months. This requires that we have six control and six experimental groups each tested before and after an assigned period of counseling to determine the optimum improvement rate based on length of counseling.

One instance which demonstrates the complexity of time series designs is in the medical field when medications are tested for their optimum effectiveness. We are accustomed to doctors telling us to use the entire bottle of antibiotics for an infection. Time series studies have been used to determine how large a dose of medication taken over a certain period of time will produce optimum effectiveness. This type of finding requires very sophisticated research and statistical approaches since people vary in their ability to metabolize medication by weight, age, and their individual level of physical health, all factors that must be considered in time series designs. In medical research, we also want to know the correct dosage per day and when, during the day, the medicine should be taken. We're accustomed to taking two or three antibiotic pills per day for 7 to 10 days. But some people believe that this dosage is used more for convenience than effectiveness. A doctor who helped develop the antibiotic for whooping cough (48 Hours, 2001) and who now, at age 103, still treats children believes that the correct way to take antibiotics for children (and presumably for adults) is to take one tablet every three hours for three days. It's not very convenient for those of us who like to sleep during the night but, in her opinion, it's the correct way to treat infections. She believes that the current way of taking antibiotics is the primary reason many childhood infections, such as ear infections, reoccur; the infection was never actually cured in the first place because the antibiotic wasn't used correctly. To test this out, get the information you receive with most medications and read about the way correct usage is determined. I'll bet you won't find anything. It makes you wonder if the way we take antibiotics is more for convenience than for effectiveness, doesn't it?

Quasi-Experimental Designs

Quasi-experimental designs are less than objective from a research point of view, but they are often used when ethical or practical considerations limit our ability to do a more precisely controlled study. In mental health clinics, denying someone service for the purpose of placing them in a control group raises a number of ethical considerations that might have legal repercussions. If someone placed in the control group commits a crime or injures someone else as a result of not being provided treatment, the mental health agency could be liable. Yet, some sort of research needs to be done to determine effectiveness of treatment. Quasi-experimental designs that control, to the extent possible, for internal and external validity (to be discussed later in this chapter) are certainly better than no research at all. Many researchers who use quasi-experimental designs have pointed out that these designs have been used to prove cause-effect relationships between variables. Quasi-experimental research is not able to precisely determine cause-effect relationships. Other researchers argue that quasi-experimental designs are subjective in nature, and that internal and external validity may be so difficult to control that the design should not be considered quantitative. For our purposes, however, I've included quasi-experimental designs in this section on quantitative research. I believe that while not all controls are maintained in quasi-experimental research, many controls can be developed that permit the data we generate from the study to be used in helpful ways. Caution should be used, however, in generalizing about the findings or by making claims of cause-effect relationships. Due to design limitations, we can neither say that the findings apply to other similar situations nor that evidence exists that we found a connection between variables.

An example of a quasi-experimental design is an attempt to find out if a social program is effective without using a control group. In this type of research, often called **program evaluation,** the ethical issue of not having people placed in a control group where they are denied treatment is taken care of by simply not having a control group. Subjects are given a pre-test and a series of post-tests and the data are then compared. While no one would argue for a cause-effect relationship between treatment and rates of improvement or that findings can be generalized to other similar settings, the results might provide important evidence regarding the way a program is functioning. That evidence could prove meaningful to other agencies and might be instructive in developing treatment strategies. The findings aren't conclusive but they are suggestive and may provide guidance to others. Quasi-experimental designs are less than perfect, but they try to make up for design limitations by being very accurate in the way they describe the research process and by the way they maintain an **audit trail** (the accurate description of what was done and why it was done at every juncture in the research process). The researcher must explain the limits of the design and must indicate how those limitations have affected the results. Once that is done, consumers are free to make informed judgments regarding their value. In the applied social sciences, many people feel that some evidence of program effectiveness is better than no evidence at all.

Eileen Gambrill (1997), a social work educator from University of California, Berkeley, has applied concepts from evidence-based medicine to suggest that helping professionals must be knowledge-guided in their approach to providing help to people in social or emotional difficulty. She maintains that if research is soft or limited, we should be very careful in the way we assure clients that we have answers to their problems. Others argue that the application of research findings, however fuzzy or soft they may be, provides direction to the helping professionals when we are uncertain regarding the approaches to use in helping people in social and emotional difficulty. Seligman (1995), in a fascinating argument about the effectiveness of counseling and psychotherapy, argues that when people tell us that therapy works, we should take that as proof that it really does. He goes on to suggest that whatever it is we do and whoever it is that does it (social workers, counselors, psychologists, psychiatrists, etc.), counseling and psychotherapy work. Why? Because when clients are asked if they are satisfied with the help they receive, most indicate that they are. This information comes by the way of a large survey of client satisfaction with counseling and psychotherapy done by the magazine, *Consumer Reports* (Seligman, 1995).

Let's put aside the issue of how many poor people or people of color were involved in the study and let's focus on whether Seligman makes a valid argument. Seligman argues that we have no reason to doubt the honesty of clients when they say that therapy and counseling helped them. Because clients say that psychotherapy and counseling helped, it probably does. Gambrill might respond that Seligman's arguments are spurious and that they provide no direction for us to take in helping people. She wants harder evidence of client improvement tied to something concretely done by the therapist and the client that is observable and measurable by other researchers. The purpose of this more scientific approach is to help others learn effective counseling skills that actually lead to changes in client behavior. Seligman might counter-argue that we probably cannot quantify (measure) what is done in therapy because it is too subjective, but that whatever it is we do, bravo! Let's keep it up because it works. For those who want some evidence, even though it isn't compelling or hard evidence, quasi-experimental designs are likely to meet this need. You can see how these arguments, while interesting, give us all headaches. Suffice it to say, quasi-experimental approaches to research, while not strongly scientific, do offer us thoughtful, suggestive ideas that perhaps there are connections between variables. If enough researchers replicate a study, we may have usable and meaningful information to guide our decisions. This is particularly true when a study uses a methodology that is as rigorous and exacting as the researcher can make it. For many of us, that's certainly better than being completely in the dark.

Survey Research

Although survey research may be considered less than objective, I'm including it as a quantitative approach because it's primary purpose is to gather information in, hopefully, a very controlled way. Survey research uses a random sampling approach, valid and reliable instruments, and statistical analysis of data. However, there are a number of things that can go wrong in survey research. These include small response rates, inaccurate information given by respondents, poorly done directions for completing the survey that result in incorrect responses, and instruments that give biased information. Survey research is the most common form of research and is widely used in polling and marketing.

Survey research has become very sophisticated as sampling procedures have become increasingly accurate. With very small samples, one can now predict voting patterns, marketing strategies, future trends, and a number of events that make life more predictable for many of us. For survey research, one must have a particularly effective instrument to measure behavior. A common fault of survey research instruments is the confusing way in which questions are asked. Consider this question: "How would you rate President Bush's effectiveness as president?" Now consider the same question asked in a somewhat different way: "If you had an opportunity to vote again, would you vote for President Bush?" You may not think these are similar questions, but they really are. The effectiveness question would probably result in high marks for President Bush. The question regarding voting for him again might get lower marks. The first question might be asked by a Republican pollster intent on getting positive feedback on President Bush, while the second question would probably be asked by a Democratic pollster to elicit less favorable information. Just remember that the way a question is phrased can dramatically affect the answers in survey research.

A good example of this is an article I found recently in a California newspaper indicating that county residents supported a tax increase to build a new park (Wall, 2001, A1). 11,849 residents living adjacent to a proposed park formed the population from which a sample of 700 households was selected. Of these 700 households, 528 were visited, but only 184 completed the survey. Residents were asked how large a tax increase they would support. The study found that they would support a $70 a year increase, and the title of the article reinforced that support: "Residents Willing To Pay For Park" (Wall, 2001, A4). No such conclusion can be made. The number of completed samples is too low. The questionnaire asked the average increase residents would support ($20 to $260) but we don't know how many would support a $70 increase as opposed to a lower increase. We certainly don't know why so few people completed the survey, and we could never agree with someone quoted in the article as saying, "The study is very positive" (Wall, 2001, A4). This is a perfect example of how survey research can be used to draw false conclusions.

Threats to Experimental Designs

Making sure that we don't ruin a study by some obvious failure to control an important aspect of the research process is always a concern for researchers. The two primary ways we tend to ruin research efforts in quantitative research relate to internal and external validity issues. **Internal validity** refers to those aspects of the study that may interfere with the cause-effect relationship between the independent and dependent variable(s). Internal validity means that our ability to say that something causes something else to happen may be interfered with because of aspects of the study which were done incorrectly or which were not adequately controlled for. A cause-effect relationship occurs when something causes something else to happen. Standing out in the rain and getting wet while you're saying goodbye to your girlfriend or boyfriend may cause you to get a cold. In research, we're always trying to find out if something causes something else to happen. Does taking massive dosages of Vitamin C cause you to have lower rates of cancer? Does it mean that you're less likely to get a cold? These are typical cause-effect relationships that concern researchers. Does the independent variable, in this example the Vitamin C, impact the dependent therapy (cancer or colds)? If we are studying the effectiveness of cognitive therapy in lowering levels of depression, then cognitive therapy is the independent variable and depression is the dependent variable. All aspects of the study that might interfere with an attempt to show a relationship between cognitive therapy and decreased depression are considered internal validity concerns. The following internal validity issues may interfere with the usefulness of the data meant to show relationships between variables in experimental or quasi-experimental designs.

Internal Validity: Threats to Showing Cause-Effect Relationships

Life Events

Events or life experiences other than the treatment intervention can affect the outcome. Falling in love while being treated for loneliness is an example. If you treat someone over a long enough period of time, chance occurrences often create more change than your treatment, although some occurrences, like falling in love, may not have been possible without treatment. Some writers call this *personal history.*

Biological Changes

People change physically and emotionally over the course of treatment. The degree of physical change may be more significant than the treatment itself. Some writers call this *maturation.* Biological changes, in explaining the effectiveness of a treatment intervention, are very important, particularly when working with children, adolescents, the elderly, and anyone in the beginning phase of a serious illness who may be unaware of the illness. You can understand that biology plays a significant role in affecting behavior.

The adolescent who seems charming and lovely one moment may appear illogical and rebellious the next moment. To not factor in biological changes in our work with adolescent clients creates error. We must also consider, under the general heading of biological changes, the use of legal and illegal drugs of which the treatment person and the researcher may be unaware. Medication of any type can significantly alter behavior and can, more than even maturational changes, confuse the results of research. One could also say the same about illnesses and diseases which neither the subject nor the researcher are aware of. Thyroid problems can produce depression and anxiety. Diabetes, in its early stages, often produces labile or erratic behavior in children and adolescents when none was noted before the illness began. These very common problems are often undiagnosed or misdiagnosed by physicians and what appears to be an emotional problem is, in reality, a symptom of a physical problem.

Chance Occurrences

Subjects may drop out of the study or outside events may affect the results of a study. Press reports of domestic violence, for example, may significantly reduce family violence for a period of time. Some authors call this *instability*. You can understand that if you're treating someone who you think is a domestic violence perpetrator and suddenly the O.J. Simpson case scares perpetrators into temporary retirement from their abuse, that it isn't your treatment that produces the change, it's the chance occurrence of a high-profile crime temporarily changing the perpetrator's abusive behavior. Chance plays a large role in social science research because people, unlike mice in a research laboratory, are subject to enormous amounts of stimuli that affect behavior. I recall a news story from Israel during the Six Day War in 1967 which stated that not a single elderly person died during the war from age-related problems. Prior to the war, the average rate was one death a day. A researcher studying death rates among the elderly would never have been able to control for this chance occurrence since they would not have known that a war would take place and certainly could never have known that people wouldn't permit themselves to die until they knew the outcome of the war.

Test-Wiseness

Taking psychological tests over a period of time may make a subject *test-wise*. The results of the study may be influenced more by the knowledge of the test than by actual change in the person. A very troubling example of this comes from my own experience working in a program providing services to felons paroled from prison. I interviewed a prisoner in jail and thought that he was psychotic. In fact, he was hallucinating in my office. However, his MMPI was absolutely normal and the parole board released him against my objections. A week later, he killed someone during a robbery. It turned out that the prisoners working in the psychologist's office were selling normal profiles to other inmates who would, when they came in to take the test, look as if they were completing it. When no one was looking, they would slip the normal MMPI out of their shirt and onto the table. In general, however, researchers worry that the more familiar the subject is with the test, the more likely the subject's answers will be **socially desirable** (meant to suggest that the subject is giving the researcher a response that he or she thinks is normal rather than what he or she may actually feel or believe).

Knowing How to Take a Test

If you know that answering a question in a certain way might reflect on how others view your mental health, you'll usually provide an answer suggesting that you're healthier than you really are. You may be seeing bats flying around when there are none, but if asked if you often see bats flying around when others don't, the wise person says, "No sir, I never see bats flying around." This is also called *social desirability* and it plagues researchers. You can only get accurate measures if people give you accurate and honest answers. To create some control over the social desirability of responses, many instruments include reliability checks in the form of the same question asked in a number of different ways. The honest test taker will answer a question in the same way, regardless of how the question is phrased. The test taker who is trying to manipulate the test may get tripped up and score badly on the reliability of responses. The wise researcher would throw that person's test results away since the responses suggest an intentional desire to manipulate the answers.

Same Test, Different Meaning

Testing instruments change over time. The researcher who is trying to compare test results over a long period of time may not be able to do so. Renorming the SAT is one example. Changes in the way the GRE (Graduate Record Examination, commonly used in graduate school admissions) is given is another example (the GRE is now computerized). Some authors call this *instrumentation*. As an additional concern, some researchers wonder if a number of the tests they give have a bias against certain groups of people. In an attempt to make a test more culturally sensitive, the test may become very different from its original construction and intent. Comparing results from an earlier instrument with those of an instrument developed at a later point in time may provide meaningless, confusing, or contradictory information.

Those Darn Statistics

Extreme scores move toward the mean over time. This means that extreme indications of improvement in treatment may be more a statistical anomaly than an actual occurrence. This is sometimes called *regression artifacts.* One example is that children of immigrants often tend to be taller and heavier than their parents, while the children of the children of immigrants may be smaller and lighter than their parents. Did that make sense? No? Ask people you know to compare the height and weight of three generations of people in one family to see if the gains in height and weight of the first generation continue to increase in the second and third generation. If this doesn't happen, then you have an explanation: extreme biological changes will be offset in future generations because growth patterns tend to move back to the norm.

Whoops, We Chose the Wrong People

Errors in the selection of subjects can greatly affect the results of an experiment. Just by keeping certain people out of a study, you can get very biased results. This was the case in a recent study showing that most research on the effectiveness of psychiatry kept the most dysfunctional people out of the study. This is also called *selection.* We like to think that selection is done objectively by researchers, but even giving researchers the benefit of the doubt, so many large errors are made in sample selection that you have to start wondering if incorrect selection isn't done to produce findings that are highly favorable to the researcher.

Drop Outs

Participants may drop out of a study at rates that affect the outcomes. This is also called *experimental mortality,* and it can greatly confuse the results of a study. What typically happens is that members of the control group drop out in greater numbers than those in the experimental group. This leaves two groups with unequal sample sizes. Statistical tests can be run to make up for the difference in group size, but most researchers wonder if this results in truly accurate information. Ideally, the control and the experimental groups should end with the same composition. When control group members drop out, you always worry that the dropouts are the ones who are most important to the study. In a small sample, just a few important dropouts (by race, ethnicity, or religion) can dramatically affect the findings.

Some Folks Are More Resilient

Certain people improve in treatment, not because of the treatment, but because of their inherent ability to *use* treatment. This occurs because they might be more cognitively able, have better language skills, be more intelligent, and so forth. Some researchers call this *selection-maturation interaction,* and most researchers tend not to give it enough credence. In a democracy, we like to believe that everyone is equal in their ability to improve themselves socially, emotionally, educationally, and financially. That is no more the case than for people getting better medically at the same rate. Some people are more physically and emotionally resilient than others. Consequently, treatment can be a very limited explanation as to why people improve.

External Validity: Threats to Generalizing Findings to Other Similar People, Situations, or Events

External validity refers to the assumption that our findings may be applicable to other places, people, or situations. While we may have a good cause-effect relationship between the dependent and independent variable, mistakes may have been made in our study that limit our ability to generalize the results to other places, people, or situations. The following external validity issues may interfere with our ability to generalize findings.

Testing Interferences

The use of an instrument to measure changes in behavior as a result of some treatment input (for example, training to sensitize workers to other cultures, ethnic groups, races, and gender differences) may increase the sensitivity of respondents to occurrences of prejudice and may lead to a reduction in bigotry. The reduction in bigotry is less a function of the training and more a function of the impact the test questions had on the awareness of problems we face with gender, racial, ethnic, and cultural bias. This is also called *pre-test treatment interference.*

If You Know You're in the Study, You Try Harder

This can happen when subjects know that they are either in a control or an experimental group, and it may lead to changes in behavior that have nothing to do with the experimental input. For example, depressed clients, on finding out that they're in the control group, may try to prove that they can get better without the help of therapy. This effect can be controlled for by a double blind design in which neither the subjects nor the researchers know which group they are in. Of course, if we're providing some form of social or psychological treatment, a double blind design may be very difficult to use unless we're such non-directive therapists that neither we, nor the client, have any real sense that we're doing any-thing. But you can understand that knowing you're being studied increases your desire to do better (or, if you have a rebellious nature, to do worse).

Problems with the Sample

Sometimes the difficulty in finding a setting that allows us to do a study re-sults in a sample of people who are somewhat different from those we had originally intended to study. If ten organizations providing mental health services turn us down and the eleventh allows us to do our study, there may be something so different about the eleventh organization that the findings prohibit us from generalizing to the other ten settings. This is sometimes called *selection-treatment interaction.* Being turned down to do a research study in the public sector is a considerable problem for social re-searchers. We need to be very adamant with our public servants that they allow access to their organizations to carry out needed research studies. Otherwise, we all experience sampling problems that result in incorrect or highly limited information.

A Biased Sample

One way to prove something is to take a small sample of people who have certain skills, measure those skills, and then let people assume that the sam-ple represents everyone in the larger population. We do this all the time. We may test a high school with very high achieving students and use the findings to represent the overall functioning of everyone in the school dis-trict. Or we may test the successful graduates of a job-training program and profile them, but fail to note what happened to everyone else in the pro-gram. This is sometimes called *specificity of variables,* a particularly confusing name, for my money.

It's Not the Treatment, It's Something Else

This occurs when subjects are exposed to a number of treatment inputs. One example is residential treatment where it is difficult to know which of the many interventions offered actually account for social and emotional changes in the subjects. One ill effect of professionalism is the belief that one and only one treatment is responsible for the subject's improvement when, most likely, it is the overall impact of everyone working together to help the client that results in improvement. But sometimes it isn't anything so specific. It just may be the friendly receptionist at the desk, or the friendly janitor, or a beautiful view from the client's window that does the most good. This is also called *multiple-treatment interference,* and it suggests how difficult it is to determine which, of the many treatment inputs a client may experience, actually causes the improvement in social and emotional functioning.

Meaningless Relationships (not to be confused with anyone's love life)

Many instruments contain questions that are "fillers" and are meaningless. The responses to these meaningless questions may suggest cause-effect relationships that are actually spurious (accidental and without validity). This is also called *irrelevant responsiveness of measures.*

Too Many Reasons to Know Why Something Happened

Because treatment is so complex, the actual aspect of the treatment responsible for client change may not be measured in the study. If you consider why people change their behavior, there are literally thousands of reasons, most of which we haven't even thought about in our study. A statistical test called *regression analysis* may show that while 20 percent of the reasons someone gets better in treatment are because of the use of a certain type of therapy, fully 80 percent of the reasons have to do with other variables, most of which we haven't included in our study. This is also called *irrelevant replicability of treatment,* but who knows why?

The Researcher's Bias

While we like to think that researchers are unbiased, sometimes their egos get the better of them and the study is compromised. I went to a meeting recently in which a researcher was discussing an on-going study concerning the use of radioactive seeds in the treatment of prostate cancer (small radioactive particles placed in the prostate for a certain length of time). The study was supposed to be a double blind study in which the names of those receiving various types of treatment (surgery, radiation, radioactive seeds, etc.) were unknown to the researcher. In the meeting, however, the researcher assured us that the patients receiving radioactive seeds were doing better than the other groups. How did he know? Obviously he knew everyone's name and the treatment they were receiving. Did that knowledge lead to the provision of other services for the sake of proving that radioactive seeds work best in the treatment of prostate cancer? You could hardly come away not believing that. And now knowing the researcher's bias, how could we possibly accept his findings?

Summary

In this chapter on quantitative methods, we briefly covered some issues related to designs and the types of errors that sometimes affect the findings in a quantitative study. As noted in the internal and external validity sections of the chapter, it is very difficult to control for all of the internal and external validity concerns we have in research. For that reason, some researchers have argued for a less stringent approach to social research. That approach, known as the *qualitative approach to research,* will be discussed in the next chapter. Most researchers believe, while acknowledging the difficulty in doing a quantitative study, that quantitative methods are the benchmark of good research. Before using qualitative designs, they might argue, students must master the more stringent expectations of quantitative methodologies. I hope that this brief discussion has been helpful. If you need more detail, I would refer you to one of the many excellent texts in the reference section of this chapter. Many of those books discuss the complexities of quantitative research in much more detail.

REVIEW QUESTIONS

1. Isn't a flawed quantitative study still useful in terms of providing important information, particularly when the researcher points out the flaws in the study and is very honest about the study's limitations?

2. Why should we know quantitative methods when it's so hard to control for the internal and external validity errors that seem to crop up in even the best designs?

3. None of the designs mentioned in this chapter, with the exception of survey research, seem even remotely possible for a student research project. Do you think that's the case?

4. Time series studies seem so complex that it would be very unlikely that they could ever be used in applied social science research. Do you agree?

REFERENCES

48 Hours. (2001, May 25). *Use it or lose it.* Originally aired May 25, 2001, CBS.

Alwin, D. F. (1977). Making errors in surveys. *Sociological Methods and Research, 6,* 131–150.

Alwin, D. F., & Krosnick, J. A. (1985). The measurement of values in surveys: A comparison of ratings and rankings. *Public Opinion Quarterly, 49,* 535–552.

Babbie, E. (1998). *Survey research methods.* Belmont, CA: Wadsworth.

Bausell, B. R. (1994). *Conducting meaningful experiments: 40 steps to becoming a scientist.* Thousand Oaks, CA: Sage.

Bohrnstedt, G. (1992). Validity. In E. Borgatta & M. Borgatta (Eds.), *Encyclopedia of sociology, Vol. 4* (pp. 2217–2222). New York: Macmillan.

Bostwick, G. J., Jr., & Kyte, N. S. (1985). Validity and reliability. In R. M. Grinnell, Jr. (Ed.), *Social work research and evaluation, 2nd ed.* (pp. 161–184). Itasca, IL: Peacock.

Campbell, D. T., & Stanley, J. C. (1963). *Experimental and quasi-experimental designs for research.* Chicago: Rand McNally.

Carmines, E., & Zeller, R. (1979). *Reliability and validity assessment.* Beverly Hills, CA: Sage.

Cone, J. D. (1977). The relevance of reliability and validity for behavioral assessment. *Behavior Therapy, 8,* 411–426.

Cook, T. D., & Campbell, D. T. (1979). *Quasi-experimentation: Design and analysis issues for field settings.* Chicago: Rand McNally.

Creswell, J. W. (1994). *Research design: Qualitative and quantitative approaches.* Thousand Oaks, CA: Sage.

Epstein, I. (1985). Quantitative and qualitative methods. In R. J. Grinnell (Ed.), *Social work research and evaluation* (pp. 263–274). Itasca, IL: Peacock.

Fischer, J. (1981). A framework for evaluating empirical research reports. In R. M. Grinnell (Ed.), *Social work research and evaluation* (pp. 569–589). Itasca, IL: Peacock.

Fowler, F. J., Jr. (1992). How unclear terms can affect survey data. *Public Opinion Quarterly, 56,* 218–231.

Gambrill, E. (1997). *Social work practice: A critical thinker's guide.* New York: Oxford Press.

Gillespie, D. F., & Glisson, C. (1993). *Quantitative methods in social work.* Binghamton, NY: The Haworth Press.

Glock, C. Y. (1987). Reflections on doing survey research. In H. O'Gorman (Ed.), *Surveying social life: Papers in honor of Herbert H. Hyman* (pp. 31–59). Middletown, CT: Wesleyan University Press.

Gordon, J. E. (1984). Creating research-based practice principles: A model. *Social Work Research and Abstracts, 20,* 3–6.

Grinnell, R. M., Jr., et al. (1994, July). Social work researchers' quest for responsibility. *Social Work, 39(4),* 469–470.

Hegtvedt, K. A. (1992). Replication. In E. Borgatta and M. Borgatta (Eds.), *Encyclopedia of sociology, Vol. 3* (pp. 1661–1663). New York: Macmillan.

Kercher, K. (1992). Quasi-experimental research designs. In E. Borgatta and M. Borgatta (Eds.), *Encyclopedia of sociology, Vol. 3* (pp. 1595–1613). New York: Macmillan.

Kidder, L. H. (1982). Face validity from multiple perspectives. In D. Brinberg and L. Kidder (Eds.), *Forms validity in research* (pp. 41–57). San Francisco: Jossey-Bass.

Medeva Phamaceuticals. (Rev. 2000).

Nelson, R. O. (1981). Realistic dependent measures for clinical use. *Journal of Consulting and Clinical Psychology, 49,* 168–182.

Seligman, M. E. P. (1995). The effectiveness of psychotherapy: The consumer reports study. *American Psychologist, 50(12),* 965–974.

Spector, P. E. (1981). *Research designs.* Beverly Hills, CA: Sage.

Swanborn, P. G. (1996). A common base for quality control criteria in quantitative and qualitative research. *Quality and Quantity, 30,* 19–35.

Thyer, B. A. (2001). What is the role of research on social work practice? *Journal of Social Work Education, 37(1),* Winter.

Traub, R. E. (1994). *Reliability for the social sciences.* Thousand Oaks, CA: Sage.

Tripodi, T., Fellin, P., & Meyer, H. J. (1969). *The assessment of social research.* Itasca, IL: Peacock.

Wall, B. (2001). *Residence willing to pay for park.* San Bernradino Sun, Dec. 17, 2001, A1, A4.

Wilson, T., LaFleur, S. J., & Anderson, D. E. (1996). The validity and consequences of verbal reports about attitudes. In N. Schwarz and S. Sudman (Eds.), *Answering questions* (pp. 91–114). San Francisco: Jossey-Bass.

Yu, J., & Cooper, H. (1983). A quantitative review of research design effects on response rates to questionnaires. *Journal of Marketing Research, 20,* 36–44.

RECOMMENDED INTERNET SITES

Social Work Resources, Smith College
    <http://sophia.smith.edu/~jdrisko/>
Inter-University Consortium for Political and Social Research
    <http://www.icpsr.umich.edu/>
Solomon Four-Group Designs
    <http://www.fammed.ouhsc.edu/tutor/solomon.htm>
NES (National Election Studies) Core Time-Series Questions
    <http://www.umich.edu/~nes/studyres/datainfo/nes_core.htm>
Online Survey Research/Public Opinion Centers: A Worldwide Listing, University of Kansas
    <http://www.ukans.edu/cwis/units/coms2/po/>

CHAPTER

9 Qualitative Designs

Introduction

In the past few years, increasing numbers of social researchers have concluded that quantitative designs using a positivist paradigm are too large, too difficult to manage, and are frequently too expensive. They have also come to believe that quantitative designs may actually inhibit the researcher from obtaining information about important issues. Not all issues in social research, they believe, lend themselves well to quantitative design. An example of how quantitative designs may not be the best way to approach certain research questions can be found in the important work that Margaret Hughes (1997) is doing on why gang members transition out of gang life. By interviewing gang members at random, Hughes has begun to believe that gang members transition out of gang life when the safety of their children is at risk. This is an important finding and it comes from a qualitative study in which she randomly interviewed gang members in Los Angeles and Boston.

Qualitatively oriented researchers like Hughes believe that the research quest should be driven by the desire to find small truths. The rules of quantitative research, they believe, make finding small truths, possible connections, and subjective links between variables quite difficult to achieve. Tyson (1992), for example, believes that "the positivist paradigm that has defined scientific social work from 1949–1981 has failed to engender research that most practitioners find useful" (p. 541). She goes on to note that the positivist paradigm places limits on inquiry that stifles the research effort and often fails to provide needed information to those in the applied social sciences. She argues for the use of a more flexible approach, which she calls *heuristic,* but which most social researcher would consider to be a type of *qualitative* or *post-positivist research* approach.

Qualitative research doesn't eliminate research rules completely, but it does open the playing field to very creative pieces of research that do not attempt to show a cause-effect relationship or to generalize to other situations, places, or people. The researcher using qualitative designs believes

151

that the role of the researcher is to provide small pieces of information that have been studied in less constrained but more creative ways than might be possible using a quantitative approach. Because qualitative research is less stringent in its application of research rules, in a sense, most of us can become researchers. As a result, the amount of information developed on topics that are usually not feasible to study with more demanding and complex methodologies, can be greatly increased.

Qualitative researchers also believe that if enough people study similar problems using research designs uniquely and creatively attuned to that problem, enough small studies will begin to suggest connections between variables that form larger meaning. The accumulation of small findings may lead us to see connections that might be applicable to other people, places, and situations. However, the point isn't so much to encourage researchers to replicate one another's studies, as it is to encourage a massive amount of small, inexpensive pieces of research using less demanding designs to study important social issues that exist and require inquiry.

Qualitative should not be taken to mean non-numerical. Statistics are often used in qualitative research. But in qualitative research, the stringent, objective rules that govern quantitative research may not always be followed. For many social researchers, it makes more sense to do single subject research to determine treatment effectiveness than no research at all. Rather than deciding that a study is not feasible because sample size is too small or a sample is too difficult to locate, a qualitative study may be infinitely better than not doing a study. Knowing is always better than not knowing even if the study isn't as objective or scientific as we would like it to be. And remember that qualitative research doesn't intend to show cause-effect relationships among variables. Rather, its intention is to show trends, possible associations, and interesting findings that might otherwise be impossible to report using more empirical methodologies.

The Rules of Qualitative Research

As with all research, in qualitative research you must have a problem formulation and a literature review. Where the rules change somewhat is in the methodology used for the study. Here, you must clearly describe what you intend to do. You need to be very specific about your sampling approach. You need to clearly describe the research problem and state the objectives of the study. Qualitative research is often not thought to be good at hypothesis testing because it cannot, by the nature of its more subjective methodology, prove or disprove a hypothesis. You must clearly describe the instrument(s) you intend to use and report their validity and reliability. And, you must explain why the instrument is appropriate for your study. You must have, what Yaffe (1999) calls, an *audit trail*. That is, you must provide clear, reliable information on all aspects of the research process, including the sampling approach and its rationale and limitations; the data collection process; the instruments used and their validity and reliability; the way the data have been analyzed; and a description of the statistical analysis and its relevance to the goals and objectives of your study. You must also provide a section on your findings that describes the limits of the study and cautions the consumer not to make more of the findings than are warranted. While a qualitative study might report some interesting findings, it must be noted in your report that the study has limitations. These limitations must be clearly noted in the audit trail you describe at every juncture of the report.

The Role of the Qualitative Researcher

Neuman (1994) has suggested that qualitative researchers do the following:

1. they observe life situations in their natural setting;
2. they experience the lives of the people they are studying;
3. because they begin to know and understand the people and the setting they are studying, they acquire an "insiders point of view";
4. they use very flexible research methodologies geared to the issue they are studying;
5. their data may include voluminous notes or outlines, "diagrams, maps or pictures";
6. they understand that people live within a social context and they factor the social context into their findings;
7. they begin to develop personal relationships with their subjects and are thus able to report on the lives of their subjects in a way that projects a caring attitude;
8. they are able to report the subjective interactions of people, which permits a more inductive approach to data collection;
9. they are able to deal with high levels of uncertainty in the process of studying events, situations, and people and;
10. they are able to recognize events, interactions, and social processes without interfering. (p. 121)

You may want to dwell on Neuman's description of the qualitative researcher since it differs in fundamental ways from the role of the quantitative researcher. Most quantitative researchers worry that developing personal relationships with research subjects might lead to a lack of objectivity in reporting information. Furthermore, as all too many cultural anthropologists will admit, it's difficult to study social processes without affecting them, particularly if those processes are destructive. Researchers studying gang violence have a very difficult time not wanting to stop the violence from taking place. That's a natural human response but it does suggest that interacting with research subjects and maintaining an aloofness that permits objectivity may be very difficult. Having an "insider's view" of events may just contaminate the findings. How objective can one be if the views of the people studied become the views of the researcher? Do voluminous notes suggest that the notes are accurate and trustworthy? Possibly not and, therefore, quantitative researchers might suspect a high degree of inaccuracy in what is reported. Finally, flexibility in the methodologies used in research has limitations. Is there a point at which a methodology is so flexible that it produces meaningless results? Some quantitative researchers worry that this might be the case.

And yet, there is something very idealistic and positive in Nueman's description of the functions of the qualitative researcher. It is this idealism that attracts many social researchers to the qualitative approach; idealism, and the ability to use highly creative and flexible approaches to inquiry that make the research exciting.

Types of Qualitative Designs

Naturalistic Research

While, to some degree, all research observes and studies behavior, naturalistic research observes behavior with the least amount of tampering by the researcher. Robert Emerson (1983) defines naturalistic research (field research) as a way to study people in their "natural environments as they go about their daily lives. It tries to understand how people live, how they talk and behave, and what captivates and distress them." (p. 8). Emerson believes that the role of naturalistic research is to understand the meaning of "people's words and behaviors." (p. 4). Naturalistic research places the researcher in the role of objective observer of people, situations, and events. The naturalistic researcher takes copious notes, reports any unusual interactions between people, and keeps daily records of what she sees, hears and, most importantly, what she feels about the situations she is studying.

Cultural anthropologists observing the behavior of people and events in various cultures often use naturalistic research. The researcher may count, interpret, inquire about or analyze behavior and events as they are happening. In naturalistic research, the researcher must describe the procedures that he or she is using to study an event and then follow those procedures to maintain maximum objectivity.

Perhaps a good example of naturalistic research is a study that I conducted in which I observed the interactions of prison guards with inmates at a medium security prison. As part of an early position I held at a social agency, I made bi-monthly trips to the facility, a prison for less seriously adjudicated felons between the ages of 18 and 25. As anyone who knows about legal technicalities might guess, the words "less seriously adjudicated felons" only meant that the felons were younger and had committed less serious crimes. As far as their psychosocial functioning, many of the prisoners were headed for some very serious crime once they were released from prison. My job was to go to the prison every two weeks and interview prospective parolees who were going to enter a program contracted to a local social service agency. The purpose of the project was to try to rehabilitate parolees by offering them vocational evaluations, subsequent vocational training and job placements, and the case management services necessary for them to re-enter the outside world (housing, financial help, family reconciliation, etc.).

While visiting the prison over a period of a year, I became fascinated by how friendly the guards and the prisoners were with one another. It became apparent to me that, in many ways, both groups were more similar as people than different. And so I began to collect information about those interactions. What I noted was the use of first names, the pride many of the guards had in their access to prison services (the food was great and it was free to the guards), the fact that guards often had prisoners do personal work for them outside of the prison, and that the prisoners were often able to get money, extra food, or other special favors as a result. I recorded my observations of prison life on the train ride back from my visits to the prison. During my travel time, I would organize my notes under various categories, changing and refining the categories of observation as I went along. I would then note how often I saw the same behaviors and ultimately came to a point in time (one year of observed behavior) when there were a sufficient number of repetitive observations to suggest the following conclusions:

1. Almost any test taken in the psychology department was faked (two packs of cigarettes would get you a falsified personality test).
2. The treatment staff (counselors, social workers, psychologists) spent most of their time "shmoozing" (sitting around talking about nothing in particular with one another). They seldom saw or provided services to even the most emotionally troubled prisoners even though there were a fair number of psychotic and otherwise deeply disturbed prisoners in the prison, many of whom I interviewed and who then became clients in our project.
3. Most parole decisions were made with such limited information about the prisoners that the parole hearing had almost nothing to do with the way the prisoner might function in the community upon release. Faked psychological tests and overly generalized prison staff psychosocial reports, which, when looked at over a period of time, might

seem to apply to anyone in prison, were the most frequently used criteria for release.

4. In notes I made after the prison interviews with over 100 parolees, I predicted that most of my clients (60% of them) were too unmotivated, troubled, or impulsive to benefit from the training our agency was about to offer, and that most would return to prison within six months after release, often for more serious crimes than they'd originally committed. I was almost always right.

5. I found little overt abuse of prisoners. In fact, a high number of prisoners liked prison life better than life on the outside. Many prisoners, in my observation, did better in prison than in the community. Perhaps they felt better treated and cared for in prison than on the outside and the structure and controls of prison life kept their impulsive behavior in check.

6. Prison did little to teach prisoners simple living skills. A surprising number of parolees entering our program had been in prisons so long that they didn't know how to use the bus, get a haircut, or have a telephone installed in their apartments. The lack of knowledge on how to deal with simple life problems often led to frustrations that ended in acting out behavior.

7. Even the prison officials I worked with were very sure that most of the parolees would return to prison in a short period of time (and they were right). Half of my client load was composed of very dangerous parolees who did dangerous crimes after they were released, while the other half were just impulsive, not too bright, and prone to making bad decisions that continually got them into small trouble. The first half should not have been released and belonged in prison with treatment. The second half belonged in halfway houses where they could be taught daily living skills and impulse control under supervision.

Can I be sure that I was correct in these observations? Yes, I think so. Over a year of visits, I kept careful notes on what I saw. I read those notes continually, organized what they said, tried to see ongoing themes in my observations, let others read my notes and organize them, and observed that others came to the same conclusions that I did. As it turned out, our clients in treatment did worse than those in the control group who were released to the community without any particular assistance. Why? Probably because we were in close contact with parole officers. If the parolee violated the rules of the agency or of his parole, he went back to prison. It led me to conclude that parole officers are much more likely to revoke parole if an outside agency serves as a watchdog. Maybe they have such large caseloads that it's impossible for them to do the job correctly, or maybe they have more faith in human nature and believe that small violations, if ignored, will ultimately permit parolees to change as they mature. I came away from the experience certain that prisons do little to help or rehabilitate prisoners. Their primary function it seemed to me was to warehouse people and prevent crime from taking place for the short time felons were in jail.

This is an example of naturalistic research. While very time-consuming and certainly subjective in nature, a good deal of meaningful information was collected that was passed on to the agency when I left. The contract to continue services to parolees was not renewed. Prisons should not be warehouses and efforts ultimately have to be made to transition parolees from prison back to the community. One of the research agendas for the past twenty years, as prison populations have swelled, is how to do this with some degree of effectiveness. The research goes on and while nothing definitive has been found thus far, it is important research on an important subject. You can only wish the researchers who work with the correctional facilities of America the best of luck.

Participant–Observer Design

This design is used when we are observing a situation in which we may also be part of that situation. Participant-observation differs from naturalistic research. In naturalistic research, we are assuming the research role of someone from outside of the setting we are studying. In effect, we are maintaining the objective and scientific role that permits us to view the events as they unfold in a reasonably objective way. In participant-observation research, we are part of the situation or the institution that we are studying. The work that was ultimately published in *On Being Sane in Insane Places* (Rosenhan, 1973) is a good example of this design. A group of researchers (sane, we think) got themselves admitted to a state hospital for trumped up and unsubstantiated emotional problems. While in the hospital, they acted no differently than ever but were viewed by the treatment staff as being mentally ill. While in the hospital, they witnessed the brutal treatment of patients who were often physically and sexually abused by the staff. They observed how little time the treatment staff actually spent with patients and determined that the state hospital in which they were posing as patients merely warehoused the mentally ill. Very little significant treatment took place. Virtually no time was spent trying to work individually or in groups with patients for the purpose of community placement or release to family. Interestingly, although the goal of the researchers was to blend into the patient population, the patients knew almost immediately that the researchers were not actual patients, something the treatment staff failed to observe throughout the research study.

While this is exciting sounding research, the methodology used requires strict adherence to research guidelines and a research protocol that includes a way to identify, report, and quantify behavior. It also requires an audit trail that helps maintain the objectivity of this approach. Maintaining objectivity in participant-observation can be problematic because we may develop friendships with the subjects we are observing. As a result, we may be reluctant to say anything negative about someone we like. Our feelings of allegiance to an institution may affect the way we interpret the information we are collecting. And there are ethical considerations, as well. Is it unethical to fool people into thinking that we are loyal members of the institution being studied? Many research subjects who believe that researchers are colleagues and friends think this approach is highly unethical. And while some meaningful results may be obtained with the participant-observation approach, the ethical imperative that we seek the consent of our research subjects to study their behavior may be violated. But clearly, from an scholarly point of view, a good deal of important data can be gathered using this approach, some of it impossible to collect using other methodologies. If we want to find out how child protection agencies handle child abuse cases, what better way to do this than to become a child welfare worker and casually observe the intimate interactions of an agency's workers, administrators, and clients?

Ex-Post Facto Designs

Ex-post facto designs look at past behavior to explain current behavior and, in some instances, to try and anticipate future behaviors. One of the best-known types of ex-post facto studies are those done to show a connection between lung cancer and cigarette smoking. Patients with lung cancer are interviewed to determine their lifelong level of smoking and to see any connection between smoking and lung cancer. The findings, as we well know by now, show that the more cigarettes smoked over a long period of time, the more likely the smoker will be to develop lung cancer. This approach has been used with many other common physical problems to show cause-effect relationships between two or more behaviors.

This design is used in situations when there may not be other ethical ways to study certain events. It would be unethical and highly unsafe to introduce smoking to a group of children, follow their health over the years, and interview them after they've developed lung cancer. When the outcomes of certain events are too cruel or unkind to create in a lab (on humans, at least), then looking backward from the point at which a problem (such as lung cancer) is recognized and trying to see connections between the problem and the cause of the problem is one of the few research approaches we can use that does not violate ethical constraints.

The problem with this design is that what may appear to be a cause-effect relationship may, in reality, be extraneous or not relevant. If smoking is the primary reason for lung cancer, then the overall lung cancer rates in the country should go down as smoking decreases. While smoking has decreased, lung cancer rates have not declined appreciably (Lung Cancer,

2002). Might the environment, diet, or any number of other reasons be at play that give better explanations for lung cancer in smokers? Perhaps, but until we determine what they are, I certainly advise against smoking.

That's really the problem with ex-post facto research. Sometimes the relationships shown in ex-post facto designs are just plain silly. Any number of ridiculous links can be made using ex-post facto research including the harm done by apples (a recent ex-post facto scare showing serious medical problems in children linked to consumption of apples). With statistics, you can prove just about anything, and in ex-post facto research, the chances of showing relationships that really do not exist can be considerable. If people who are violent eat bread, isn't there a link between eating bread and being violent? Think that's ridiculous? Ex-post facto designs have been used to show links between hyperactivity and the intake of sugar. They've been used to show relationships between aggression and eating too much red meat and junk foods. Until we have some definitive information that correlations exist and that eating sugar, junk food, and red meat cause hyperactivity and violence, I would suggest caution in eating all three, except that giving up Baby Ruth candy bars and spare ribs is just asking too darn much of this researcher. In fact, Tuesday in Mt. Pleasant, Michigan, is all-you-can-eat rib night. If you think those of us who partake are violent, you'd need to see the slow, ponderous gait of the patrons of the Mountain Station Restaurant in Mt. Pleasant to know that these folks aren't going to hurt anyone but themselves.

When using ex-post facto designs, we have to show, through our literature review, that there is a good reason to think that a link exists between the variables being studied. These links need to be rational and, most importantly, we need to maintain a commitment to objectivity in our study so that we don't try to prove connections between variables for our own highly personal reasons. This happens all too often when researchers have strong personal beliefs about the importance of their outcomes. In more cases than we care to note, researchers have found links between variables that don't hold in replicated studies. Having strong convictions that other people can't shake is generally good in life, but not in research. If you have a personal bias against sugar or red meat and see them as massive culprits of chaos and violence, fine. But you can't take that bias into a research design that is often used to prove connections among variables when none may exist.

Focus Groups

In the focus group, a sample of people is brought together to discuss an issue and then reach agreement about that issue through consensus statements. Getting people together to discuss issues and developing consensus statements about events, attitudes, and opinions is frequently done in research. This process of using groups to provide information has many names, but the most commonly used name for this approach is the *focus group*. Focus groups are qualitative because the design makes it impossible to adequately control for many important variables. It is a useful way, however, to gather data.

Some researchers use videotapes to record group interactions. Linguistic techniques to analyze the interactions among the participants might also be used to factor in subjective, but meaningful, non-verbal communications. There is usually a second person present with the researcher to run a video camera or to record written observations of group interactions as a way of making the researcher's conclusions more objective. Focus groups are beneficial because a great deal of important data can be collected in a short period of time. However, if several people take over the group and push their opinions so hard that it influences the way others in the group respond, or if the focus group facilitator has a certain point of view he or she wants to stress, the information that results from a focus group session can be fairly biased. Watching focus groups of undecided voters in the 2000 presidential election evaluate the three presidential debates gave new meaning to the term *useless information*. The focus groups listened to a 10-minute analysis of each debate by television commentators who uniformly agreed that President Bush had won the debates. Before the start of the focus groups, the results of telephone polls were flashed across the television screen, showing a strong majority of voters who watched the debates thought that President Bush had won, hands down. Then the focus group met. Does it surprise anyone that the groups also thought President Bush won the debates?

Focus groups, if handled correctly, provide a wealth of information. Nicholas Leman (2000), writing about the use of focus groups to compensate for inaccuracies in political polls, notes that political focus groups are meant to "pick up on aspects of voter unconsciousness that lie outside the questions asked in polls" (p. 107). Leman goes on to say that under the "prodding" of the group leader, members of focus groups should be able to "free associate" and that such a process will "reveal the shadings of opinions within a single category of voters" (p. 107). In other words, focus groups permit one to define terms and to better understand feelings and thoughts that are often outside of the narrow questions asked in surveys and polls. To a large extent, they break down social desirability and capture core concerns, beliefs, and confusion about issues. Focus groups narrow down opinions in a way that polls and surveys can never do because they permit focus group members to clarify, for themselves and others, what they really believe. This permits political scientists and pollsters to define for politicians subtle and emotional issues that have meaning for voters but are seldom captured in polls. The term *quality of life*, for example, in a focus group Leman observed, came out not to mean personal happiness or the availability of a safety net, but the amount of money the participants had. This definition of quality of life would very likely be at odds with the way most of us define life quality and would apply to a very small segment of the population. None-the-less, if trying to understand that small segment of the population was important to the social scientist, the information would be profoundly important.

A good focus group has random selection of subjects. Everyone's opinion in the group is sought. The questions asked come from a well thought through protocol developed by the researcher in an objective and thoughtful way. The researcher should have specialized training in focus group procedures and should know how to introduce questions, allow for discussion, summarize the various points of view, and move toward consensus statements. Some researchers use linguistic and group behavioral techniques to measure non-verbal behavior and to monitor the dynamics of the groups, all for the purpose of increasing the information provided by the focus group.

If during the consensus statement phase, non-verbal behavior suggests a greater margin of disagreement with the consensus statement than the vote to accept it, this would certainly affect the results. A well-trained group leader would stop the vote and cycle back to the discussion bringing all group members and the subjects discussed into the debate until, non-verbally, it appeared that everyone had his or her say and that the vote was ready to be taken. This ability to use non-verbal behavior (the head shake, the look of disappointment, the inability to look at the leader at a crucial moment, the flash of joy or anger at what someone says) can make a group very dynamic and the information retrieved very useful. If it takes seven levels of questions to get at honest feelings about a subject, then the focus group needs to use every available strategy to get at honest and freely chosen beliefs, feelings, and opinions. You can see, however, that focus groups can suffer from social desirability and that consensus statements may be agreed on that aren't really indicative of what people believe.

The focus group approach can also suffer if participants have great concerns that what they say might get them into some degree of trouble. If you ever get a group of child protective service workers together who come from the same agency, you'll note how careful they are in the discussion not to say anything that might get back to a source capable of causing trouble for the workers. If the workers come from very different geographic locations and are unlikely to ever see one another again, the discussion might proceed in a much more objective and informative way. Choosing the participants correctly for a focus group is vital. Selection should consider diversity of opinion and representation by race, ethnicity, gender, income and educational levels, to mention just a few important factors to consider when choosing members of a focus group.

Analyzing content from focus group discussions can be painful because so much of the material is subjective. The researcher must have a methodology in place for data analysis. Some researchers leave the analysis of the data to people who weren't involved in the focus group. This can be done by video taping the session and letting other researchers analyze the findings and evaluate the objectivity of the techniques used by the focus group leader. As a way of collecting very important data in a short period of time, focus groups can be a tremendous amount of help to the researcher.

A few suggestions: keep the group size within controllable limits. The groups of forty to fifty people you see on television are just too large for effective discussions. Two or three people will take over the group and the discussion will be limited to their input. The group should only have that number of people who are able to contribute to the discussion an equal number of times. My suggestion is that fifteen people are about the limit for a good focus group. It's wise to leave about two hours for discussion and to limit topics to perhaps five to seven questions. I also recommend that a second person video tape or record the proceedings in writing.

Single Subject Studies with Goal Attainment Scaling

In single subject research, we are only interested in studying one subject. Another name for single subject research is *N=1 designs.* There are a variety of common single subject designs, only two of which will be discussed here: the AB design and the ABAB Reversal design.

AB Design. The most common single subject design is the AB Design. A steady state is determined that indicates how long the condition we are treating has existed. Then a baseline measure or pre-test is taken before the treatment input begins. The treatment input is described, a time-line indicating how long the treatment input will be given is determined, and when treatment is completed, a post-test is taken to measure change. Further post-tests might also be given to determine how long the change lasts. The steady state, if long enough, suggests that changes taking place are a result of the treatment input and not some intervening or capricious variable(s). This is because change that does not occur over a long period of time without treatment (the steady state) and now changes with treatment can logically be thought to have occurred because of the treatment input. As we will explain, this isn't easy to prove, but there is at least some strong reason to believe that the longer the steady state, the more likely change will be related to the treatment input. Single subject research is often done in conjunction with goal attainment scaling which will be described later in this chapter.

ABAB Reversal Design. But how do we know for certain, in such a simple design, that change is really due to the treatment input? One way to determine this is to use an ABAB Reversal design in which the treatment is given for a short period of time and then, for the same amount of time, it is taken away, and then given again. If we are correct that treatment is the reason for the change, we should see an improvement in behavior when treatment is initially provided, a worsening of behavior when we withdraw the treatment, and an improvement when the treatment is provided again. Physicians sometimes use this approach to determine the effectiveness of a medication, but in the applied social sciences, it may be difficult to find an ethical way of using the ABAB Reversal design since it may lead to deterioration in the client and some very unwanted side effects.

In the medical field, many conditions are borderline conditions for the use of medication. High blood pressure is an example. In patients with a steady state of borderline high blood pressure (not quite high enough for the use of medication but moving ever higher every year) physicians will test a number of treatment strategies. Medication and diet with exercise are two commonly used strategies. Medications have unwanted side effects but are used when the patient is unwilling, or unable, to use diet and exercise. To see which strategy might be most useful, the physician might place the patient on a hypertension medication for three months to lower blood pressure. Getting a steady state and a baseline measure, the physician might track the blood pressure for three months, note the change, take the patient off the medication for three months, and then reintroduce the medication for three months. Change may take place or it may not. After this attempt to see the effectiveness of medication, the physician might place the client on a strict regimen of diet and exercise tracking changes and using the same process noted above with the medication. In this way, the physician and the client can see which approach works best. Because so much high blood pressure in America is stress- and weight-related, physicians sometimes shy away from using medication in borderline cases although cautious physicians may be unwilling to substitute diet and exercise for medication fearing a worsening of the condition. The risk of side effects of medication sometimes outweighs the benefits of the medication. You can see how an ABAB Reversal design might help show patients with certain conditions that life style changes are more effective than medication and have the benefit of few unwanted side effects.

Goal Attainment Scaling. Goal attainment scaling is used when the researcher or therapist works with the subject to outline goals that all parties recognize as feasible and then monitors the progress and attainment of those goals. Goal attainment scaling is used for measurable and, therefore, observable behaviors. Goal attainment scaling is an easy way to determine the improvement rate of clients in treatment. While considered qualitative in nature, goal attainment scaling is a simple way to determine, with the client, the "hoped for" rates of improvement as a result of treatment. Because these "hoped for" rates of improvement (or goals of treatment) are fairly subjective, it is best to set treatment goals based on what the literature considers realistic improvement rates given the severity of the problem and the length of time available to see the client in treatment. Goal attainment scaling is often used with single subject designs in which we are only interested in the improvement rate of an individual subject. In single subject designs, we are not comparing people against one another. Rather, we are only interested in the progress of one client. However, if enough clients are evaluated using a single subject design, we might be able to suggest a weak association between what we do in treatment and its impact on similar clients.

Steady State. One way to determine whether the client has changed as a result of the treatment as opposed to some extraneous event (like falling in love, inheriting a great deal of money, etc.) is to measure how long the condition existed before the client sought help. The longer a depression lasts, for example, the less likely it is that something capricious will happen to change the client's behavior after treatment begins. Yet it could happen and trying to show a cause-effect relationship between treatment input and any degree of improvement using a qualitative approach such as a single subject design with a goal attainment scale, isn't really possible. Change in the client's behavior during treatment not noted during a very long steady state might suggest, however, that the longer the steady state, the more likely it is that treatment input was responsible for the client's improvement.

Baseline Measures. A baseline measure can be likened to a pre-test. It is the set of behaviors the client wants to change over the course of treatment as measured before the first treatment session begins. Baseline measures should all lend themselves to easy measurement and should be behavioral in nature. Weight, blood pressure, grades, exercise regimens, and blood-alcohol content are all examples of easily measured behaviors. Happiness, morale, or work satisfaction are examples of difficult to measure behaviors unless a valid and reliable measurement is used. Even then, goal attainment scaling is more concerned with changes in behavior that are directly observed in the person's life and can be measured. The depressed client who gets up in the morning, dresses, goes to work, and does his or her job reasonably well demonstrates measurable behaviors that indicate an ability to function even though the tests used to measure the level of depression may suggest a high rate of depression in the subject. Conversely, a person who has improved scores on an instrument measuring depression may also have poor social functioning. Consequently, to the extent possible, goal attainment scaling tries to measure changes in actual behavior rather than using instruments to measure levels of emotional dysfunction. Furthermore, while we trust the client to give us correct information, goal attainment scaling often uses primary ways to determine change. The client with a weight problem is weighed every session. The client who agrees to walk two miles a day must have a card signed by someone from a health facility who has observed the two mile walk and will verify it on paper. **Independent verification** is a strong point in measuring change.

Post-Tests.   As with any type of measurement to determine improvement as a result of any treatment input, one should also use a post-test. On a goal attainment scale, this is the level of improvement reached after a specific period of treatment as determined in the contract set between worker and client. The same set of goals outlined by the worker and client at the outset of treatment can be used to determine how long the improvement lasts after the initial post-test. One might want to do two or three post-tests over an 18-month period of time to determine whether the improvement is lasting or whether additional treatment is necessary.

Goals of Treatment.   In goal attainment scaling, the goals we set for improvement in functioning are determined conjointly with the client in the contracting phase of treatment, usually at the first session of ongoing treatment. The goals must be behavioral in nature (easily measured with minimal reliance on subjective client feedback) and they must be 1) directly related either to the process of change (the new behaviors the clients must practice to change the presenting problem) or 2) a direct measurement of the amount of change in the client's presenting problem(s). For example, it might be a goal in clinical work for a depressed client to have improved social functioning. Therefore, social functioning is the most important measurement of success in the treatment of depression. Does the client get up in the morning, dress, go to work, remain independent, have sufficient social contacts, or does the client deteriorate, lose his or her job, become dependent on some form of financial help, and succumb to the depression as a way of life? Improved social functioning is the end goal of treatment, and goal attainment scaling is a simple way to determine the level of social functioning.

You may disagree. You may think that happiness is always the end goal of treatment. But happiness is highly subjective. Lance Armstrong, four-time Tour de France bicycling champion who suffered from testicular cancer writes, "I become a happier man each time I suffer. Suffering is as essential to a good life and as inextricable, as bliss" (2001, p. 64). Does this sound like your definition of happiness? John Perry Barlow writes, "Extolling the virtues of happiness was a toxic stupidity entirely unworthy of our greatest American hero, Thomas Jefferson. Indeed, the pursuit of happiness is a poison that sickens our culture. I wish he'd never said it" (2001, p. 96). How does that relate to your feelings about happiness? Owen Edwards writes, "I now know what you knew when you wrote those famous words [speaking of Thomas Jefferson]: Happiness is a mirage, a chimera, no more catchable than a unicorn" (2001, p. 56). I should mention that all of these quotes come from an excellent *Forbes* magazine special edition on happiness. *Forbes* is a magazine that celebrates happiness as the end result of the attainment of wealth and the accumulation of material goods. How ironic that they would publish such thoughtful if downright antagonistic arguments against the magazine's primary purpose: to encourage the accumulation of wealth for the purpose of achieving happiness. None-the-less, you can see how difficult it is to define happiness and how each of us has very different definitions of happiness that make its use in treatment a very complex proposition. So, until we can agree on what constitutes happiness, much less how to measure and control it, we will stick with our standard procedures for setting goals and getting depressed people back to improved social functioning.

Examples of Goal Attainment Scales

In the following example of a depressed client, we use the Beck's Depression Inventory (BDI), hours of sleep, and work loss as dependent variables. The independent variables are exercise and social contacts. If the client exercises and improves the number of social contacts as a positive result of our treatment, then all three dependent variables (sleep, work lost, and the BDI score) should improve, we hope.

When you decide on goals, choose five goals of which at least two goals are dependent variables and three are independent variables. The following example of a goal attainment scale uses dependent and independent variables that are easy to measure. You may have other ideas about what needs to be done in treatment, and the goals you choose might differ from the ones I've suggested here. The best way to determine goals jointly with the client is to use the research literature as your guide.

Directions for Creating a Scale: Intervals and Weightings. On a goal attainment scale, 0% represents the baseline measure or the pre-test. This is a measure of the client's functioning at the start of treatment. Each increment of 25 percent represents our "hoped for" levels of improvement as the client progresses in treatment for a serious depression. The intervals between the percent of gain must be equal and increase by 25 percent from a baseline of 0 percent to the point of having fully achieved a goal of 100 percent. In the following goal attainment scale, intervals on the BDI are 15 points and the interval for hours of sleep per night is one hour. There are three additional goals: work lost per month, exercise, and social contacts. The intervals for each of these goals may be found on the goal attainment scale in Table 9.1. 100 percent represents our "hoped for" improvement rate after six months of once-a-week treatment. Another way of putting this is that 100 percent improvement is our contracted improvement rate when treatment begins.

W represents weighting or the importance of each variable we are using to measure improvement. Total weighting cannot surpass 1.0. The BDI is a measure of depression. It should show improvement as the other variables also improve. Sleep and missed days at work should decrease as the depression lessens. Increasing social contacts (movies with friends, church attendance, eating with friends, dates, etc.) and exercise should also help reduce depression. I have given higher weighting to the dependent variables (the depression scale, hours of sleep, and work lost) than the independent or treatment variables (exercise and social contacts). My reasons for doing this is that I want a number of ways to show that the depression is lifting. You may have other ideas about how this could work. That's fine. I'm giving two additional examples of goal attainment scaling in this chapter to help you better understand the process.

Determining the Amount of Improvement.   Multiply the weighting for each variable times the percentage of actual change in 6 months. For the Becks' variable, if 100 percent achievement of the goal is made, multiply .3 times 1.00 (100%) for a 30 percent improvement rate. If a 75 percent gain is made on the Becks', multiply .3 times .75 (75%) for a 22.5 percent gain on the depression inventory variable. Do this for all the variables, add them

TABLE 9.1   A Goal Attainment Scale Related to the Treatment of Depression

Score on the Becks Depression Inventory		Hours of Sleep per Day	Work Loss (days) per Month	Exercise (walking) per Day	Number of Social Contact per Week
W = .3		W = .2	W = .2	W = .15	W = .15
0%	80	12	12	0 miles	0
25%	65	11	8	.5 miles	1
50%	50	10	6	1.0 miles	2
75%	35	9	4	1.5 miles	3
100%	20	8	2	2.0 miles	4

up, and you'll get an overall improvement rate for all the variables combined.

Example One: Calculating Overall Gain on a Goal Attainment Scale

I'm going to give some possible improvement rates with this client so that you might better understand how to calculate the overall rate of improvement. Then I'll give my interpretation of what it all means.

1. *Improvement rate on the Becks Depression Inventory (BDI) = 75%.* $.75 \times .3 = 22.5\%$ gain.
2. *Improvement rate in the hours of sleep = 50%.* $50 \times .2 = 10\%$ gain.
3. *Work loss per month improvement rate = 25%.* $.2 \times .25 = 5\%$ gain.
4. *Exercise improvement rate = 0.* 0 times $.15 = 0\%$ gain.
5. *Social contacts improvement rate = 75%.* $.15 \times .75 = 11.25\%$ gain.
   Add all the percents of improvement together for a total improvement rate after six months of treatment for depression as follows:

   Becks = 22.5%
   Sleep = 10%
   Work = 5%
   Exercise = 0%
   Social = 11.25%
   _____
   Total = 48.75%

48.75% of the contracted for goals were achieved after six months of treatment.

What Does This Tell Us?

What can we make of this data? The client has an almost 50 percent gain in the goals agreed upon at the start of treatment. The BDI looks good. There is a 75 percent improvement rate but scores on psychological tests are notoriously prone to the halo effect. The depression might still be there but at the moment the test was given, the subject may have had an emotional high and scored better than he or she might really feel most of the time. The client is still missing a great deal of work. This isn't a good sign at all. Missing so much work places the client in jeopardy of losing his or her job. The client is sleeping less and has more social contacts. These are good signs, but exercise hasn't improved. Overall, it looks as if the client's depression is lifting and that some of his or her relevant behavior is better. But in the important area of work, improvement is marginal and one would probably conclude that while the depression is lifting somewhat, the depressed behavior is still affecting social functioning. It is social functioning, after all, that mainly concerns us. While the client may *feel* better, if that doesn't translate into better functioning at work, or with family, or in other important areas of behavior in a social and emotional context, then we can't be very positive about the impact of our treatment. We might conclude that more treatment is necessary and that the therapeutic approach we are using needs to be modified.

Example Two: A Goal Attainment Scale to Measure Weight Loss

In the next example, we are using a goal attainment scale (GAS) (Table 9.2) to determine the improvement rate of a client who has a weight problem but is also suffering from a weight-related problem of essential hypertension (high blood pressure without an organic cause). We have two dependent variables: weight and blood pressure. Our three independent variables are: fat grams eaten per day, calories eaten per day in the client's diet, and time spent walking per day. All three independent variables should impact our two dependent variables. Less fat grams, fewer calories, and more exercise should all have a positive impact on weight loss and lowered blood pressure.

Directions.   Zero percent represents the baseline measure or the pre-test. It is a measure of key behaviors at the start of treatment. Each increment of 25% represents where we hope the client will be as he or she progresses in the treatment. The intervals between the percent of gain must all be equal. 100% is our "hoped for" goal in treatment after 6 months of once-a-week treatment. The therapist and the client have agreed on the improvement rate before treatment begins. The improvement rate must be realistic and it

TABLE 9.2   A Goal Attainment Scale for Weight Loss

Weight		Fat Grams per Day	Calories per Day	Walking per Day	Blood Pressure
W = .3		W = .15	W = .15	W = .2	W = .2
0%	220	60	4000	0 miles	170/100
25%	210	50	3500	.5 miles	160/95
50%	200	40	3000	1.0 miles	150/90
75%	190	30	2500	1.5 miles	140/85
100%	180	20	2000	2.0 miles	130/80

must be consistent with what the literature suggests to us about probable client improvement rates after six months of weekly therapy. *W* represents weighting or the therapeutic importance of each variable we are using to measure improvement. Total weighting cannot surpass 1.0. The client's weight and blood pressure will be checked each week when they come for treatment. The client will keep calorie and fat intake records in a log. The amount of walking per day (five days per week) will be verified by a health club staff member.

Determining the Amount of Improvement. Multiply the weighting for each variable times the percentage of actual change over six months. For the weight variable, if 100% achievement of the goal is made, multiply .03 times 100% for a 30% improvement rate. Do this for all the variables, add them up, and you'll get an overall improvement rate for all of the variables combined.

Example Three: A Goal Attainment Scale to Improve Grade Point Average

In the following example (Table 9.3) of a client with problems in school, we are using grade point average (GPA) as the dependent variable and the other four variables, study time alone, absences, tutorial meetings, and study group meetings, as the independent variables. My theory is that the four independent variables, if done with motivation, will improve GPA. Note that I'm trying to make the improvement in GPA reasonable. I may be overly optimistic or overly pessimistic, but a change in GPA from 1.5 to 2.7 in six months seems like quite a bit to me. You may feel differently. I've also placed a check (✓) next to those levels of improvement that I think might be attained so that we can practice the math again.

TABLE 9.3 A Goal Attainment Scale to Measure Grade Point Average Improvement

Grade Point Average (GPA)		Study Time Alone/Day (in minutes)	Class Absences/ Week	Tutorials/ Week	Study Hours/ Group
W = .4		W = .2	W = .15	W = .15	W = .1
0%	1.5	10	10	0	0
25%	1.8✓	40✓	8	1	1
50%	2.1	70	6✓	2	2✓
75%	2.4	100	4	3✓	3
100%	2.7	130	2	4	4

Determining the Amount of Improvement. Multiply the weighting for each variable times the percentage of actual change in six months noted on the previous goal attainment scale (see where the "✓" is placed). The actual improvement rates are calculated below.

> Grade Point Average: .25 × .40 = 10%
> Study Time Alone: .25 × .20 = 5%
> Absences per week: .15 × .50 = 7.5%
> Tutorials per week: .15 × .75 = 11.25%
> Study Groups per week: .01 × .50 = 5%
> *Total Goals Achieved = 38.75%*

Discussion. This goal attainment scale shows some promising changes in the student's work. GPA is up slightly, the student is spending more time in tutorials and group study, but absences from class are still too high, and the student is not making much improvement in working alone. My guess is that after six months of work, the student isn't achieving at a level to give us confidence that once treatment stops, improvement will continue. In fact, my guess is that underlying study habits are still poor and that the increase in GPA is a function of learning from the study group and the tutorials. I'm not optimistic, even though over one-third of the goals have been achieved. In the two variables most important to our goal attainment scale, grades and absences, the student has only made slight improvement. I could be wrong. Perhaps this is the start of a gradual climb. I doubt it, but what do you think?

Summary

Qualitative designs seem ideally suited for student research studies. While they are less stringent than quantitative studies, by explaining our methodology and by keeping and reporting an audit trail, we are often able to approach a research problem in ways that provide for considerable creativity. Qualitative studies are not thought to provide cause-effect relationships nor are they usually thought to be generalizable. They do, however, provide links and weak associations and are ideal for small studies, particularly initial studies where the goal is to explore new issues or to develop new methodologies.

REVIEW QUESTIONS

1. If you were to use a focus group, how might you go about collecting the information developed through the group interaction? How might you check for reliability and validity?

2. How would you handle the ethical issues related to the use of a participant-observer approach to data collection so that it would receive human subjects approval?

3. What are some arguments against the use of single subject research as a way of determining client change?

4. The use of qualitative designs is sometimes cited as an excuse for badly done research. What are the steps necessary to ensure that a qualitative design is used correctly?

5. When we ask a subject to keep a log or to record his or her behavior during treatment, how do we counter the argument that client logs tend to show improvements in behavior that may be false or inflated?

REFERENCES

Armstrong, L. (2001, December 3). Back in the saddle. *Forbes, 64.*

Barlow, J. P. (2001, December 3). The pursuit of emptiness. *Forbes,* 96–97.

Edwards, O. (2001, December 3). Dear President Jefferson. *Forbes,* 56–58.

Emerson, R. (1983). Introduction. In R. M. Emerson (Ed.), *Contemporary field research* (pp. 1–16). Boston: Little Brown.

Grinnell, R., Jr., et al. (1994). Social work researchers' quest for respectability: Points and viewpoints. *Social Work, 39(4),* 469–470.

Hughes, M. J. (1997, June). An exploratory study of young-adult black and Latino males and the factors facilitating their decisions to make positive behavioral changes. *Smith College Studies in Social Work, 67(3),* 401–414.

Leman, N. (2000). The Word Lab. *New Yorker, October 16 and 23, 2000,* 100–112.

Lung Cancer. (2002, April 24). [Online]. http//www.oncologychannel.com/lungcancer/.

Neuman, W. L. (1994). Social research methods: Qualitative and quantitative approaches. Needham Heights, MA.: Allyn & Bacon.

Tyson, K. B. (1992). A new approach to relevant scientific research for practitioners: The heuristic paradigm. *Social Work, 37(6),* 541–556.

Tyson, K. B. (1994). Author's reply: Response to "Social Work Researcher's Quest for Respectability". *Social Work, 39(6),* 737–741.

Rosenhan, D. L. (1973). On being sane in insane place. *Science, 179,* 240–248.

Yaffe, J. (1999, July). Personal conversations with Dr. Yaffe. Salt Lake City: University of Utah School of Social Work.

ADDITIONAL READINGS

Adler, P. A., & Adler, P. (1994). Observational techniques. In N. Denzin and Y. Lincoln (Eds.), *Handbook of qualitative research* (pp. 377–392). Thousand Oaks, CA: Sage.

Allen, K. R., & Walker, A. J. (1992). A feminist analysis of interviews with elderly mothers and their daughters. In J. Gilgun, K. Daly, and G. Handel (Eds.), *Qualitative methods in family research* (pp. 198–214). Thousand Oaks, CA: Sage.

Altheide, D. L., & Johnson, J. M. (1994). Criteria for assessing interpretive validity in qualitative research. In N. K. Denzin & Y. S. Lincoln (Eds.), *Handbook of qualitative research* (pp. 485–499). Thousand Oaks, CA: Sage.

Atkinson, R. (1998). *The life story interview.* Thousand Oaks, CA: Sage.

Barlow, D. H., & Hersen, M. (1984). *Single-case experimental designs: Strategies for studying behavioral change.* New York: Pergamon.

Becker, H. S. (1970). Problems of inference and proof in participant observation. In W. J. Filstead (Ed.), *Qualitative methodology: Firsthand involvement with the social world* (pp. 189–201). Chicago: Markham.

Becker, H. S., & Greer, B. (1982). Participant observation and interviewing: A comparison. In W. J. Filstead (Ed.), *Qualitative methodology* (pp. 133–142). Chicago: Markham.

Becker, H. S., & Greer, B. (1982). Participant observation: The analysis of qualitative field data. In R. G. Burgess (Ed.), *Field research: A sourcebook and field manual* (pp. 239–250). Boston: Allen and Unwin.

Berg, B. L. (1998). *Qualitative research methods for the social sciences.* Boston: Allyn and Bacon.

Bernard, H. R., Killworth, P., Kronenfeld, D., & Sailer, L. (1984). The problem of information accuracy: The validity of retrospective data. *Annual Review of Anthropology, 13,* 495–517.

Bouchard, T. J., Jr. (1976). Unobtrusive measures: An inventory of uses. *Sociological Methods and Research, 4,* 267–300.

Burgess, R. G. (1982). Approaches to field research. In R. G. Burgess (Ed.), *Field research* (pp. 191–194). Boston: Allen and Unwin.

Creswell, J. W. (1994). *Research design: Qualitative and quantitative approaches.* Thousand Oaks, CA: Sage.

Denzin, N., & Lincoln, Y. (1994). *Handbook of qualitative research.* Thousand Oaks, CA: Sage.

Feldman, M. S. (1995). *Strategies for interpreting qualitative data.* Thousand Oaks, CA: Sage.

Fine, G. A., & Glassner, B. (1979). Participant observation with children: Promise and problems. *Urban Life, 8,* 153–174.

Fink, A., & Kosecoff, J. (1998). *How to conduct surveys.* Thousand Oaks, CA: Sage.

Gold, R. L. (1969). Roles in sociologist field observation. In G. J. McCall & J. L. Simmons (Eds.), *Issues in participant observation* (pp. 30–39). Reading, MA: Addison-Wesley.

Goodsell, C. B. (1983). Welfare waiting rooms. *Urban Life, 12,* 464–477.

Griffin, L. J., & Ragin, C. (1994). Some observations on formal methods of qualitative analysis. *Sociological Methods and Research, 23,* 4–22.

Grinnell, R. M., Jr. (1997). *Social work research and evaluation: Quantitative and qualitative approaches* (5th ed.). Itasca, IL: F. E. Peacock.

Heckathorn, D. D. (1997). Respondent-driven sampling: A new approach to the study of hidden populations. *Social Problems, 44,* 174–199.

Hersen, M., & Barlow, D. H. (1984). *Single case experimental designs: Strategies for studying behavior change (2nd ed.).* Elmsford, NY: Pergamon.

Kazdin, A. E., & Hussain, A. (1982). *Single-case research designs.* San Francisco: Jossey-Bass.

Kiresuk, T. J., & Sherman, R. E. (1968). Goal attainment scaling: A general method for evaluating comprehensive community mental health programs. *Community Mental Health Journal, 4,* 443–453.

Krueger, R. A. (1988). *Focus groups: A practical guide for applied research.* Beverly Hills, CA: Sage.

Krueger, R. (1994). *Focus groups.* Beverly Hills, CA: Sage.

Krueger, R. (1997). *Moderating focus groups.* Beverly Hills, CA: Sage.

Layder, D. (1993). *New strategies in social research.* Cambridge, MA: Polity.

Marshall, C., & Rossman, G. B. (1995). *Designing qualitative research (2nd ed.).* Thousand Oaks, CA: Sage.

Maxim, P. S. (1999). *Quantitative research methods in the social sciences.* New York: Oxford Press.

Miles, M. B., & Huberman, A. M. (1994). *Qualitative data analysis* (2nd ed.). Thousand Oaks, CA: Sage.

Mitchell, R. G., Jr. (1993). *Secrecy and fieldwork.* Thousand Oaks, CA: Sage.

Morgan, D. (1997). *The focus group handbook.* Thousand Oaks, CA: Sage.

Morrow, R. A. (1994). *Critical theory and methodology.* Thousand Oaks, CA: Sage.

Morse, J. M. (1994). Designing funded qualitative research. In N. Denzin and Y. Lincoln (Eds.), *Handbook of qualitative research* (pp. 220–235). Thousand Oaks, CA: Sage.

Olicker, S. J. (1994). Does workfare work? Evaluation research and workfare policy. *Social Problems, 41,* 195–211.

Olsen, V. (1994). Feminism and models of qualitative research. In N. Denzin and Y. Lincoln (Eds.), *Handbook of qualitative research* (pp. 158–174). Thousand Oaks, CA: Sage.

Reissman, C. (Ed.). (1994). *Qualitative studies in social work research.* Thousand Oaks, CA: Sage.

Rodwell, M. K. (1987). Naturalistic inquiry: An alternative model for social work assessment. *Social Service Review, 61(2),* 232–246.

Rubin, A., & Babbie, E. (1989). *Research methods in social work.* Boston: Wadsworth Publishers.

Sherman, E., & Reid, E. (Eds.). (1994). *Qualitative research in social work.* New York: Columbia University Press.

Silverman, D. (1993). *Interpreting qualitative data.* Thousand Oaks, CA: Sage.

Strauss, A., & Corbin, J. (1990). *Basics of qualitative research.* Thousand Oaks, CA: Sage.

Swanborn, P. G. (1996). A common base for quality control criteria in quantitative and qualitative research. *Quality and Quantity, 30,* 19–35.

Yegidis, B. L., Weinbach, R. W., Morrison-Rodriguez, B. (1999). *Research methods for social workers.* Boston: Allyn & Bacon.

Yin, R. (1994). *Case study research.* Thousand Oaks, CA: Sage.

RECOMMENDED INTERNET SITES

The Qualitative Report
<http://www.nova.edu/ssss/QR/web.html>
The Institute for Community Research
<http://www.hartnet.org/icr/>
International Institute for Qualitative Methodologies
<http://www.ualberta.ca/~iiqm/>
Participatory Action Resource Net, Cornell University
<http://www.parnet.org/>
Narrative Psychology Internet Resource Guide
<http://maple.lemoyne.edu/~hevern/narpsych.html>

CHAPTER

10 Sampling

Introduction

While the concept of sampling may seem complex at first, it really isn't. **Sampling** is the process of selecting a smaller group of subjects to tell us essentially what a larger population might tell us if we asked every member of the larger population the same questions. In fact, the science of sampling has become so refined that national samples as small as 500 can tell us how people will vote in a presidential election. Are they always right in basing a prediction on such a small number? Not always, but they're right an amazing number of times. Obviously, this ability to use small numbers of people to predict the way larger numbers of people will respond is fraught with methodological quicksand. If your sample is incorrectly drawn or if it somehow forgets to include sub-groups of the larger population (by gender, ethnicity, and race, for example), the results of the study may be almost useless. We saw this happen in the 2000 presidential race where polls had one or the other candidate ahead by large margins when, in reality the election could not have been closer.

Typically, well-understood populations produce fairly exact samples. Caucasian voters who have voted in the past are an easy population from which to draw a sample. This is a fairly predictable and homogenous group and, while they may vote either democrat or republican, their beliefs are relatively easy to predict because the range of their behavior, based on their past behavior, is fairly predictable politically. But as new voters whose culture and race are unknown to researchers enter the picture, the ability to draw accurate samples and to predict outcomes becomes more difficult. My guess is that as these new voters begin to vote in large numbers, pollsters will scramble to refine their sampling techniques. Before this happens, however, you will see some patently inaccurate predictions of voting outcomes similar to the 2000 presidential election where polls had President Bush ahead by as much as 10 points only days before the election. As we now know, the popular vote resulted in an almost dead heat between the two candidates with Al Gore winning the popular vote by 200,000 votes but losing the electoral vote.

Pollsters often base predictions on prior voting patterns, but what happens if some wise politician pushes hard to get the voters out in populations that haven't voted in the past? What happens is chaos. Remember that sampling is only as good as the information about the larger population from which the sample is drawn. Leaving out certain groups of people because we haven't included them in the past can result in very large error rates. We haven't had a terribly bad prediction of an election outcome since Harry Truman beat Dewey in the 1948 presidential election. In that election, the pollsters were so inaccurate that some newspapers incorrectly printed the results indicating that Dewey won the election before it was actually decided. The next day when Harry Truman was declared the winner, he held up a copy of the *Chicago Tribune* in his hand with the front-page headline reading, "DEWEY WINS ELECTION." It wasn't one of the brightest days for pollsters or for scientific sampling.

Sampling requires that we have accurate knowledge of the number and characteristics of our larger population so that we can select enough subjects to effectively represent that larger population. Two additional sampling issues must also be dealt with to obtain respondents representative of the larger population from which we are drawing the sample: **sampling bias** and **sampling error.**

Sampling Bias

Sampling bias is a result of planned or unplanned changes that take place in the sampling process that may lead to an unrepresentative sample. In general, the smaller the population from which the sample is drawn, the more likely we are to introduce sampling bias. In important ways, all samples differ from the population regardless of how accurately the sample is drawn. There are just too many variables to control for, and a small population may not permit an accurate sample, particularly if the larger population includes excessive differences among its members. Further, the less we know about the membership of the larger population, the more likely we are to introduce sampling bias. Government census data are sometimes thought to be inaccurate because certain groups are not included in the census. Those who are often excluded from census data are recent immigrants, illegal aliens, the homeless, men who avoid paying child support by becoming invisible, people in temporary housing, and a host of others. This degree of inaccuracy in the census has negative consequences for communities in terms of state and federal funding based on population size and diversity. Voting districts are also based on population and can be incorrectly drawn. To make up for sampling bias, the census people have statistical models that try to include people who may have been inadvertently left out of the sample. You can understand, however, that these models are general in nature and may be unhelpful to individual communities. Once again, sampling bias leads to an incorrectly drawn sample that is not representative of the larger population from which the sample was drawn.

Sampling Error

Sampling error refers to the almost inevitable fact that the sample will differ in some subtle way from the population from which it is drawn. This leads to a *margin of error* which refers to the fact that all sampling brings with it a certain error rate explained by the fact that the only totally accurate way to get perfect data is to seek information from every individual member of the larger population. The trade off is that while all sampling brings with it a certain level of error, seeking the opinions of every member of a larger population can be impossible or, at the very least, highly impractical. Given our recent experience with the U.S. census, trying to get information from every member of the population is difficult in the extreme. Many people just won't cooperate. Sampling, for all of its potential problems, is still a very good way of getting information quickly and inexpensively. As we note later in this chapter, even though sampling inevitably brings with it some error, the amount of error may be acceptable because the issue we are studying doesn't necessarily require absolutely accurate data. Finding out how people feel about the future of America, for example, requires far less demanding results than predicting how people might vote or how they might react to a product marketing campaign. The future of America is a vague concept and opinions vary greatly with the exact moment in time the question was asked. No one expects great accuracy. We might expect a margin of error of plus or minus five percent and find that perfectly acceptable. To find out margins of error by sample size, you can look at the tables in the back of most statistics books. In general, however, the larger the sample size in relation to the population it represents, the smaller the margin of error.

There are several additional terms related to sampling often used by researchers: statistic, parameter, universe, and sampling frame. **Statistic** describes the identifying characteristics present in a sample. Examples include race, ethnicity, gender, and age. **Parameters** describe the distribution of variables, or those characteristics in the larger population. Ideally, the ratio of statistics to parameters should be the same. If 20% of the population we are studying are bald men (and heaven knows that bald men should be highly valued in any study for their intelligence, wisdom, and sexiness), then twenty percent of the sample should be comprised of bald men. A **universe** is defined as that group of people who share similar identifying characteristics. Let's say that twenty percent of the population of American men are bald. One could then say that twenty percent of the universe of men would be bald using America as our universe. A **population** is that portion of the universe that is available for us to study, and a **sam-**

pling frame is that smaller segment of the population that is available for us to study but is also very much like the population. One example is a much smaller group of bald men who are seeking hair transplants but who may also differ in some important ways from the larger population of bald men (perhaps only a handful of bald men want hair transplants while the rest of us are ecstatic, happy as clams, find it just plain peachy being bald, although heaven only knows that bald jokes do get tiresome and some of us bald guys have had it up to our . . . but that's another story). I'm going to bypass all of these terms and just use the terms *population* and *sample* in this chapter. For our purposes, a population is the large group we are try-ing to study and a sample is the smaller portion of that population who we hope are representative of the larger population. Got it?

Probability and Non-Probability Sampling

There are two primary approaches to sampling: **Probability sampling** where the population is known to us and **non-probability sampling** where the population is unknown. Individuals questioned by census takers are an example of a probability sample since the census taker goes from home to home to interview individuals. People who are homeless, illegal aliens, criminals on the run, and others who live in places not accessible to the census taker and who do not want to take part in the census, are an ex-ample of a non-probability sample. One group we know while the other group is unknown to us. It is the unknown quality of any population that often creates such conflict whenever census data are used for political pur-poses. A significant undercount of a population might permit a district to become so gerrymandered (split into a voting district where certain domi-nant characteristics such as a large Latino population are ignored for the purpose of negating the Latino vote by placing Latino voters in adjacent voting districts) that the districts fail to adequately represent the desires of the Latino population. This is an old political trick. Ever wonder why we have such an under representation of people of color in the political arena? That's a primary reason.

The fact that large numbers of people are unknown to us wreaks havoc with social research. Of what value, anymore, is research done on standard populations when large numbers of people aren't included? Cen-sus data can be very inaccurate because millions of people who feel outside of the social contract to participate in the census refuse to cooperate in the process. As the Latino population continues to grow in size in many states, a greater number of Latinos will define life in America. This also includes people from many parts of Asia. Attempts to factor their presence into sam-pling efforts are often in error because most researchers not only haven't a clue about their numbers, they also have little idea about how these groups of people might be added to the sample. Imagine mounting a public health campaign to eliminate tuberculosis, a disease considerably on the rise in America, when large numbers of the people most at risk of getting the disease are unknown to public health administrators and are unlikely to be seen by doctors should they have serious and potentially infectious diseases?

It isn't just a little ironic that while the government seems unable to correctly count people and often has difficulty locating them, as may be the case in parents who default on child support payments, Publishers Clearing House, the company that sells magazines through much criticized rewards campaigns, knows where each defaulter is at any moment in time and can track one down regardless of how many times he moves or changes his name. Ever wonder how? I do.

Consequently, all sampling efforts begin with a desire to accurately identify the populations we are using to select our sample. We will discuss ways of selecting a sample when populations are unknown to us through the use of non-probability sampling, but for now you can understand that vaguely understood populations often result in poorly drawn samples.

Sampling a Population Whose Members Are Known: Probability Sampling

In probability sampling, every member of the larger population has an equal or random chance of being selected. Their inclusion in the sample represents the fact that what they have to say about an issue is generally felt to be similar to what people like them, in the larger population, would also say. Selecting a sample is not only less time-consuming than seeking information from every member of the population, it also saves a great deal of money. The more homogeneous (similar) the population, the smaller and less sophisticated the sample size and selection process needs to be. What we are required to do is to decide on the absolute number of people needed in our sample to give us an acceptable margin of error (a plus or minus number indicating how close we've come to knowing how everyone in the entire population we are studying would respond), and then we can use any number of approaches to select our sample size. Those approaches follow.

Simple Random Sampling

In this approach to probability sampling, the researcher selects a certain number of names to represent his sample. He takes the population he's drawing from (let's say the student body phone book at your college), and chooses a small number of people to form the sample (perhaps 2% of the total names in the phone book). This can be done by taking every 10th or 15th name until the sample size has been achieved. As a variation, he could also put names in a hat and draw his sample that way, or he might find a statistical computer package in which the names are randomly selected by a series of random numbers. In simple random sampling, if you choose enough people at random, the hope is that you will select a sample that closely represents the larger population in all of the important characteristics of that population. There is, however, a risk in a simple random sample: some people might be left out of the study whose characteristics might be important to the study. This occurs either because a large enough sample isn't chosen or because certain people will not be available to us when we select the sample and will therefore, be excluded. For example, it's possible that certain people important to our study are not listed in the student phone book. While simple random sampling will give us a fairly accurate representation of the larger population, the margin of error is likely to be somewhat larger than a random stratified sample described later in this section. Something to remember: Choose a larger sample than you actually need just to anticipate that not everyone chosen will agree to be part of your study. It's sad to say, but people often don't like to be included in research studies. Often they won't take the time to complete a survey or they'll complete only a small part of the study making the data unusable. Having a cushion of alternative subjects in your sample is a way to make up for subjects who refuse to be in the study, drop out of it, or fail to complete the instrument.

Systematic Random Sampling

This type of sampling uses a formula to select the sample. Let's say that we want to choose fifty names from a list of 500 names, thus providing us with a ten percent sample. We divide 500 by 50, giving us the number ten. We then arbitrarily choose a number between one and ten as our starting point (let's say the number is five) so that our first selection is the fifth person on the list. Then, using ten intervals between names, our second selection is the fifteenth name, then the twenty-fifth name, and so on until we have 50 names.

Stratified Random Sampling

Making sure that a sample includes the many elements of a larger population by race and/or ethnicity, gender, and other important characteristics, requires us to break the population down by strata or sub-groups and then select a sample to proportionately equal the sub-groups within the larger population. For example, we have a population of 1,000 clients receiving services from an agency. Forty percent of the clients are Caucasian, thirty percent are Latino, and thirty percent are African American. To make certain that the same proportions exist in the sample, we take the 1000 clients in the larger population and divide them into three subgroups, 400 who are Caucasian, 300 who are Latino, and 300 who are African American. We then randomly select three samples (the sample size is up to the researcher and depends on the acceptable margin of error) knowing that each of the three samples will have a proportionately equal number of members from all three ethnic groups. If we want to be even more accurate, we can break the sub-groups down by gender and age. Researchers often fail to stratify samples and it's not unusual for the number of women and minorities to be disproportionately smaller on samples than the population would indicate. There are many examples of women being ignored in research studies. Until recently, women were thought to experience lower rates of heart disease than men. This turns out not to be true, but for a very long time they were just not included in studies on heart disease. You can see what a disservice this is to women, and how a bias on the part of researchers can lead to important populations being left out of research studies.

Some students argue that if the sample size is large enough, then the characteristics we have in the larger population have an equal chance of being chosen just by using a random sample. This may not necessarily be true because it's incorrect to assume that all people in any population have a realistic chance of being chosen. If you are using a telephone book to choose a sample, people with a low income may not be in the book because they cannot afford a phone. Some people choose not to list their names and numbers. Some people new to town do not as yet have their numbers listed. Immediately, we have a problem with the phone book failing to represent the population of a community. This is why a random stratified sample, even though we may not precisely know every characteristic of a population, is superior to a simple random sample.

Let's consider an example of random stratified sampling. We are attempting to study the opinions of registered nurses in the state of Michigan on the quality of medical care in Michigan. In our example, the board that licenses nurses has provided us with a list of RN's in Michigan, their work addresses, their gender, and their ethnicity. From that list (Table 10.1), we have a total of 10,000 RN's.

I've consulted a statistics book and have found out that a sample of ten percent will give us a margin of error of about plus or minus four percent. That means that the opinions of medical care by nurses in our survey will either be 4 percent higher than is indicated if we asked all 10,000 nurses in our study, or it is 4 percent lower. No matter what size sample we use, not asking all the nurses in the state their opinions about quality of medical care is going to result in some margin of error. I'm willing to accept a plus or minus four percent error rate since quality of medical care is a very subjective concept subject to frequent changes of opinion and exact data are not absolutely necessary. Okay. Following me so far? To find out the number of people in the random stratified sample (10% of each subgroup), let's look at the larger group of 10,000. The sample size breaks down as shown in Table 10.2.

The total sample size is 1,000 RN's (10% of the population selected at random). We have correct proportions of people in our sample based on

TABLE 10.1 Total RNs from Michigan in Our Population

Caucasian Women	4,000
Caucasian Men	1,000
Latino Women	2,000
Latino Men	500
African American Women	1,000
African American Men	500
Asian Women	500
Asian Men	500
Total= 10,000	

TABLE 10.2 Sample Size of RNs from Michigan as a Random Stratified Sample

Caucasian Women: 10% of 4,000 = 400
Caucasian Men: 10% of 1000 = 100
Latino Women: 10% of 2,000 = 200
Latino Men: 10% of 500 = 50
African American Women: 10% of 1,000 = 100
African American Men: 10% of 500 = 50
Asian Women: 10% of 500 = 50
Asian Men: 10% of 500 = 50

Total= 1,000

their gender and ethnicity and a margin of error of 4%, plus or minus. What we do not have are variations among the sample by age, degree of idealism, size of family, their income, levels of career aspirations, and many other important variables. What we *will* have, however, is a sample broken down by race/ethnicity and gender and the hope that any variations within the sample by level of idealism, age, and so forth, will be included by the random nature of our selection process. You can see that the selection of participants in a study requires a very refined ability to include an almost endless number of characteristics defining the population and then, the sample drawn from that population.

Cluster Sampling

Sometimes we can't locate names of subjects to form our larger population. Instead, we have to rely on groups or clusters of organizations. To better understand this concept, let's assume that we're trying to measure the level of depression in new clients receiving services from community mental health facilities in a certain region of the country. We don't know the clients' names, but we can locate community mental health facilities that form a cluster of agencies. From within that cluster of agencies, we can create a random sample of clients. While this is certainly one way to select clients, remember that clusters of agencies may not give us an accurate sample of all depressed clients seeking mental health services in a certain region. The cluster of agencies may provide services to more affluent clients or clients who are primarily Caucasian. This leaves us with minimal information about depressed clients who are poor or of color. However, cluster sampling, like the non-probability sampling approaches we will discuss next, are sampling approaches used only when we are unable to access the larger population. While there are methodological issues of importance to be considered when using cluster sampling, many researchers argue that providing data, even if the data fail to give us the entire picture, is better than providing no data. Other researchers argue that tainted or somewhat incorrect data create stereotypes and ultimately do harm to certain populations. As you can see, researchers are a tough lot to please.

Alternate Selections

Because not everyone we choose to be in our sample may agree to take part in our study, we usually have to choose three to five percent more participants than are actually needed. This is done to make up for dropouts, people who flatly refuse to be in the study, or people who provide incomplete information on an instrument. These additional people in the sample are chosen randomly and exist as alternates in case something happens to lower our pool of respondents. Alternates are particularly important if we are using a control group since people not receiving the treatment input may be unwilling to continue to participate in our study. In fact, uneven sample sizes between control and experimental groups is a serious problem in scientific research. In the laboratory, it is essential that control groups and experimental groups are the same exact size. To understand this, let's say we're using mice to determine aspects of memory loss related to the aging process. The experimental group is being given a memory enhancer while the control group is just getting old and forgetful (like your research author who promised in the preface not to ever mention mice). If the size of the control group is appreciably smaller than the size of the experimental group at the end of the experiment, we may not be able to statistically extrapolate data to compensate for the decrease in the size of the control group. The importance of maintaining an equal number of subjects in the experimental group cannot be over emphasized.

Sampling a Population Whose Members Are Not Known: Non-Probability Sampling

Non-probability sampling is used when we have no idea about the number or location of those people who comprise the population from which we intend to draw a sample. Consequently, we must first go through a series of steps to identify the population and then determine a suitable sample. An example of a non-probability sample might be determining the number of people in a geographic area from a specific ethnic group so that a census can be taken. From the census we might have a more accurate count of people that could possibly require some form of social service. We frequently undercount certain ethnic groups who may have serious health and social problems because we have no way to identify their numbers since we may not know where they live. In non-probability sampling, we might begin counting the number of people in our population by first finding one name and asking that person to give us additional names. We would then ask those people for additional names, and so forth, until we have a reasonable guess as to how many people comprise a special population. Keep in mind that we have no real way to determine an accurate sample until we know more about the larger population.

Researchers often use the following types of non-probability sampling when they are unable to identify a population for the purpose of using a probability sample:

Convenience Sampling

Sometimes a population is so difficult to locate that we find only a few people to use for our study. We use those people in our study because they are the only people available. We hope that in most respects, their involvement in the study will give us similar information had a larger population been available. Of course, this is a dubious assumption in some cases, and convenience sampling, while yes, convenient, may not give us an accurate picture of the larger population. It will provide us *some* picture, however representative, of the larger population. Researchers who use convenience samples must be very careful not to make more of their findings than are supported by their sampling procedures.

I'm reminded of a study of autopsies of Latino men in which four men were autopsied at random and all four had cirrhosis of the liver. The results were used repeatedly in other studies to show the high level of alcoholism among Latino men, a very subjective and harmful finding based on a dubious sampling technique. In repeated literature reviews on Latino alcoholism, the study was reported as evidence of Latino alcoholism. The study was particularly harmful because it supported stereotypic beliefs about alcoholism among Latino males that are neither true nor supportable in the research literature. You can understand that before statements could ever be made about alcoholism based on autopsies, hundreds of bodies would need to be included before we could draw a usable sample. The reported study took the first four bodies available and found evidence of liver damage, a highly unscientific and pejorative way of determining alcoholism rates in any population.

Snowball Sampling

Snowball sampling is an extension of convenience sampling. We start out with a small group of people and hope that others will join the sample until our sample is complete. By asking subjects if they know of others who would join our study, we may be able to add respondents to our sample until we have enough subjects to complete our study. Scientific? Well, not very. Practical? Sure. Can we generalize our findings to the larger population? Probably not. Does it help us understand the larger population in some important ways? Maybe. However, if we start out with a biased person, one who will provide self-serving or politically correct responses, then it's quite likely that the additional people suggested by our original person will recommend others with similar biases. While it may be the only approach we can use, we need to beware of making too much of the findings. The original respondent should be encouraged to give us names that represent a range of opinions within a population.

One of my students did a study involving a newly immigrated group of Southeast Asians who were experiencing much higher than expected numbers of child abuse complaints. She used a snowball sampling approach only to discover that everyone in the sample had been forewarned by the original person, a highly placed member of the community, to give only very limited information about child abuse in the community. The result of her study, or should I say the non-result of her study, was that there was no child abuse among this population, and any perceived problems were related to language differences. Of course, the child protective service agency dealing with child abuse accusations had a very different idea, but you get the point, I'm sure. A snowball sample is only as good as the people who provide names and are willing to give accurate information. When my student discovered the problem, she found other subjects, assured them of confidentiality, and found that child abuse was not a problem. Parents were practicing old folk remedies to help children who were ill. When these practices were described and explained, the entire issue of child abuse was resolved and there were no further complaints of child abuse from the authorities.

Purposive Sampling

This is a sampling approach used when a population consists of subjects who have a special quality we want to study. One of my students studied Latino day workers to learn about their level of stress, their salaries, their legal status, and so forth. Day laborers often congregate in specific areas of a community and are hired by companies or private citizens for short-term work. The student chose only people available to him from several locations in the community who were willing to talk to him (many weren't willing to talk to him because they thought he worked for the INS). Ultimately, his sample consisted of people who were willing to share important information that many of them were concerned might actually be used against them in citizenship challenges. He was able to do a purposive sample by recognizing qualities in the potential subjects that made them likely to agree to an interview (gentleness, good eye contact, a positive disposition). In this sense, the sample was purposive, but you can see that agreeable subjects aren't necessarily subjects who represent all day workers. In fact, the people who refused to be included in the study might be more representative of day workers than those who were included in his study. Obviously, you have to use the group available to you, and recognize the limits this places on the researcher not to give more meaning to your findings than may be warranted.

Quota Sampling

Let's assume that we've decided to interview a sample of people from a community about a certain issue. We use a shopping mall to locate our subjects. We know that the breakdown of the community of 50,000 is 40 percent Caucasian (60% female, 40% male), 40 percent Latino (55% female, 45% male), 10 percent Asian (60% male, 40% female), and 10 percent African American (60% female, 40% male).

Let's further assume that we choose a 2 percent overall sample requiring us to interview 1000 people. Within that sample of 1000, 400 will be Caucasian. Of the 400 Caucasians, 240 will be female and 160 will be male. We do the same for other ethnic groups until we interview 1000 people. Neat? Very. Scientific? Maybe. It's possible that the shopping mall caters to a more affluent or less affluent group who are not representative of the larger community. However, as an easy way of getting a quota sample that has elements of stratification, it's about as simple as it can be. How do you know people's ethnicity? Well, you can use face recognition, of course, but on the questionnaire, you might ask them their ethnicity as an additional check.

Error Rates as a Result of Sampling

Most statistics books explain how large a sample size must be to lower the potential rate of error. All samples contain a certain error rate since we could only know the correct answer to a question asked of the population if every member of the population answered. By using a smaller sample, we introduce the possibility that the sample may only marginally represent the population. Consequently, one of the most common errors made in research is selecting a sample that is unrepresentative of the larger population. Error rates may happen when the sample is too small or when a random sample doesn't include particular characteristics of a population (not enough people of color, new residents or immigrant groups are included, for example). It can also escalate when the population we draw from isn't correctly identified and people are missing from the population (remember our earlier discussion about using the phone book to select a sample?) so that we underrepresent their numbers in the sample. Finally, error rates can make our data unusable when the error rate associated with a sample is too high to be acceptable, as in an election poll where a plus or minus 5 percent error rate may be too high because the vote may be determined by a 1 percent margin.

When you select a sampling approach for your research study, keep in mind that your sample might provide unproductive data. Even though the sample may be correctly drawn, problems in your methodology might affect the return rate yielding a larger than useful error rate. Possible problems affecting error rate include: incomplete information on surveys because the survey was overly long or unclearly written; the poor response rate of mailed surveys; random samples correctly drawn, but responses that come from only one particular sub-group of the sample completely eliminate the random aspects of the sample.

In your study, you should seriously consider using probability sampling with known population characteristics. When one member of the sample fails to return a questionnaire or doesn't show up for an interview, you can use alternate subjects and still retain the integrity of the study. You can also do your study with fairly similar or homogeneous groups. Clients receiving assistance from a social agency and who share many social and emotional characteristics is a good example of the type of population from which to draw a random sample. Psychologists, social workers, or academics in a certain field of study, are other good examples. Remember, the more heterogeneous (dissimilar) the sample, the more error is introduced. Even though a random sample generated by a table of random numbers is supposed to include all the characteristics of the population if the sample size is large enough, frequently, even a random approach leaves out important members of a population and introduces error.

A very well-done discussion of error rates can be found in a text by Allen Rubin and Earl Babbie (1989, pp. 207–208). The following is a distillation of an example they provide to help us determine error rates in sampling.

> If we do a pre-test to determine the opinions of people in a community of 50,000 about whether a new community center should be built, and we use a random sample of 100 community residents, the greater the agreement in the random sample of 100 people about building the community center, the fewer peo-

ple we need in our larger sample to get a smaller margin of error rate. With 80 percent of the people in favor of the community center in our pre-test and only 20 percent opposed, a sample of 500 would give us a margin of error of +/−3.6%. If opinion was split evenly in our pre-test, a sample of 500 would give us a margin of error of +/−4.5%. Increasing the number of people in our sample would reduce the margin of error only slightly. Therefore, to produce a sample with an acceptable error rate, many researchers do a small pre-test to determine the actual number of subjects necessary for the larger sample. The more agreement about an issue in the smaller pre-test, the smaller the sample size needs to be in the large study to keep margins of error within acceptable limits. The greater the disagreement in the pre-test, the larger our sample size needs to be. Remember that the sample in the pre-test must be drawn randomly to obtain usable data.

Reading the Table

In the following example (Table 10.3), use of a random sample of 100 people in the pre-test to determine homogeneity/heterogeneity of the population as it relates to building a new community center is demonstrated. Based on the initial results in the pre-test using 100 people in our sample, the top line represents the homogeneity of the initial random sample of 100. If the homogeneity is very high (90% are in favor of the new building with only 10% against) a sample size of 500 will give us a margin of error of +/−2.4%. However, if the initial sample indicates only 50 percent agreement, a sample of 500 will give us a margin of error of almost twice as much (+/−4.5%).

As you can see, the more people in our original sample of 100 that agree about building a new community center, the smaller the second sample in our larger study needs to be to get acceptable margins of error. With 90% of our initial sample in favor of building a community center, a sample size of 500 in our second and larger survey would give us a margin of error of only +/−2.4%, a very good error rate for this type of survey. Adding another 500 people to our sample to give a sample of 1000 decreases the

TABLE 10.3   Margin of Error Rates

	Sample Size	Margin of Error				
Agree/Disagree	X	50/50	60/40	70/30	80/20	90/10
	100	10%	9.8%	9.2%	8%	6%
	500	4.5%	4.4%	3.6%	3.0%	2.4%
	1000	3.2%	3.1%	2.9%	2.5%	1.9%

error rate from +/−2.4% to +/−1.9%, a very marginal difference that wouldn't justify increasing the size of the sample.

Understand that margin of error is most important when the results need to be highly accurate. A sample that gives us a +/−5% margin of error related to the outcome of a medical treatment is just not acceptable. The spread of 10 percent (+/−5%) is just too great for us to have confidence in the findings. However, if our sampling approach attempts to find the opinion of people regarding how well a politician seems to be doing at a particular time in his or her tenure, no one expects these results to be particularly accurate; a +/−5% margin of error might be good enough to get some basic sense of how well that person is doing. Therefore, the more important the results need to be, the smaller the margin of error required. Yet, there is a limit in even the most sophisticated sampling approaches as to how small a margin of error one can achieve. Perhaps a +/−1% error rate is about as close as most researchers can realistically come. For most things in life, that's pretty good. For your purposes in student research projects, a 5% error rate might be realistic and acceptable. To lower the error rate might require a much larger sample, one that requires more money, time, and sophistication in sampling than you may have. However, let your instructor be the judge of that. He or she may have a good reason to expect a very low margin of error rate because of the sensitivity and importance of the study or for some other reason.

To Sample or Not to Sample, That Is the Question

Okay, Dr. Glicken, you've thoroughly confused us. First you tell us that sampling is easy and that it's a good thing to do. Then you fill us full of doubt by telling us about all the things that can go wrong. How about making up your mind?

Good question, all you wonderful students out there in readerland. The fact is that, even though sampling can cause errors for new researchers and although there are some methodological complications, I tell my students to use sampling in their research studies. Observe the problems, identify the potential errors, and use sampling as a learning experience. Most social research today uses sampling procedures. Sometimes samples are elegantly drawn using very sophisticated mathematical models and the results are pretty amazing. But sometimes people who should know better, in fact who *do* know better, use sampling procedures that are full of mistakes and the results of those studies confirm our belief that a good deal of social research is full of baloney. In order to become a sophisticated consumer of research, something all social science majors should be, you first need some practical experience in choosing samples, even non-probability samples. If you think about the cost and time it saves to use a sample, you have to be convinced that it's a logical way to go for social researchers. But, and this is an important but, you need to be painfully honest about the limits imposed on your findings in using sampling procedures, particularly those that are less than objective and have known methodological concerns. Tell consumers what you think is wrong with the sampling approach, report your findings, and have faith that they will make wise choices about how best to use your findings.

Sometimes, even flawed samples give us astonishing results. Two of my students decided to study the way Arab Americans treat elderly family members and to compare that treatment to that of an Arab Israeli population of caregivers. To begin with, Arab Americans are a vastly understudied population in America. Furthermore, while accurate data are unavailable, they are certainly as large a group as other well-known minority groups, including Jewish Americans. My students did something very useful in studying this population and then something surprisingly useful by comparing two groups of caregivers. That the Arab American group suffered some slippage in the quality of elder care when compared to an Arab Israeli group is of no real surprise. Assimilation often brings with it changes in the treatment of elderly family members. However, the slippage was minimal and both the caregivers and the elderly were happy with the arrangements, but both were very concerned about finances, a practical and predictable issue for almost all caregivers of elderly family members. What is so wonderful about this small piece of research is that Arab Americans are often thought of as an invisible population, one that doesn't like the intrusiveness of researchers coming into their homes. Yet, both students were able to interview caregivers and the elderly in their homes and in the process, provide us with an early look at a very understudied group. The sample was certainly a convenience sample and yet, this is the type of study one applauds students for doing, methodological problems and all.

Summary

This chapter on sampling procedures notes the two widely used sampling approaches, probability and non-probability sampling. The discussion of the use of each approach suggests that sampling, even when flawed, is a less expensive and time-consuming way of including people in a study than trying to get information from every member of the population. Special attention was given to the problems associated with each form of sampling, and the issue of sampling error was discussed in relation to the degree of importance of the study.

REVIEW QUESTIONS

1. Given the problems related to the snowball approach to non-probability sampling, how might you avoid using someone to give you names of potential members of the sample who will also give you inaccurate information?

2. Isn't it less trouble and about as accurate to increase the size of your random sample rather than stratifying the sample?

3. Since a certain segment of any population will choose to remain hidden, of what value is it to concern oneself with their inclusion in any research study?

4. A great deal of time was spent discussing populations who are under-represented in studies. If those people who are under-represented play a marginal role in the social fabric of our society, why should we be concerned about their inclusion in social research studies?

5. Probability sampling assumes a certain logic in the way people of similar ethnic, racial, gender, or social class composition will respond in any study. Isn't this assumption false, and don't most people have very independent views that are difficult to categorize?

REFERENCES

Berk, R. A. (1983). An introduction to sample selection bias in sociological data. *American Sociological Review, 48,* 386–397.

Henry, G. T. (1990). *Practical sampling.* Newbury Park, CA: Sage.

Kish, L. (1965). *Survey sampling.* New York: John Wiley & Sons.

Rubin, A., & Babbie, E. (1989). *Research methods in social work.* Belmont, CA: Wadsworth.

Scheaffer, R. L., Mendenhall, W., & Ott, L. (1986). *Elementary survey sampling (3rd ed.).* Boston: Duxbury Press.

Solomon, P., & Paulson, R. I. (1995). Issues in designing and conducting randomized human service trials. Paper presented at the *National Conference of the Society for Social Work and Research,* Washington, DC.

Sudham, S. (1976). *Applied sampling.* New York: Academic Press.

Yegidis, B. L., Weinbach, R. W., & Morrison-Rodriguez, B. (1999). *Research Methods for Social Workers.* Boston: Allyn & Bacon.

RECOMMENDED INTERNET SITES

Allyn & Bacon's Sociology Links
   <http://www.fsu.edu/~crimdo/soclinks/research.html>
American FactFinder
   <http://factfinder.census.gov>
Center for Demography and Ecology
   <http://www.ssc.wisc.edu/cde>
CSAC Ethnographics Gallery Software Archive
   <http://lucy.ukc.ac.uk/archives.html>
Mathematical and Statistical Software
   <http://www.portal.research.bell-labs.com/cgi-wald/dbaccess/32>

11 Sadistic Statistics: Part I. Measures of Central Tendencies

WITH JOSEPH GREENE

Introduction

Thank goodness for computerized statistical programs like the Statistical Package for the Social Sciences (SPSS). All you have to do now to run statistics is enter the data from your study and click the correct button at the prompt. Well, that does it for this chapter on statistics.

Unfortunately, it's not quite that easy. Even though you can now run statistics in a flash, you still have to know what each statistic is called, what it is intended to show, how it can best be used, and its level of power, statistically speaking. Like everything else in life, some statistics are better and more powerful than others. You also have to know those obnoxious little Greek signs that look like someone from a fraternity has been playing a bad joke. Most statistics are reported using Greek letters. Whose idea was that, anyway? Obviously, somebody who knew Greek. Maybe a person from Greece. What an idea!

Greek symbols aside, when all is said and done, statistics have three functions: to describe, to generalize, and to show relationships (Franzblau, 1958). In presidential elections, it's important for candidates to know how various groups in America will vote. A pollster might want to give a candidate the breakdown of his or her support by race, ethnicity, gender, age, socio-economic class, and so on. This type of statistic is used to describe a candidate's base of support. The candidate might then be interested in shoring up his or her base of support or might want to approach those groups for whom there is little support and try and woo them to his or her side. Statistics, and knowing how to read them, can make or break a candidate's bid for office. Now, since you're most likely not running for office, let's look at how statistics can help you get a firmer grip on the social research process.

Statistics are widely used to *describe* a subject. Statistics are numbers giving us a snapshot of any given subject. The U.S. Census Report is a good example of the use of descriptive statistics. How many people live in America? What is the breakdown of America by race/ethnicity? What is the average income of Americans? We are accustomed to the use of descriptive statistics in America and almost always think that descriptive data are useful to us in our everyday lives. What does the average college education cost? How long will it take to get a degree, on average? What is the average salary for newly graduated students in certain fields? These data are quite often used by many of us to make important decisions about careers, places to live, and the advanced education we choose to pursue after we receive our undergraduate degrees.

The ability to *generalize* is a much more complicated issue. We're now asking whether the data we've collected are applicable to other populations. We may know how people in North Dakota feel about a presidential candidate but will the people in Florida feel the same way? Probably not, because people from North Dakota are a pretty serious lot and voter fraud isn't considered good citizenship in the Dakotas, as it seems to be in an unnamed Southern state. Generalizability is a key issue in social research. It determines whether our findings are applicable to other groups outside of our sample. The more generalizable the findings, the more important they become since they can now be used with other people and situations beyond our original study. There is considerable debate among researchers about whether a study done in one area of the country applies to people in another part of the country. Looking at the polls before an election, you begin to realize that there are wide differences among people along geographic, racial, and gender lines. Can we say that the way a sample responded to our study in Arizona will be the same for the people in New York? Almost certainly not, since the people in each state are quite different along many complex indicators. That is why generalizability is difficult to assert when trying to compare a sample in one locale to a sample elsewhere.

Finally, statistics can be used to understand the existence of *relationships* between variables. Does something cause something else to happen? This question constantly intrigues social researchers. If we provide preschool child care services to children of impoverished families, will those children do better educationally over their life-span than children of impoverished families who are not provided pre-school child care? To be able to answer that question definitively would completely modify the way we look at the use of pre-schools in America. If there were a strong relationship between these two variables, then we would be highly inclined to provide free day care to children of poor families. But, as we will learn in Chapter 12, showing strong relationships between variables is anything but easy. Using the pre-school example, how would we know for certain what the absolute reasons would be for children doing better educationally if they attend pre-school day care? Might there be other compelling reasons? Might children do better educationally because of strong parental interest or better choices in schools after pre-school? Showing relationships is absolutely the toughest issue in social research.

The Statistics We Cover in This Book

In the following two chapters, I'm not going to cover a wide range of statistics or teach you how to do calculations because it would bore you and it isn't necessary. The computer can run statistics for you in almost a fraction of a second. Instead, what I'd like to do is to help you understand and use very common statistics of the kind you will use in your research projects. There are any number of excellent statistics books that you can consult for a more thorough understanding of statistics, particularly more complex statistics that won't be covered in this book.

The statistics that are essential for you to understand and that will in all likelihood be used in your research projects are measures of central tendency, including mean, median, mode, standard deviations, and z-scores. You will also need to know about connections, associations and relationships between variables and the various statistics used to make this determination as well as their level of strength. Beyond that, you need to take statistics courses to learn about the elegant but complex statistics available to the researcher. Our job in these two chapters is to simply explain the most likely statistical tests you will possibly use in a research project, to note their function, and to suggest their level of usefulness.

Measures of central tendency are among the simplest statistics used in research. They can be invaluable even though they're simple. For example, if we evaluate job satisfaction in an organization having morale problems leading to workplace violence, it helps a great deal to identify the characteristics of the workers most likely to be violent. Once we do that, perhaps we can initiate organizational changes to negate the potential for violence in the workplace. If you're the one working in an organization with severely disgruntled workers who might become violent, you might find statistics more than invaluable. Keep in mind that social science research has "real world" applications that are possible only because of statistical analysis.

In this chapter we also discuss statistics that are very weak indicators of connections among variables, such as the Chi-square and the T-test. We will also talk about a few other subjects related to statistics, and we will try to use terms that are comprehensible and don't sound as if someone is sneezing in Latin. Let's now consider an important issue in statistics: The three types of data we work with in social science research.

Types of Data

The word *data* can be simply defined as a "number signifying information." In statistics, we usually think of three types of data: **nominal, ordinal,** and

interval continuous data. Simply stated, in nominal data there are no distinct differences in the value of the data. The researcher assigns a number to a non-mathematical category solely for the purpose of coding it for an eventual statistical analysis on the computer. The researcher may give women in the sample the number 1 and men in the sample the number 2. This is done so that the computer can keep track of the subjects who are women and the subjects who are men. Consider gender or race/ethnicity as value neutral examples of nominal data. Nominal data do not have a naturally occurring order. If you gave Caucasians the number 1, for computational purposes, and African Americans the number 2, what meaning would 1.5 have? The answer is that it would have no meaning. Nominal data are value neutral and can be translated into numbers for the purpose of counting or doing statistical analysis (as in the opinions regarding an issue by gender or by race/ethnicity). Fractions of the numbers have no meaning. Students reading a computer printout of nominal data may be confused by what the number 1.5 may mean under the gender category. It has no meaning because gender is a value free concept in statistics. The important thing to remember is that the values assigned by the researcher using nominal data are arbitrary and have no numerical superiority. If women are assigned the number one, it doesn't mean they're better than men who are assigned the number two, even though women may argue that they are clearly better. Numbers in nominal data represent categories and have no numerical superiority.

Ordinal data are data in which the categories we create can be ordered in any way we wish. Think of a Likert Scale in which we've ordered the responses on the scale from high to low. In one survey *good* may correspond with the number one, while in the next survey *good* may correspond with the number five. We may give each response a number, but the data only have meaning because of the meaning we've provided. Like nominal data, ordinal data are value free, but unlike nominal data, ordinal data might have a classification in which fractions do make sense. For example, people may be asked to respond to a survey asking them to rate their satisfaction with a newly purchased CD. When the data are calculated, it turns out the CD earned an average rating of 4.5 with 5 being the highest and 1 being the lowest possible rating of satisfaction. You can see that a rating of 4.5 is moving in the direction of a very positive level of satisfaction with the CD. In ordinal data, fractions have meaning because we've provided that meaning by the way we rank order the choices subjects can make on an instrument.

Interval continuous data are data that are classified and rank ordered. Think of SAT scores or scores on an examination. An SAT score of 1500 is far better than an SAT score of 800. The value of the test score is predetermined by the test maker. A score on an examination of 100 is worth more than a score of 70 on the same examination. In interval continuous data, the researcher is using an instrument in which numbers may indicate the level of comprehension or achievement. The higher the number, the more likely it is that the subject comprehends the material.

For computational purposes, we convert everything in statistics into numbers. That's because the computer can calculate numbers, but cannot calculate letters. We've already talked about assigning numbers to categories of ethnicity, but there are many other ways to tell the computer how to look at the data. For example, the category *age* can either be the exact age of the respondent or an age range to which we give each range a number. 18–25 might be given the number 1. Twenty-six to thirty-two might be given the number 2, and so on. When the computer package, such as SPSS, runs your data, you get numerical results. The average age of your respondents might be 27 or, if you use a range, it could be 2.2. As with all numbers, you, the creator of the numbers, must know what they mean. A tutorial in SPSS will help you learn how to label all of the numerical information you enter into the computer so that you don't forget, or get confused, about the actual meaning of the numbers you've created. Do students forget what the numbers they've created actually mean? Constantly. I've read computer printouts where statistical tests have been run and the student can't seem to remember what information the number represents. Make certain that you save this information and that you have it with you when you run your data. If you don't, the information on your computer printout will be of absolutely no value.

Measures of Central Tendency

Measures of central tendency are the statistician's attempt to find out a series of statistics related to average scores. That's putting it simply, but the statistics we discuss here, as measures of central tendency, are all related to the notion that we can find data that describe a sample by such variables as age, ethnicity, gender, and so forth. Knowing averages can be very important in understanding the data. The primary measures of central tendency are mean, median, mode, range, standard deviation, and z-scores.

Let's start with the concept most of us know best, the **mean** or average score. To calculate the mean or average score, we add all of the scores on a measurement together and then divide by the number of people who have taken the measurement. Let's take the scores on a quiz in which 60 points is the highest score anyone can get. By adding the following ten scores and dividing by the number of people taking the test (10), we calculate the mean score. The scores to add are: 29, 16, 33, 47, 31, 27, 51, 55, 23, and 35. If you added correctly and divided by 10, you should come up with a mean score of 34.7. The **range** of the scores, or the lowest score to the highest score, is: 16–55. What we know about this test is that most people didn't do very well, although a few people did quite well and a few did quite badly. We can't say anything about the quality of the test or about the quality of the students taking the test. We have no data to answer either of those questions. Consequently, mean scores tell us what happened but do not help us understand why it happened. This is a crucial issue in understanding measures of central tendency and helps us recognize the limitations of this type of statistic.

The **median** score refers to the point at which exactly half the scores are higher and the other half of the scores are lower. To find the median score, we place the scores in the order they were achieved starting with the lowest score and proceeding to the highest score. Using the same numbers we used to calculate the mean, those numbers are: 16, 23, 27, 29, 31, 33, 35, 47, 51, and 55. We calculate the median score by taking the two scores on either side of the mid-point (31 and 33), adding them together, and dividing that number (64) by two. The median score for the ten numbers is 32. The reason we have a higher mean score (34.7) and a somewhat lower median score (32) is that the mean scores were influenced by some very high scores: 51 and 55 are much closer to the highest score attainable (60) than the lowest score (16) is to the lowest score attainable (0). Frequently, mean and median differ but, in general, as in this case, they tend to be fairly close to one another.

The modal score or **mode** is the score that appears most often. In the range of numbers of 17, 23, 45, 33, 45, 55, 27, 44, 21, 16, you can see that the score 45 occurs twice. 45 is our modal score. When two or three sets of numbers occur the same number of times, we refer to these scores as being bi-modal or tri-modal. This indicates that the range of scores is not going to be a typical **bell shaped curve** with equal distribution but a **skewed curve** since the scores are not evenly represented.

Standard deviation is another measurement of central tendency. Imagine a bell shaped curve with a vertical line drawn right down the middle of the curve (Figure 11.1).

Half of the scores on the curve are higher than the mean and half of the scores are lower than the mean. Standard deviation tells us the distance a score is from the mean. Standard deviation is also measured by plus or minus numbers. For example, on a normal curve, 68.26% of the scores occupy one standard deviation, plus or minus, from the mean. Think of the normal distribution of IQs. On a normal distribution or bell shaped curve, IQs range from 90 to 110. We use 100 as the mean IQ score for the total population. Consequently, 34.13 percent of all IQs are higher than the mean and fall in the IQ range of 100.6 to 110, while 34.13 percent of the IQs are lower than the mean and range from 90 to 100.5. The higher scores have a standard deviation of +1.0 from the mean; the lower IQ scores have a standard deviation of −1.0 from the mean.

You will note on Figure 11.1 that if we add two standard deviations from the mean, we increase the number of IQ scores to 95.46 percent of all

Normal Curve

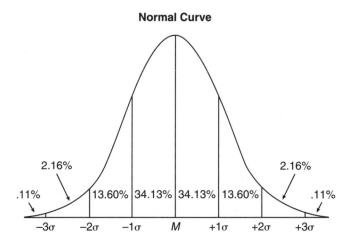

FIGURE 11.1 Normal Curve

the possible IQ scores. Let's say that the IQs at two standard deviations from the norm are now 111 to 120 on the positive side of the mean and 89 to 80 on the negative side of the mean. Three standard deviations, plus or minus, give us very high and very low IQs and would include 99.79 percent of all IQ scores. At three standard deviations from the mean, we have a +2.16% and −2.16% of the total IQs. This gets us into very high and very low IQ scores. Four standard deviations from the mean provides an additional .11% of the highest and .11% of the lowest IQs. It gives us very high, perhaps immeasurably high IQs while four standard deviations of the lowest IQs gives us almost immeasurably low IQs. We can string standard deviations out to infinity to cover the few cases of people whose IQs are absolutely so high that we can't be certain of their actual IQ and, similarly, people with IQs so low that we are fairly uncertain of their actual IQ.

On a skewed curve (see Figure 11.2), the IQs are more highly prevalent on one side of the mean or the other. If we were looking at the IQs of a gifted class of high school students, the IQs will probably start at 120 and go higher. Looking at the positively skewed curve in Figure 11.2, the mean will start well above the mean of 100 on a normal curve, perhaps as high as an IQ of 135. Consequently, one negative standard deviation from the mean on a skewed curve will probably have IQs from 120 to 135. One positive standard deviation from the mean might find IQs from 136 to 150. The higher the positive number of standard deviations, the higher the IQs. Conversely, if we are looking at the IQs of a developmentally disabled group of high school students where the IQs begin at 70 and go lower, we will also have a skewed curve but on the minus side of the mean (see the negatively skewed curve in Figure 11.2). The mean IQ will probably be around 55. One positive standard deviation from the mean represents IQs in the 55 to

Positively Skewed Distribution

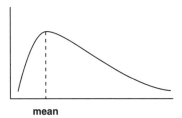

mean

Negatively Skewed Distribution

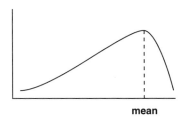

mean

FIGURE 11.2 Skewed Distribution

70 range and will fall on the plus or right side of the mean. IQs below 55 will fall on the left or negative side of the mean. A grouping of IQs from 40–54 will have one minus standard deviation from the mean.

A **z-score** shows the number of standard deviations an individual test taker might score from the average score of everyone taking the test. It will also tell us a test taker's percentile rank on the examination when compared to the larger group taking the examination. Therefore, z-scores give us a way of comparing an individual score to a group score and help the test taker know how well or how badly he or she has done on an examination when compared to others in the class.

Chance

In research, there is always the possibility that unwanted events can affect our findings. This can be caused by some aspect of the design that we've neglected to control for, or it may have occurred as one of those random events in life that no one really expects. Nothing in life is ever completely predictable, and before we use our findings to support our hypothesis, we need to check our data to determine whether chance has played more of a role in the outcome of our findings than is considered acceptable. These chance occurrences are referred to in statistics as the probability of error. The **probability of error** is a number that is usually reported as more or less than five chance occurrences out of 100.

Probability of error, or the *p* value, is also referred to as the **level of significance.** The *p* score tells us whether our results are within acceptable limits for chance occurrences or whether they are affected by outside extraneous events that render our findings unacceptable. In social research, no more than five chance occurrences out of 100 are considered acceptable. If more than five chance occurrences take place, we conclude that chance played too much of a role for the findings to be meaningful. As *p* increases in size (for example, *p* might be 10 or 15 out of 100), so does the possibility that the researcher will draw erroneous conclusions about his or her findings because chance has played such a significant role. That is why we are only willing to accept a 5% chance of error in social research and would prefer even less.

Some social researchers report *p* as an absolute number, as in (p = .03), signifying that only three chance occurrences took place out of 100 and that the findings are now considered acceptable. Or they may report the findings by noting that the level of significance (*p*) was greater than five times out of 100 ($p < .05$) or less than 5 out of 100 ($p > .05$). The smaller the number, the better the level of significance and the less chance has played a role in our findings. So $p = .0000$ is far better than $p = .05$ because it indicates that chance has played no role in the findings at the one in ten thousandth level. $p = .05$ merely means that chance has affected the findings 5 times out of 100. Acceptable, but not as good, by a country mile, as $p = .0000$. Got it?

The element of chance is always a killer in research findings. As we discuss statistical tests to determine chance occurrences in the next section, we need to be clear about the concept of chance. It isn't necessarily some demonic event in the life span of a research study: It usually occurs because of a flaw in our research design. Internal and external validity issues are usually the cause of a higher degree of chance interference than is acceptable in social research. But chance is a concept that is badly understood by many of us. If you toss a coin a hundred times, the statistics teacher I had said that 50 times out of 100 the coin will come up heads and 50 times out of 100 the coin will come up tails. But in reality, when coins are tossed a few thousand times or more, the coin comes up heads or tails more or less than 50 percent. To achieve a coin toss of an equal number of heads or tails, one would have to toss the coin hundreds of thousands of times. Even after a few hundred thousand coin tosses, the coin might not come up heads or tails precisely 50 percent of the time. The reason for this is that chance plays a role in most research efforts to a greater extent than most of us like to believe.

Again, there is no demonic reason for this. Rather, the study of people is always complicated by the fact that most behavior is completely unpredictable. No research design can ever adequately control for the fact that the unexpected may occur. When it comes to coin tossing, many factors contribute to chance. The coin may be subtly weighted more on one side or the other. The way the coin is tossed and variation in air currents when the coin is tossed can affect the outcome. I've seen people who can predict the outcome of the toss before they toss it (heads or tails), at an astonishing rate of accuracy. When you think about the multiple ways a study can go wrong, you begin to realize that chance is always a factor to contend with. Even the most carefully controlled for study has chance elements that cannot be predicted or completely eliminated.

Human behavior is often very chaotic and while **chaos theory** suggests that even randomly occurring and unpredictable events have a logic that helps us understand behavior at its most unstable, in reality, no one ever knows how a study will turn out or how a group of people will act under certain conditions. As a social worker, that thought gives me comfort. I'd rather think that behavior is unpredictable, and that the human condition is always able to astonish us, even at its most chaotic. But as a researcher, the very need to order events so that results have validity and reliability makes me believe that research studies using people as subjects face incredible difficulties in reaching logical conclusions. Yes, certainly we try, but a close look at most research findings in the social sciences should convince us that the study of people is always laden with unpredictable, highly unordered, and very chaotic possibilities that increase the probability that chance plays a significant role in much of the data we collect. That realization is comforting and a little unsettling at the same time. It suggests that much of what we think we know about people, societies, and culture, may not be true. In fact, I think that's the case. It doesn't stop us from trying to order behavior and understand it, but the fact is that the human condition is so complex that however hard we try to rationally construct a research study, something or the other will usually interfere with our ability to generalize the findings to other people, places, events, and situations. That is why most social researchers are reluctant to make strong statements about their findings. They know, all too well, that generalizing from one study to a larger population is often likely to result in incorrect predictions of future behavior.

Because of the difficulty in controlling for chance occurrences, many social researchers are moving in the direction of what Tyson (1992) calls the *heuristic paradigm*. As she notes, "the positivist paradigm communicates unwarranted assumptions about science" (p. 54b). Positivism believes that the only possible way to achieve "valid knowledge" is through the empirical approach to knowledge. Tyson, like many social scientists, believes that small studies that may not be conducted under highly rigorous research controls are often capable of producing great insight into the human condition. Like most post-positivist researchers, Tyson doesn't believe that knowledge is only legitimate when the approach used to attain it is undeniably empirical. Knowledge comes in many forms. The wise researcher is always willing to accept that creativity and flexibility are sometimes more likely to astonish us than well controlled for designs which, despite our most careful attempts to factor out chance, end up badly flawed. People, unlike molecules and atoms, are difficult to order and are almost never willing to act in rational and predictable ways. I suspect the same can be said of molecules and atoms, but this is a book about social research. Molecules and atoms should go elsewhere to find a suitable audience, perhaps central Michigan where the sun hasn't shined in six months and where molecules and atoms must certainly be to blame.

Chi-Square

One frequently used statistical test to determine the level of chance is the **chi-square** test represented by the symbol X^2. The chi-square is probably the most commonly used test in statistics. It is a very weak statistical test, and its purpose is to show the level of chance between variables that might suggest a weak association or link between those variables. I'm using the words *link* and *association* because the chi-square is not a powerful statistical test and is unable to show relationships between variables. Before doing the more powerful statistical tests to show relationships between variables (referred to as **correlations** in statistics), we first run the chi-square test. Once again, the chi-square test cannot be used to show a cause and effect relationship, but it will suggest whether the links and associations between variables are strong enough to run measurements of correlation.

The chi-square measurement tells us whether the link or association between variables is caused by random chance. If the level of chance is at a .05 level or better, we could then infer a weak association between variables. The smaller the degree of chance (the smaller the number using .05 as a baseline acceptable level of chance), the more it suggests a stronger link between variables, but never an absolute cause and effect relationship.

This is often confusing for students who want to believe that the chi-square measurement shows relationships. It doesn't. All the chi-square measurement tells us is the role chance plays in the interaction between two or more variables. The less chance plays a role, the better the association between variables is thought to be.

Let's consider an example of the use of the chi-square. One of my students wanted to determine the link between the level of trauma of coming out for gay/lesbian subjects and the degree to which they thought their families would accept them after they disclosed their sexual identity. She found that, in general, the link between the two issues was strong. The chi-square measurement gave her a level of significance of .001, which suggested that the link was a very good one. When she ran correlations to determine if the link indicated a strong relationship, she found that the correlation was weak ($r = +.20$) and that chance played an unacceptably high role in the relationship ($p = .21$). How is it possible to have such a good level of significance on an initial test for the chi-square measurement and such a poor correlation?

It's possible because the chi-square is a weak and unreliable statistic while tests to determine correlation are of a much higher order of rigor. Determining a relationship between the two variables (coming out and the perception of the level of family acceptance) requires a very precise and exacting statistic. The chi-square is neither. What the chi-square does is give us a rough idea of whether two variables are linked. It helps us determine whether the level of chance (if good) would warrant the use of a higher order statistic such as a measurement of correlation. Consequently, be aware that the chi-square, while a good statistic for the beginner to use, is often considered a weak and unreliable statistical test for more complex social research purposes.

But doesn't it make sense that there should be a relationship between the traumatic impact of coming out and the perception of family acceptance? It certainly seems so and yet, when my student ran measures of correlations, she failed to find any acceptable level of relationship between the two variables. Could it be that the lack of a relationship had more to do with her design or something related to the way the questions were asked than the actual lack of a statistically significant relationship? Probably. The reality is that because so many gay and lesbian clients tell us how traumatic it is to disclose their sexual identity to their families, we are inclined to anticipate a link between the two variables. This points out something all researchers recognize. When relationships among variables fail to materialize, even in those relationships that should be obvious, the reason often has to do with chance interference, bad designs, or the existence of other reasons we haven't controlled for in our study.

Once again, the concept of chance is often referred to as the *level of significance* by researchers. It may also be called *probability of error.*

T-Tests

We've noted that the chi-square doesn't allow us to conclude a cause-and-effect relationship. The t-test, however, is one of the statistics that does allow us to draw inferences about cause and effect. It is intended to be used in comparisons between two groups.

The t-test is not a particularly complicated statistic and is certainly less complicated than the tests for correlation that we discuss in the next chapter. However, there are several important things to remember about the t-test, and these have to do with what the t-test is actually testing.

When we run a t-test, what we're actually testing is the difference between the means of two groups. In a t-test, we're trying to determine whether the two groups are different, statistically speaking. The t-test is a comparison of whether or not the means of the two groups are different enough for the two groups to be considered "significantly" different.

It is also important to understand that there are different kinds of t-tests. One type of t-test is the **between-groups t-test.** This is the type of t-test you run if you are using a control group and an experimental group. Your concern is whether there is a difference between the two groups. If there is a difference, you've selected your groups incorrectly. Remember that the control group and the experimental group should be exactly similar to one another at the point of selection so that you can determine the impact of treatment.

Another type of t-test is the **within-groups t-test.** We run a "within-groups t-test" if we are using a pre-test/post-test design where we test a group, apply a treatment, and test again. With this type of t-test, we operate without a control group. This t-test helps us determine whether the group improved because of the treatment input or whether it improved because of chance.

The other types of t-tests are the **one-tailed t-test** and the **two-tailed t-test.** The "one-tailed t-test" is used when we think we know the direction of the difference between groups with one group likely to score either higher or lower than the other group. A "two-tailed t-test" is used when we're not sure about the direction our findings might take.

When you run a t-test using a statistical package for computers, such as SPSS, you see a great many numbers. The only numbers that should interest you are the t value and the p value. The t-value is what you get by actually computing the t-test. If you were doing this test by hand, you would go to a statistics book and look for a table in the back of the book called the *Critical Value table.* This value is based on the level of error you have selected as acceptable (the p value) and the number of subjects in your study. If your t-value is greater than the critical value, your means are significantly different. It's important to keep track of that t-score, since you will need to report it when you write your results. Remember that the level of error and the level of significance mean the same thing and are two terms used to explain the degree to which chance affects your outcomes.

To rephrase what I've just said, the t-test is used to determine whether the means between the two groups are statistically different. If we use a control group and an experimental group to determine the impact of treatment and want to know whether the two groups are different in their level of improvement after a certain period of time, the t-test provides that information. The critical value tells us whether the difference between the two groups is statistically significant or whether it is unacceptable because of chance occurrences.

In a computerized statistical package such as SPSS, the critical value for a number of subjects is known. SPSS automatically tests at different levels of error and tells us the best p value at which the means are sufficiently different to exceed the critical value. First it tests at the .05 level. If it's significant at the .05 level, it then tests at different values less than .05 to see if the differences are also significant. When it reaches a result that isn't significant, it stops and gives you the exact p value as the level of significance.

The important thing for you to know is that the p level needs to be less than .05 in order for there to be significance. If the p value is greater than .05, there isn't a statistically significant difference between the two groups because chance plays too powerful a role in the outcome.

Assuming we have achieved a level of significance of five chance occurrences out of one hundred ($p < 05$), we can say, with some degree of assurance, that the difference between the groups is due to the impact of the independent variable (the treatment input). If that value is very small, let's say no chance occurrences in one and ten thousand times ($p < .0000$), then it's possible that our results are really caused by the factors for which we are testing. The t-test, as we have indicated before, is only intended for tests between two groups. If we want to test more than two groups, we have to use a different statistical measure. Care should be taken to discuss the use of the t-test in your study with your instructor. Be sure that it's the correct statistical test for your purposes and that more is not made of the findings than may be warranted.

Summary

This chapter covered some very basic statistical concepts and included discussion of measures of central tendency, chi-square, and t-tests, and the importance of chance occurrences in statistical measurements. The chapter was not meant to provide an in-depth discussion of statistics but rather, and in keeping with the focus of this book, to provide a very simple explanation of some commonly used statistical concepts and tests. For a more complete discussion, there are any number of excellent statistics books for the social sciences. Your research instructor and your statistics instructor can help in this regard. If statistics are difficult for you, and they are for many people, there are programmed statistical packages available for the computer that help students understand statistics. Again, your instructors or the computer center at your university can make suggestions.

REVIEW QUESTIONS

1. The beginning level of chance acceptable in the social sciences is 5 times in 100. Would you take a medication that could make you sick 5 times out of

100 or would you go for a surgery that could worsen your condition 5 times out of 100? Isn't the number used in social research to determine chance occurrences much too low? Shouldn't we have a higher expectation for our research so that chance plays little, if any role, before we accept the findings?

2. The concept of a normal curve is confusing. Aren't all populations skewed in some way?

3. Why doesn't an almost completely chance free chi-square (p = .00000) indicate a relationship between two variables?

4. What is the point in knowing very much about statistics? SPSS or some other statistical package does all the work. All we need is for someone to tell us what tests to run and then someone else to tell us what the test results mean. Why do we need to know about statistics?

5. Statistics often confuse issues more than they clarify them. Isn't there a better way to find out about social events than using statistics?

REFERENCES

Bartko, J. J., Carpenter, W. T., & McGlashan, T. H. (1988). Statistical issues in long-term follow-up studies. *Schizophrenia Bulletin, 14(4)*, 575–587.

Bohrnstedt, G., & Knoke, D. (1994). *Statistics for social data analysis* (3rd ed.). Itasca, IL: Peacock.

Craft, J. (1990). *Statistics and data analysis for social workers* (2nd ed.). Itasca, IL: Peacock.

Dey, E. (1993). *Qualitative analysis: A user-friendly guide for social scientists.* New York: Routledge.

Franzblau, A. N. (1958). *A primer of statistics for non-statisticians.* New York: Harcourt, Brace and World, Inc.

Hall, L. D., & Markshall, K. P. (1992). *Computing for social research: Practical approaches.* Belmont, CA: Wadsworth.

Hasse, R. R., Waechter, D. M., & Solomon, G. S. (1982). How significant is a significant difference? Average effect size of research in counseling psychology. *Journal of Counseling Psychology, 29(2)*, 59–63.

Herrnstein, R., & Murray, C. (1994). *The bell curve: Intelligence and class structure in American life.* New York: Free Press.

Katzer, J., Cook, K. H., & Crouch, W. W. (1991). *Evaluating information: A guide for users of social science research* (3rd ed.). New York: McGraw-Hill.

Miles, M., & Huberman, M. (1994). *Qualitative data analysis.* Thousand Oaks, CA: Sage.

O'Brien, R. M. (1992). Levels of analysis. In E. Borgatta and M. Borgatta (Eds.), *Encyclopedia of sociology,* Vol. 3, (pp. 1107–1112). New York: Macmillan.

Tyson, K. B. (1992, November). A new approach to relevant scientific research for practitioners: The heuristic paradigm. *Social Work, 37(6)* 541–556.

RECOMMENDED INTERNET SITES

Doing chi-squares by hand
<http://www.uea.ac.uk/~w088/Researchmethods/Chi-square.htm>

Chi-square analysis in Microsoft Excel
    <http://www.analyse-it.com/default.asp?source=goto.com&keyword=chi%20square>
Graph-pad's free t-test calculator
    <http://www.graphpad.com/calculators/ttest1.cfm>
SPSS Help Archive, University of Colorado at Boulder
    <http://sobek.colorado.edu/LAB/STATS/SPSS/>
SPSS for Windows: A Brief Tutorial
    <http://www.psych.utoronto.ca/courses/c1/spss/page1.htm>

12 Sadistic Statistics: Part II. Correlations

WITH JOSEPH GREENE

Introduction

A statistical **correlation** is a relationship between variables. Correlations are determined on a continuum from minus (−) 1.00 to plus (+) 1.00, which means that it is possible for two variables to be either positively or negatively related to one another. A positive correlation indicates that one variable has a positive impact on another variable. For example, as you increase the amount of medication given for an illness, the health of the patient improves. Negative correlations indicate that the variables move in opposite directions of each other; as you increase the amount of medication given for an infection the amount of bacteria in the body increases and the patient becomes more ill.

The idea of a positive correlation is easy to understand because we're used to thinking of the beneficial impact of an experimental input. A negative correlation just means that the opposite of what we thought would take place is what actually happens. If we take an antibiotic for an infection and we get better, that may indicate a positive relationship between curing the infection and taking the antibiotic. But what if we get sicker? That may mean that taking the antibiotic for the type of infection we have is negatively correlated. Instead of making us better, the medication either makes us sicker or we become more ill because the antibiotic has no impact on the illness. In either case, a negative relationship would exist between the use of the antibiotic and our health.

In terms of understanding the meaning of correlations, the closer the correlation is to +/−1.00, the stronger the relationship is between variables. A positive correlation between taking an antibiotic and getting better of +.95 is an exceptionally good indicator that the antibiotic works. It's important, however, to remember that correlation does not prove causation. Just because two things occur together does not mean that one causes the other to happen. The two variables could have a third, unstudied catalyst.

While we still can't infer that the antibiotic causes us to get better, it does appear that most of the time we will get better if we take the antibiotic even if there are other hidden variables that affect the outcome. If the correlation between taking the antibiotic and getting better is only +.10, that means it's unlikely the antibiotic will have any positive impact. If the correlation is −.20, it means that there is a real chance that we will get sicker if we take the antibiotic. This, of course, does not mean that the antibiotic makes us sicker. It only means that we tend to get sicker when we take it. There might be other factors that cause us to get sicker. Until we run statistical tests that control for those other unknown factors, we won't know for sure if the antibiotic will make us healthier or more ill.

Understanding the Meaning of Correlation Scores

The following explanation of correlations might help you better understand the meaning of correlation scores (Franzblau, 1958).

1. A reliable (free of unacceptable chance error) correlation of 0 to +/−.20 indicates no correlation or a very negligible correlation. A score this low does not show a cause-effect relationship and is considered too low to suggest any useful relationship between variables.
2. A reliable correlation of +/−.20 to +/−.40 suggests a low level of relationship between variables and, again, does not suggest a cause-effect relationship.
3. A reliable relationship of +/−.40 to +/−.60 suggests a moderate level of relationship between variables and does not suggest a cause and effect relationship.
4. A reliable correlation of +/−.60 to +/−.80 indicates a marked degree of relationship between variables. One would now be able to suggest a beginning cause-effect relationship between variables.
5. A reliable correlation of +/−.80 to +/−.100 is regarded as a very high correlation. One could certainly suggest that a cause-effect relationship exists among the variables being tested.

However, and this is important to understand, even when a correlation is perfect, there may not be a cause-effect relationship. You can have a perfect positive correlation of +1.00 between the highest number of admissions to psychiatric facilities and the time of the month when the moon is full, but still lack a concluding cause-effect theory that the full moon causes people to become psychotic. The real reason for increased admissions during full moons could be a third variable such as higher police vigilance during a full moon for erratic behavior in people. Or it might be caused by increased caregiver sensitivity during the full moon to psychotic behavior. Even very high correlations between variables can have hidden reasons that negate a cause-effect relationship.

To make this point even more clearly, there can be a perfect (+1.00) correlation between people who commit violent acts and eating bread. Does bread cause violence? It's unlikely unless it's the mushy, doughy kind you can smush into a ball but, even then, it's pretty unlikely. And while there can be a perfect correlation between opening up a small package wrapped in a cellophane wrapper and lung cancer, we all know that it's smoking the cigarettes inside the small package that causes the cancer and not the cellophane wrapper.

So what *does* correlation tell us? It only tells us that two variables seem to be related. It may or may not suggest a cause-effect relationship. This is where common sense and an objective frame of reference come into play. We might know that certain medications seem to make people feel better. We might even find that taking a medication results in people feeling better at a high correlation (r = +.90). Logically, it appears that the medication works. The scientific approach, however, demands that every other possible reason we can think of (the placebo effect, the patient possibly getting better without medication, etc.) must be carefully examined before we accept a cause-effect relationship between taking the medication and getting better. And more importantly, the long-term effects of the medication must also be studied. If, in the long run, people develop medical problems that might not have happened without the use of the medication, a high initial correlation between getting better and using the medication is meaningless. So unfortunately, correlations, while a powerful statistic, do not necessarily lead us to conclude the existence of a cause-effect relationship. One way to look more effectively for cause-effect relationships is using the statistical concept known as *variance*.

Variance

Using the previous example of the antibiotic, **variance** tells us how much of the reason we get better is because we took the antibiotic. To determine variance, we multiply the correlation times itself. If the correlation is +.95 then the variance is .95 × .95 or 90 percent. In other words, it is fairly accurate to say that 90 percent of the reason we got better is because we took the antibiotic. Notice that I'm not saying that the antibiotic itself is responsible. I am saying that *taking* the antibiotic seems to have a strong connection to our getting better. We still need to rule out other reasons for getting better (the placebo effect, spontaneous remissions, we would have gotten better anyway, etc.), but a variance of 90 percent is considered very good. Most of us would feel quite optimistic about taking an antibiotic that seems to make us better 90 percent of the time.

Statistics can help us make sense out of seemingly contradictory information. Here's an example. Let's say that we're going to try to show that there is a relationship between examination scores in a sociology methods class and the teacher's ability to teach. To do this, we create a test and give it to all students taking methods from every sociology professor teaching the course during a semester. We give the test to all methods students on the same day. By now you know all about intervening variables and biased samples. Sure, one section of methods might have better students, but for the sake of discussion, let's say that the students are all pretty equal in ability. We then compare the mean (average) scores on the examination and discover that there is, wonder of wonders, a pretty big difference in the average scores for each section taught. Can it then be said that the reason for these differences in scores has to do with the ability of the teacher to teach the material? This is the point at which statistics can be helpful. The average scores on the tests tell us something, but there may be a variety of reasons why some groups did better than others. Could it be, perish the thought, that the later in the day the test is given, the higher the test scores? Sounds like a little information exchange is going on. Either that, or perhaps the later classes are just more awake. Perhaps the classes later in the day had the time and the wisdom to organize into study groups. Perhaps they gave each other practice exams or had a tutor.

While the average scores might suggest that the test results are influenced by the ability of the teacher to teach the material, the fact is that the often-times overlooked third variable of chance, that unpredictable interference in research, may explain the difference in scores much better than the instructor's teaching ability. There are statistical tests that can help us determine how much of a role chance plays in the outcome of any statistical measurement. Aren't you happy for your poor instructor who taught methods at 8:00 A.M. and had such dismal examination results?

Making decisions about whether someone is an effective teacher is really a good deal more complex than it sounds, but the correct statistical measures can clear up those complexities quickly. The proper statistical test not only tells us how much chance plays a role in the findings, but the strength of the relationship between test scores and the teacher's ability to teach can also be established through use of the correct statistical measurements. What might look, on the face of it, like a clear indication of a relationship between scores on an examination and the teacher's ability to teach the material, might look a good deal different once correct statistical measurements are utilized.

But doesn't that confuse the issue? If there can always be a third explanation to explain the data, or if you can always chalk the results up to chance, can't statistics be used to defend bad teachers? Nope. Statistics are a way of determining whether the data we've collected is useful. In the real world where every manner of manipulation goes on when examinations are given, it's an important distinction to remember. Statistics can help us understand the meaning of the data we've collected. They can't cover up bad teaching. What they can do is to show us the importance of every single reason for test score differences that we can think of: Time of day the test was given, the years of experience of the teacher, the relationship between student satisfaction with the teacher and examination scores, the scores students had on their SATs, the grade point averages (GPAs) of students in each section, and so on until we've considered every logical reason for test score variability. But finally and hooray, once we've established the importance of all of the other reasons for examination score results, statistics can help us know how much of a role the teacher played in the examination scores. To help us do that, it is useful to look at a fairly sophisticated statistical test called a *regression analysis.*

Regression Analysis

One statistical measure used to find more relevant correlations is a **regression analysis.** It's certainly one of the most useful statistical measures we have, and it is one of several very strong statistical measurements used to *predict* relationships among many variables. It also tells us how much of a role chance plays in each and every piece of data generated by a statistical test. By analyzing the way in which variables seem to relate to each other over time, we can eventually predict, to some degree, the way in which they will relate to each other in the future. This assumes that the variables will remain relatively constant in the future. Regression analysis is not the same as correlation, but it's similar. While correlation simply shows the general trend of the relationship, regression analysis helps us understand the exact role each individual variable seems to play in our outcome.

In the real world, the relationship between the ability to teach and examination scores is very difficult to determine. The reason is that there are an infinite number of reasons to explain how well or how badly someone did on an examination. We may not even know all of the reasons much less include them in our statistical analysis. In regression analysis, when all of the reasons we can think of are accounted for, the actual amount of variance (how much of a role the teacher played in the examination results) may be very small. For the sake of understanding the impact of teaching on examination scores, let's assume that we've included the following variables in our regression analysis: The time of day the test was taken, the current grade in methods of each student in a class section, the gender of each student, the hours spent studying for the examination, the number of methods classes previously attended before the examination, a voluntary pre-test questionnaire asking students to rate their general mood and confidence level for the specific examination, and the number of years the teacher has taught the methods course. These are only a few potential variables of the many hundreds of reasons for test score differences. I'm sure you can think of others.

Once we've coded the data and entered it into the computer, using a regression analysis we can compare variables against one another seeking significant correlations. We also run a test for variance. Having done this, let's assume that of the 100 percent of the reasons someone did well or poorly on the examination, the teacher's impact on test score performance is only 20 percent. Even though the variance may be small in this case, we can still compare the separate correlations between test scores for each teacher and compare them to other variables included in the regression analysis.

Practically speaking, this lets us evaluate the impact of each individual teacher's effectiveness on the performance of students. Let's say that the best correlation between test scores and an individual teacher is +.50. In other words, when we look at instructor A, who has been teaching the longest, we find that the scores her students made on the test were higher than anyone else teaching the course. In fact, as we look across the correlations between teaching effectiveness and student scores on the methods examination, we discover that the correlations are linked to the length of time teachers have been teaching methods. Let's consider the ten instructors who teach the methods classes and compare each of them with student scores on the methods examination (see Table 12.1). Remember that the higher the correlation number, the better students did on their examinations. The lower the number, the worse they did. If the number is negative, it means that the teacher seems to have been responsible for lowering the test score.

The correlation between the length of teaching and the results on the student examination is: $r = +.71$ ($p = .0006$).

TABLE 12.1 Correlations between Examination Results and the Instructor

Instructor			No. of Years Teaching Methods
1	+.52	p = .0000	23
2	+.37	p = .0001	18
3	+.24	p = .0000	16
4	+.10	p = .0002	8
5	+.03	p = .0000	4
6	−.03	p = .0004	1
7	−.12	p = .005	Never taught methods before
8	−.21	p = .0000	1
9	−.37	p = .0007	Never taught methods before
10	−.56	p = .003	Never taught before

From these scores, we readily see that the length of time the instructor has been teaching methods *does* play a role in the scores on examinations ($r = .71$). Not a particularly strong role since 80 percent of the examination score is influenced by other variables, but even if only 20 percent of the score seems to be influenced by the instructor, we still see that many of the instructors have a very low impact on examination results. In fact, a number of instructors (five to be exact) have a negative impact. Several of them *appear* to have a very negative impact. They certainly need to consider their style of teaching and their ability to present the material in the future but, clearly, length of teaching seems to correlate with results on examination scores. I should add that all the correlations shown are statistically significant at much better than the .05 level.

The data we generate doesn't specifically tell us what experienced teachers do in the classroom that differs from what inexperienced teachers do, nor does it tell us anything about the overall ability of the ten instructors to teach anything more than the material tested in a sociology methods course. Does this mean that some of the lower scoring teachers can't teach? No. It just means that, *in general,* the students taking these instructors for a sociology methods class did not do well on one examination. We certainly can't say anymore about the results, although it is reassuring to know that instructor experience, in this one case, seems to correlate with better student results on an examination. Might another test suggest different results? Certainly. An instructor may know the material covered better on a second test or may be better prepared for a second test and teach students the material covered in that test in a more effective manner.

ANOVAS and Beyond

We've already discussed the concept of variance and how it can be viewed as part of the reason for differences in correlations. In some ways, the t-test is a way to analyze the variance between two groups. But if we want to compare more than two groups, we have to use a statistic that is just what it says it is, the **analysis of variance, ANOVA** for short.

In some ways, an ANOVA is much like a t-test in that it compares means while taking the variance into account. But the ANOVA is intended to be used with more than two groups. If you want to get really complicated, you use a variant of the ANOVA, the **MANOVA,** or the **multiple analysis of variance.** You'll probably never need to know the formula for the ANOVA, but you do need to understand the answers that you'll get from SPSS or some other statistical program.

The ANOVA output is very similar to that of the t-test. You'll still be looking for a *p* value of less than .05, but the actual score being calculated is an **f-score.** Once again, you'll need to keep track of it, since it will be reported in your results.

Let's assume for a moment that we ran our ANOVA with three groups (one control group and two different treatment groups), and we got an *f*-score that the computer reports as being significant at the .01 level (*p* = .01). But we have three groups! Are they all significantly different from one another?

Not necessarily. It's possible that the two treatment groups are different from the control group but not different from one another. This can be good or bad, depending on what we're looking for. But the only way we're going to know for sure is to use one of two methods, each of which have their strengths and weaknesses.

Planned Versus Unplanned Comparisons

In order to determine exactly which groups are different from one another, we have to choose between two testing methods. It is important to remember this: You can't use both methods and choose the results you like best. Doing so will cumulatively increase your chance of error. This is also the reason we don't do just multiple t-tests; we have the exact same problem. There's a very good chance that your level of significance (*p*) will go over the .05 level if you do.

The two types of tests you can use are **planned (orthogonal contrasts)** and unplanned **(post hoc)** comparisons.

Planned comparisons are used when you think you have a pretty good idea where some of the differences may exist among the groups you are comparing. Planned comparisons are a little more complicated to set up, but they give you a greater chance for significance because you are planning them. Let's consider the example I used earlier of a control group with two treatment groups. We are reasonably certain that some treatment is better than no treatment, so we plan to compare both treatment groups together against the control group by itself. Then, we want to compare the treatment groups to each other. The important thing to remember is that we cannot compare each individual treatment group to the control group anymore. That's part of the trade-off since we're treating the two treatment groups as if they are the same.

But what if we want to compare the treatment groups to the control group because we suspect that there are differences in each of the two treatment groups? To do this we set up a post hoc test which is a way of comparing all groups against one another. This is a test to use when you're not entirely sure how significant the results will be.

There are a number of different post hoc tests and you will probably find one that you like. Some people like the **Tukey's LSD test** just because they like the name "Tukey." Which test you use doesn't make a great deal of difference, though, and your software package may dictate which statistical test you use.

How to Report Statistics

Eventually, you'll need to put statistics into your research report. Reporting statistics is really pretty easy, in fact; once you get the hang of it, you'll find that it's much easier than writing the literature review.

When reporting statistics, we tend to go from the simplest data to the most complex data. The first thing we report is the number of subjects in our groups. We further break that figure down by reporting the number of males and females in our study, the race/ethnicity of our subjects, their ages and educational level, and other descriptive data that we find relevant (religious preference, income, marital status, etc.). This is often called *sociodemographic information.*

Next, we report measures of central tendency. Mean and standard deviation are commonly reported. Report the numbers concisely as in this example: "Tennis playing males between the ages of 55 and 60 who grew up in the great state of North Dakota and who saw alien life forms reported a mean life satisfaction level of 10 (with 10 the highest score possible), and a standard deviation of 4.7."

If we ran a chi-square, we note only those chi-squares with a level of significance at the .05 level or better. This is an example: "The chi-square notes a level of significance between life satisfaction of male tennis players ages 55 to 60 and higher levels of intelligence at the .0000 level." In other words, there appears to be evidence of a link between male tennis players ages 55 to 60 and high intelligence. There is also a probable link between older male tennis players and low cholesterol, low blood pressure, higher levels of sexiness, and a greater ability to tolerate bad music, but it's beyond the scope of the current study to indicate that any of this has been found in the current study. Perhaps some wonderful student researcher will see the wisdom of completing such a study for a high number of extra points on their grade in a methods class.

If we ran correlations, the next thing we report is any correlations that were important. "Important" doesn't necessarily mean a high correlation; something that has a very low correlation might be important to report. This is particularly true if you expected to find a high correlation or a significant relationship but discovered instead that your correlations were either very low or were, in fact, negative. Consider this way of reporting a correlation: "Male tennis players ages 55 to 60 were found to have very healthy blood pressure readings. The correlation between male tennis players ages 55 to 60 and very healthy blood pressure readings (120/70 to 130/80) was very high ($r = .874$). Further evidence of the good health of male tennis players ages 55 to 60 was noted in high correlations with life satisfaction ($r = .934$), low blood sugars ($r = .879$), and high levels of intelligence ($r = .997$). All data reported were significant at the .0004 level or better." Anyone for tennis?

Finally, we need to report inferential statistics (t-tests, ANOVAs, post hocs or orthogonal contrasts). It's important that we report both the actual score and the level of significance (the probability of error, or p). We also need to report something called the *degrees of freedom,* or df. Degrees of freedom should be on your SPSS printout, but it's essentially (n − 1), or the number of subjects in each group minus one. If using a between-groups design, subtract one from the total number of subjects for each group in your study.

Our report of a t-test might look something like this: "A between-groups t-test was performed to examine the relationship between gender and life satisfaction among male and female tennis players ages 55 to 60 as reported on the Glicken Intensely Interesting Scale (GIIS). A t-value of 4.3124 was found, suggesting that tennis playing males tend to experience higher levels of life satisfaction than tennis playing females ($p < .05$, df = 83)." This can be explained by the fact that females play doubles, a boring and completely useless form of tennis, while warrior male tennis players stick to singles even if they experience breathing problems and chest pains because they need to prove how macho they are. This final sentence is an aside and would not be reported in this section but might be appropriate for a section explaining the findings.

Be complete in reporting your statistics because they are your proof. Make sure that you report completely and accurately, and make sure that any statements you make are supported by the data. Don't editorialize; you have the opportunity to discuss the meaning of the results later.

The most important thing to remember about reporting statistics is to completely report every statistic that is relevant to the hypothesis being testing. Even if it's not statistically significant, report it. What is not significant from a statistical standpoint may be significant from a research standpoint. It's often as important to know which variables *do not* relate to one another as it is to know which variables *do* relate to one another. That's part of the scientific process.

My rule of thumb on what data to report is that it should support or refute our hypothesis. Additionally, report data that may be of relevance to the study. Do the data suggest something so unusual that it begs to be noted? Going back to the discussion of instructor impact on examinations, what if the most important single finding was neither discussed in our literature review nor anticipated in our research design? What if the most significant factor affecting scores on the examination had to do with the room in which the test was taken? Or perhaps, what if the reason had to do with the colors of ink used on the various tests? Or, to make matters even more complicated, what if the main reason for test score differences had to do with the comfort of the desks in the various rooms in which the tests were taken? How would we know that since we completely forgot to say a thing about any of the three variables just listed and failed to include these issues in our research design? By asking a few simple questions after the examination, we might have been able to determine unpredictable reasons for test score differences. Colors of ink may have changed in the process of duplicating the examinations. We may have been totally unaware of the change until some alert researcher found it or our students mentioned it. To not report this finding would be to miss an opportunity to make a relevant statement about test score results that might lead to a breakthrough in theories about how the testing environment affects performance. If students do better on examinations written in red ink, then you'd hope that such a finding would be used in future test giving so that it would increase a student's chance of receiving a higher score. It would be pretty difficult to explain *how* the color of ink influences test scores, but it would certainly be of relevance to our study and all subsequent research done on student test performance.

Computerized Statistical Packages

Because of the simplicity of using computer programs like SPSS, many students run statistical tests and can neither read the findings nor understand the way the statistics generated by a test might best be used. To help you understand the data generated by a statistical package such as SPSS, let's summarize what we've said so far in the last two chapters so that after you go to the computer, input your data, tell the computer what you want, and wait the 20 seconds for the statistical package to do its magic, you actually understand what you've done, why you did it, and what the data you generated actually mean.

1. Measures of central tendency including the mean, median, mode, range, frequencies, standard deviations, and z-scores that describe a sample. They tell us how many people are in the sample and their distribution by such attributes as age, race, ethnicity, gender, educational level, and so on. They also provide averages and tell us how close or how far away a single individual in the sample is from the mean for everyone in the sample. When you use SPSS, you ask the computer to determine frequencies and you tell it the specific frequencies you want.

2. To note the degree to which chance plays a role in your findings, you use the chi-square or a t-test if you are comparing groups. The chi-square suggests links and associations while the t-test is a stronger statistic and can suggest relationships between groups. Both statistics determine whether chance plays a role in the comparisons between variables. If chance plays virtually no role in the comparison between variables (for example, chance doesn't impact our findings in one in ten thousand times), a strong link between variables is suggested. Chi-square does not directly indicate a relationship between variables (the words *links* and *associations* better describe what the chi-square provides). T-tests, considered a stronger statistical test, suggest a possible relationship between groups. SPSS permits you to run both the chi-square and the t-test(s).

3. Correlations are meant to suggest a cause-effect relationship. While we have gone to great lengths to help you see that proving a cause-effect relationship is very tricky and requires the use of critical thinking and common sense, the concept of correlation is always fraught with methodological difficulties. Bad designs are usually at the forefront of problematic correlations. More importantly, however, showing a cause and effect relationship in the social sciences is always beset by issues of chance. People are unpredictable, and how they respond in any research situation is complicated and difficult to control. Chance is always measured as part of any correlational statistic. Often studies show only moderate correlations but chance plays too large a role in the findings to be acceptable. Most studies done by students at the undergraduate level do not use correlation statistics as an option, although you can easily run correlations on SPSS.

REVIEW QUESTIONS

1. The point has been made that even though variables might be highly correlated, in fact, they may not form an actual relationship. How is the consumer of research to know this?

2. It seems obvious that if chance doesn't play any role in a statistic such as a chi-square, one should be able to say something more meaningful than the existence of a link or an association between variables. Why not set an arbitrary number for chance at the (.0000) level and say that anything that achieves that score shows a cause-effect relationship?

3. In a regression analysis, how can we possibly know how many variables to include? It seems likely that even if we make a good faith effort by reading the literature carefully, we might leave out a number of important variables.

4. If a correlation is high but the level of significance is poor, doesn't the correlation score outweigh the level of significance because it's a more powerful statistic?

5. The concept of variance seems to suggest that while a correlation may be strong between two variables, the importance of the correlation in the overall picture may be very limited. Why even run correlations if variance is the more important issue?

REFERENCE

Franzblau, A. N. (1958). *A primer of statistics for non-statisticians.* New York: Harcourt, Brace and World, Inc.

ADDITIONAL REFERENCES

Andrews, F. M., Klem, L., Davidson, T. N., O'Malley, P. M., & Rodgers, W. L. (1994). *A guide for selecting statistical techniques for analyzing social science data* (3rd ed.). Ann Arbor, MI: Institute for Social Research, University of Michigan.

Brown, R. W. (1992). *Graph it! How to make, read, and interpret graphs.* Englewood Cliffs, NJ: Prentice-Hall.

Coleman, H., & Unrau, Y. A. (1996). Phase three: Analyzing your data. In L. M. Tutty, M. A. Rothery, & R. M. Grinnell, Jr. (Eds.), *Qualitative research for social workers: Phases, steps, and tasks* (pp. 88–119). Boston: Allyn & Bacon.

Craft, J. L. (1990). *Statistics and data analysis for social workers* (2nd ed.). Itasca, IL: F. E. Peacock.

Gabor, P. A., Unrau, Y. A., & Grinnell, R. M., Jr. (1998). *Program evaluation for social workers: A quality improvement approach for the social services* (2nd ed.). Boston: Allyn & Bacon.

Grinnell, R. M., Jr. (Ed.). (1997). *Social work research and evaluation: Quantitative approaches* (5th ed.). Itasca, IL: F. E. Peacock.

Kiess, H. O. (1989). *Statistical concepts for the behavioral sciences.* Boston: Allyn & Bacon.

Krishef, C. H. (1987). *Fundamental statistics for human services and social work.* Boston: Duxbury Press.

Lewis-Beck, M. S. (1995). *Data analysis: An introduction.* Thousand Oaks, CA: Sage.

Loether, H. J., & McTavish, D. G. (1988). *Descriptive and inferential statistics: An introduction* (3rd ed.). Boston: Allyn & Bacon.

Shavelson, R. J. (1988). *Statistical reasoning for the behavioral sciences* (2nd ed.). Boston: Allyn & Bacon.

Stahl, S. M., & Hennes, J. D. (1980). *Reading and understanding applied statistics* (2nd ed.). St. Louis: Mosby.

Tutty, L. M., Grinnell, R. M., Jr., & Williams, M. (1997). Quantitative data analysis. In R. M. Grinnell, Jr. (Ed.), *Social work research and evaluation: Quantitative and qualitative approaches* (5th ed.) (pp. 475–500). Itasca, IL: F. E. Peacock.

Tutty, L. M., Rothery, M. A., & Grinnell, R. M., Jr. (Eds.). (1996). *Qualitative research for social workers: Phases, steps, and tasks.* Boston: Allyn & Bacon.

Weinbach, R. W., & Grinnell, R. M., Jr. (1996). *Applying research knowledge: A workbook for social work students* (2nd ed.). Boston: Allyn & Bacon.

Wilcox, R. R. (1987). *New statistical procedures for the social sciences: Modern solutions to basic problems.* Hillsdale, NJ: Lawrence Erlbaum.

Williams, M., Tutty, L. M., & Grinnell, R. M., Jr. (1995). *Research in social work: An introduction* (2nd ed.). Itasca, IL: F. E. Peacock.

Wright, S. E. (1986). *Social science statistics.* Boston: Allyn & Bacon.

Yegidis, B., Weinbach, R. W., & Morrison-Rodriguez, B. (1998). *Research methods for social workers* (3rd ed.). Boston: Allyn & Bacon.

CHAPTER

13 Ethics in Research

Introduction

Over the years, people have been hurt by research studies that fail to inform them of their rights. Because certain researchers have been less than honest with subjects regarding the real intent of their studies, we no longer have the right to force anyone to take part in a research study. Prior to concerns for the rights of subjects, many people, some of them in locked facilities, were involuntarily subjected to medical research studies that are now considered unethical and illegal. Under guidelines developed by the federal government, we can no longer force people to complete surveys or to be interviewed against their will. If we attempt to do research that hasn't first been approved by a sponsoring organization, we may commit a potentially unethical act.

It may seem unnecessary to many students that they must first get their research projects approved by a human subjects review board at their institutions. After all, their instructor has approved the study and it seems harmless enough. But subjects sometimes question our right to do research. They want to know if someone is sponsoring it. They want to know what the research is about before they agree to take part in the process. If you don't think they have a right to make informed decisions about participating in a research study, you're in trouble. Without duly notifying the subjects of their rights, and without telling them what the project is about and how they can obtain the results of the study, we set up a potential situation where subjects enter into a research study not fully informed and, conceivably, against their will. This is the perfect arrangement for a lawsuit or a formal grievance against you, your school, or your organization.

In response to serious complaints from research subjects about dishonest research practices, universities and other large organizations (school districts, mental health facilities, public welfare agencies, corporations, government agencies) have set up human subjects review systems. These usually consist of a committee of scholars or high-level professionals with research skills who make certain that proposed research studies include the necessary human rights protections of subjects. This might be done within a social science department, or it may be done by a larger group of scholars representing the entire organization. My former department of social work had its own human subjects review committee, but it was guided and monitored by the university-wide human subjects committee. Approval of your proposal by the human subjects committee protects you from legal issues as long as you remain faithful to the original plan approved by the committee. If you stray from the approved research procedures, or if you change your methodology in mid-stream without first informing the committee, you are libel for any legal action brought against you. It's doubtful if the university will support you. Oral approval of your project isn't acceptable. You need written approval from the human subjects review committee.

In higher education, sometimes a departmental review isn't sufficient. Research pertaining to children or confined subjects almost always requires broader review by the university committee. Although I have the right to ask for an initial departmental review of projects related to children or confined subjects, I almost always send the research proposals directly to the university human subjects review committee. I do this to protect my students in cases where, conceivably, the judgment of the departmental committee might not be correct. If there is doubt, sending it to the parent committee that directly represents the university is always a good idea.

Are we being overly concerned about protecting the human rights of subjects? It may seem that way, but there have been some egregious examples of research that is both unethical and harmful to subjects that make us mindful of the need to protect people, particularly poor, disenfranchised, or uninformed people who enter into research studies in good faith only to find that it may negatively affect them. One such study that immediately comes to mind is the Tuskegee Syphilis Studies (Jones, 1982) in which unsuspecting African American men who went for medical treatment for syphilis were given placebos that usually resulted in early death, blindness, insanity, or other severe illness. We have hundreds of years of evidence that syphilis is harmful if not treated correctly. Subjecting men unknowingly to a placebo would never be approved today because of the absolutely negative impact it would have on the health of subjects. Furthermore, such a study would certainly be racist.

The Human Subjects Approval Process

A request for approval of a project involving human subjects must contain the following information:

1. A letter(s) from any organization you intend to use to collect information stating that you have the right to conduct the research within

the organization. Someone who speaks with authority for the organization must sign the letter.

2. Instruments used in your study created by someone else must have the written approval of the author(s), or you must have evidence that the instrument is free to use. Free instruments are often said to exist in the "public domain." Instruments are sometimes created for the use of other researchers and are free to use. Sometimes they are copyrighted and their use requires the author's approval in writing. Instruments that have copyrights may require payment for use of the instrument, although a student discount is sometimes offered. You must show evidence of approval to use the instrument before you can get human subjects clearance. You must also include any instrument, developed by you or created by someone else, in the materials you send for human subject review.

3. Your methodology must be free of anything that could potentially violate human rights. An unobtrusive study in which the subject doesn't know that he or she is being studied is an example. Using people below the age of 18 without the consent of their parents is unacceptable. Using incarcerated subjects who have lost certain rights without obtaining the consent of the organization that holds those rights (prisons, juvenile courts, etc.) is unacceptable. Finally, using subjects who can't understand their rights is another example of a methodology not acceptable to a human subjects review committee. All material provided to subjects must be written in very simple language. That material must also be written in the language the subject speaks. If consent and debriefing statements are read to a subject, they must be read slowly and the subject provided with an opportunity to ask questions to clarify any statement that might be confusing or unclear.

4. You must include two additional documents in your request for human subjects approval. The first is an **informed consent statement.** This statement explains the research study and defines the rights of the subject. I've included a sample informed consent statement later in this chapter. The second document is a **debriefing statement** which is given to subjects when they have completed their part in the study. The debriefing statement explains what the research study is trying to accomplish. It also explains to subjects how they can get the final results of the study and indicates where subjects can go for help if any of the questions asked or if any aspect of the study caused them emotional pain. You will also find an example of a debriefing statement later in this chapter.

You may wonder why your small pieces of research might cause subjects discomfort. Occasionally we ask subjects questions that make them depressed or anxious because they remind subjects of early life experiences that were unpleasant or abusive. Some questions make them feel badly about their current lives. Some questions might prompt them to consider emotionally or physically self-destructive behaviors. Imagine what participation in a job satisfaction survey might do to someone close to committing workplace violence against a co-worker. The questions asked on the survey may act as an emotional catalyst for violence.

Many human subjects committees require that a form be filled out when applying for human subjects approval. That form usually explains the degree of complexity of the review and the type of information required of the applicant. I've included parts of an application form for human subjects that may, within some parameters, be similar to the forms used in many organizations and universities. Your school or organization may differ, although many schools follow human subjects guidelines and language developed by the federal government. Keep in mind that the organization is legally liable for any research study. If you've failed to get human subjects approval from the correct committee, you'll be held legally liable, particularly if you've been told to get approval first and fail to do so. Never do a study before you have approval, and no matter how small the study is, get guidance from your instructor regarding the proper approval process before data collection begins.

The Types of Human Subjects Review

There are generally three types of reviews you can request when you are ready to submit your proposal for human subjects review: exempt reviews, expedited reviews, and full board reviews. Let's consider each type of review.

Exempt Reviews

Certain types of studies (some surveys, field interviews, or standard educational testing) can be **exempt** from full review by human subjects committees. The chair of the organization's humans subjects review committee usually makes that decision. Normally, the following types of studies are the most likely to receive exempt status:

1. Research that is frequently done in educational settings to evaluate the effectiveness of certain teaching approaches. Research evaluating the predictive quality of required standardized tests such as the SAT or the GRE is an example. Remember that the chair of the human subjects committee must first make the determination of whether a study meets these standards.

2. Research involving surveys or interview procedures are often exempt unless subjects can be identified, the research deals with highly personal areas of the subject's behavior (abuse, infidelity, criminal behavior, acts of racial or gender bigotry, etc.), or the research places subjects at legal or financial risk. Surveys or interviews with public officials or candidates for public office are usually exempt if the researcher uses ethical approaches to data collection. If the researcher lies to the public official about the study or about his or her identity, the study is considered unethical and would not be approved for exempt status.

3. Research involving observation of others is often exempt unless the subject can be identified, the observation of participants place them at risk (physical or emotional), or observations deal with very sensitive and private aspects of the subject's behavior, including drug use, sexual behavior, or illegal conduct. A famous study comes to mind that would never have received human subjects approval by today's guidelines. A social researcher sat outside public restrooms and observed men entering the restroom (Humphreys, 1975). If a subject stayed for more than a few minutes and there was another subject in the restroom who also stayed longer than usual, it was assumed that the two men were having sex. Using the license plate numbers of the men who were assumed to be having sex, the researcher found their addresses and phone numbers, and contacted many of the men in hopes of interviewing them. Whether this was worthwhile research is very doubtful in my mind. The fact that people were being unknowingly observed and license plate numbers were used to track subjects down to interview them would be cause enough to say emphatically "NO!" to this study.

Expedited Reviews

An **expedited review** is often given in cases where the research involves very minimal risk and can be approved by a small sub-committee of the human subjects review committee, such as a departmental committee in sociology, psychology, criminal justice, or social work. Categories that are acceptable for expedited review and are relevant to the social sciences include:

1. Physical information that occurs naturally and does not require invasive procedures (taking blood samples, for example) to obtain information. This might include checking someone's height and weight or taking samples of sweat or naval lint. Biofeedback research might be expedited if care is taken not to place high levels of stress on subjects. The age of the person from whom information is obtained is important, and an expedited review requires subjects to be 18 and older.

2. Under some conditions, the collection of blood samples not to exceed a certain amount in an eight-week period and not more than twice a week in healthy, non-pregnant subjects above the age of 18 are permitted under an expedited review. These procedures are considered acceptable for expedited review only if health–safety factors are observed. Using students with no experience to draw blood is considered unacceptable. Similarly, using lab technicians with communicable diseases is also considered unacceptable. While I've indicated that collection of blood might be approved for an expedited review, I want to caution you that blood sampling is a highly controversial subject and seems very unlikely for social research. Losing blood samples, confusing donor samples, and incorrect data findings that must be shared with subjects, all bode badly for liability issues. I leave blood sampling to medical researchers.

3. Voice recordings to determine speech defects are acceptable for expedited review if confidentiality of the identities of subjects is maintained. Knowing that someone has a speech defect may affect the subject's ability to get gainful employment or it may affect an educational experience. The subject may want a mild hearing loss to remain confidential because he or she fears that if a classroom instructor knows about the hearing loss, it may affect how the subject is viewed educationally. This is particularly true in professions requiring communication skills including social work and psychology where a hearing loss might be thought to adversely affect the helping process.

4. Moderate exercise by healthy volunteers can be included under research seeking expedited status. The researcher must first establish that the subject is "healthy" which may require a doctor's written approval or a physical examination prior to the start of the study. It also assumes that the physician providing the approval knows exactly what level of exercise is required by the study. Just having the subject declare himself healthy, if a preexisting or unknown condition exists, can place the researcher in legal jeopardy. One of the workers in an agency I once directed was asked by a caller if moderate running was permissible for the caller even though he was experiencing mild chest pains. The worker, thinking the chest pains were anxiety-related, said yes. Upon hearing about the call, I contacted the caller, told him that under no circumstance should he run, and that he should see his doctor immediately to determine whether he had physical problems. I emphasized not running three times. I also told him that if the doctor determined that the problem was anxiety-related, we could help treat the anxiety through counseling. First, however, I wanted him to see a doctor. After determining his health status, he and the doctor could discuss continued running. I was correctly worried about a lawsuit. If we encouraged someone to continue running in the midst of chest pains, and the caller had a heart attack, the resulting cost to the agency in legal damages and fees could destroy the agency. The caller turned out to have anxiety problems and came for therapy for six months. I was his therapist and he was a wonderful, highly intelligent, and thoughtful man who taught me a great deal about cultural differences.

5. The study of existing data, documents, and records may qualify for an expedited review. This assumes that the organization holding the documents has first given its permission and that confidentiality is maintained. It also assumes that the researcher is collecting data about the topic approved by the human subjects committee and that he or she isn't collecting data for other reasons or for which they have not received approval.

An example of this comes to mind. A student wanted to find out whether children taken from parental homes due to the dangers of possible incest, were molested in foster homes. A very important subject. The agency refused to allow the study, citing the fact that the student didn't know the definitions of molestation well enough to make clear judgments. Furthermore, the agency worried that if even occasional abuse occurred in foster homes, the study might serve to keep children in their highly dangerous parental homes where abuse was almost guaranteed to continue. The agency consented to allow the student to collect socio-demographic data (race, income, number of children in the home, etc.) about the homes from which children were removed. That was the extent of the approval. The student, a child victim of incest, we discovered later, did exactly what the agency and the human subjects review board said she could not do. She used the records of child abuse victims to show high rates of continued abuse in foster care. She then gave the data to the newspaper and for months the agency had to defend itself against charges of child endangerment. The agency sued the student who was given a failing grade in her research course and was asked to appear before the university disciplinary board. Much as we can commend the student for the importance of the information she provided, to do a study at variance with the limits placed on the study by the human subjects review committee is unethical and could result in serious repercussions.

6. Studies of how people perform on specific tests where the researcher does not manipulate the subject's behavior or increase the subject's level of stress are usually approved for expedited review. There is, of course, a very fine line in the definition of the word *stress*. In the following example, you will see how the concept of stress-free testing is totally negated and how the manipulation of subjects can produce some highly volatile results.

Milgram's (1963) famous study on the subject of authority in which research subjects were given simulated shocks by other research subjects on the assumption that electric shocks would improve learning, would not receive exempt status in today's world of human subject rights. For one thing, it mislead subjects into thinking that they were helping people learn by asking the subjects to give high level electric shocks to other students who were not learning a procedure at an acceptable rate. Secondly, it left some subjects worried that, under the constant encouragement of researchers who urged subjects to increase the voltage of the electric shocks to improve learning, they had seriously hurt and even killed subjects. The purpose of the study was to see how likely student volunteers were to apply ever-increasing levels of harmful electric shock to other students playing the role of slow learners. The experiment didn't use real electric shock, nor were the subjects ever hurt. The outcome suggested that ordinary people, under certain conditions, could do some pretty awful things to gain the approval of the researchers (authority figures). The research has implications regarding the use of authority in almost any situation, and is considered to be a very important study of social behavior with significance for prisons and other confined settings where the staff has absolute control over residents and where extreme harm can be done to people. The study would never be approved today because it violates the rights of subjects to know what the research is about and to understand their right to withdraw from the study. It would also be denied approval because of the extreme stress it places on subjects to harm other subjects. Even though the study is an important piece of social science research, the numerous violations of human subjects procedures would doom it to failure in today's political and legal climate.

Full Board Review

Proposals that do not fit into either of the above categories require full organizational or departmental reviews. In my opinion, all studies of children, subjects in residential settings, prisoners, the mentally ill, and the intellectually challenged should, as common practice, receive full board review. The additional work required for a full board review is a small price to pay for the added protection this provides the researcher and the subject. A great deal happens during a research study. Be aware that you will be held liable if you haven't received proper approval. In the real world, children in residential care for serious emotional problems often make suicidal gestures when questions asked of them are too stressful. The intellectually challenged may have depressions after an interview because they feel the researcher is being condescending. When in doubt, ask for a full board review.

The Request for Human Subjects Approval Form

Many human subjects review committees ask for additional information to expedite the evaluation of the research proposal. They may ask for your complete proposal, but, more than likely, they will request limited information. The following information are examples of what might be asked of you:

Participant Recruitment

You might be asked to describe how you plan to recruit and select subjects. You might also be asked to describe physical and socio-demographic characteristics of your subjects such as age, ethnicity, gender, institutional status (e.g., whether the subjects are prisoners or juveniles under state custody in group facilities), as well as the general state of physical and emotional health of your subject pool.

Description of the Project

You might be asked to briefly describe the methodology of your study, your research objectives (including any hypothesis or research questions), your data collection procedures, and any special features of the research design. You might also need to include the instruments you will use (with approval letters) and a list of all the questions you will ask subjects including any special features of the methodology that might appear to be unusual.

Some special features in a research design became apparent when two of my students used an Internet site they had created to see if women who were anorexic or bulimic also had attachment disorders (early life difficulty in bonding with parents or significant adult care-takers). The site used a confidential e-mail system that allowed subjects to complete an informed consent form, the questionnaires, and, once having completed and e-mailed the questionnaire, a debriefing statement. I thought this was very creative but a bit out of the mainstream and suggested a full review by the university human subjects committee. The larger committee applauded their creativity and approved the project without any significant changes.

Approval Letters

Attach all letters giving you approval to use a specific physical site to conduct your research. That site could be a workplace, school, club, and so forth. The letter should come from the person in charge of the organization and should be on the letterhead of the organization. Additionally, attach all instruments you plan to use. If someone else created the instrument, you must have a letter from the author of the instrument giving you approval to use it. If the instrument is in the public domain, include evidence from articles or other sources that the instrument can be used without prior approval or payment to the authors. A letter from the author(s) of the instrument, even if the instrument *is* in the public domain and free to use, is the better way to go. The authors might provide additional information about the instrument that is not available in the literature. Consequently, I encourage my students to directly contact the authors, and ask for permission to use the instrument and for any additional information that might prove helpful in analyzing their data. Many people who create instruments include e-mail addresses in their articles, and my students are often able to contact them by e-mail. Most authors of instruments, in my experience, are extremely helpful and generous with their time and expertise.

One student was asked by a researcher if he (the researcher) could include data from the student's study in a forthcoming article the researcher was writing for a journal. The data my student collected and the information she was able to share with the researcher was so impressive that the researcher included my student's name as second author. This is pretty impressive stuff, and it helped my student move forward in her desire to pursue a career in academia.

Risks and Benefits of the Research

You need to describe any immediate and/or long-term risks to subjects that may result from the study. Risks may be legal, physical, social, emotional, or economic. Common risks include side effects from the experimental input, risks from placebos, risks due to normal delays in treatment, questions that remind subjects of prior traumatic events, or risks to subjects as they look critically (and perhaps negatively) at their lives. Indicate any precautions you will take to minimize these risks as well as any anticipated benefits to participants and others as a result of the knowledge obtained in the study. Realize that when you ask subjects emotionally charged questions, the questions may trigger unanticipated emotional responses. Asking adult children of alcoholic parents about their early life experiences may be a catalyst in precipitating a depression as the subject relives unpleasant and traumatic early experiences in which alcohol played a significant role. Other early life experiences may prompt feelings of emotional discomfort including child neglect; physical, sexual, and emotional abuse; early introductions to alcohol and drugs; sexual assault; emotional abuse; and other life experiences that precipitate feelings of sorrow and despair. If these risks are evident, you need to discuss them in your proposal. One way to do this convincingly is to cite the research by others in which unanticipated side effects, resulting from the use of a particular instrument or experimental input, were negligible.

Informed Consent Statement
and Debriefing Statement

These are discussed in the following section.

The Informed Consent and Debriefing Statements

You need to have two additional pieces of information in your human subjects application: informed consent and human debriefing statements. An **informed consent statement** requires the subject of the research study to read and acknowledge that he or she has full understanding of the nature of the study and understands that his or her participation in the study is voluntary. An example of an informed consent appears later in this chapter. A **debriefing statement,** given to the subjects once their part in the study is completed, tells the subject what the study was about and notes where and when the subject might obtain the results. It also tells the subject where to get professional help if it is needed as a result of having taken part in the study.

Following is a list of the usual topics to be covered on an informed consent statement. Remember that the informed consent is given to the subject *before* he or she begins their involvement in the research study. The debriefing statement is given to subjects *after* their participation in the study is complete.

Guidelines for the Informed Consent Statement

1. The researcher(s) must identify themselves and give their organizational affiliation.

2. The researchers must explain the nature and purpose of the research, the research methodology, the expected length of time it will take for the subject to complete his or her part in the research, a description of the procedures to be followed, and a truthful disclosure of any procedures that might be harmful. The researcher must be completely honest. If it takes most subjects twenty minutes to complete the study, you may not tell subjects on the informed consent form that it takes ten minutes to complete. Also, you must tell the subject in very clear and easily understood language what the study is really about. You may not say it's about one thing in the informed consent and about something else in the debriefing statement.

3. A description of any foreseeable risks or discomfort to the subject. If you have evidence from pre-testing the study that the study may cause subjects discomfort, or if prior published research suggests risks to subjects, you must share those risks in your informed consent statement. Not to share them is unethical even if doing so discourages subjects from taking part in the study.

4. A description of the benefits the research will provide to the subjects or to others. These benefits should either come from prior research or should be concluded after careful consideration. It's not fair to tell subjects they will benefit from involvement in the study or that others will benefit from the study results if you have absolutely no plan to use the data in any constructive way. Publishing an article or presenting the findings at a conference is a constructive way of using the data to benefit subjects.

5. A statement regarding the confidentiality of responses and the safeguards that protect the subject from being identified by his or her responses. This is very important. I was asked to fill out a questionnaire regarding how I felt about a certain issue at a university at which I formerly taught and identified myself as a member of the social work faculty. To my amazement, the response was printed verbatim in the report and no one had any trouble identifying me as the source of the comment. The instrument promised confidentiality, but the researchers failed to use common sense in the way that promise was kept. In my view, their behavior was highly questionable since it breeched confidentiality and put me at risk. Similarly, when only a few members of a gender or ethnic group are included in a study, most people can easily identify the respondents when data are presented. When you assure subjects of confidentiality, be sure that you actually provide it.

6. If injury to the subject is possible (as in the case of medical or physical experiments), include an explanation of compensation and the availability of medical care, if injury does take place. In the social sciences, emotional risk can be present because questions might negatively affect the client by bringing up traumatic experiences from the past that are emotionally upsetting. It may not be enough to suggest avenues for help if this happens. Rather, the organization sponsoring the study might be *required* to offer free services for any unintended risk.

7. The name of the contact person who can answer pertinent questions for the subject about the project, the subject's rights, and who to contact in the event of a research-related injury or an emotional problem brought about by questions asked by the researcher. This is usually your research instructor or your thesis chair. You should not use their names unless they consent to having them used.

8. A statement indicating that a subject's participation in the study is voluntary. Furthermore, the informed consent must make clear that there are no penalties to the subject refusing to participate in the study. At any time during the study, the subject may voluntarily discontinue his or her involvement. This is very important. The guarantee of voluntary involvement cannot be too strongly stated. Remember that the word *voluntary* is often a very loosely defined term. Offering failing students added points for involvement in a study, gives *voluntary* a different meaning. The same is true if a subject thinks that not taking part in a study may offend a teacher or an employer. Using the word *voluntary* means that direct or subtle pressure to be included in a study cannot be placed on a subject. If it is, involvement in a study is no longer voluntary.

9. Minors under the age of 18 cannot be involved in a research study without the written consent of their parents. If the child is above the age of 7, the child's consent is also required. Sometimes a waiver of parental approval is requested if the study involves no risks to the child and isn't about a topic that may be sensitive to the subject. In this case, the organization in which the study is being conducted contacts the parent and describes the research. They also note that the organization is giving the researcher permission to conduct the study, with the reasons why. And finally, the organization informs the parent that they can contact the school in writing to deny their child's involvement in the research study.

A Sample Informed Consent Statement

Following is an example of an informed consent statement. Be sure that your informed consent statement is similar to the one normally used at your university or organization.

> The study in which you may voluntarily participate is a study of stressors related to work on the Master of Social Work (MSW) degree. The study is being conducted by Dr. John Edwards, Director of the Upper Penninsula University Department of Social Work in Mt. Arctic, Michigan. The study has been approved by the Institutional Review Boards of the Upper Penninsula University and the Department of Social Work. The department and the university require that you give your consent before participating in this or any other research study.
>
> In this study, you will fill out a three part survey. The first part asks socio-demographic questions such as age, gender, years of education, etc. The second part contains the Beck Anxiety Measure (The BAM). The third part contains questions related to the reasons (if any) for your level of stress and whether it directly relates to being in an MSW program. The instrument you will be given will not have your name on it to insure complete anonymity of responses. Please note that you are not required to fill out the instrument, and you can refuse to take or complete it

at any time you wish. Completion of the instrument has taken most of our test respondents about 20 minutes, but it may take you more or less time to complete.

Please be assured that findings will be reported in group form only. No identifying information will be used that can identify you. At the conclusion of the study, you may, upon request, receive a copy of the findings.

Questions related to stress as a result of the MSW program may cause you emotional discomfort. The debriefing statement, which will be given to you when you have completed your part in the study, has the names and numbers of mental health and family service agencies you may contact to help discuss and resolve any emotional discomfort you may have experienced. You may also contact the university counseling center.

If you have any questions about the study, or if you would like a report of the findings, you may contact Dr. John Edwards at 012-434-6711. If you have any questions about this research study, your rights as a participant, or potential injuries or negative emotional side effects, please contact the Institutional Review Board of the university by phone at 012-434-1192.

By checking the box provided below and dating this form, you acknowledge that you have been informed of and understand the nature of the study and freely consent to participate. You further acknowledge that you are at least 18 years of age.

I agree to participate in the study _____ (Check if you agree)

Today's date is:_____

Note: If you decide to ask the participants their names rather than using a check format, you need to have your study reviewed by the University Institutional Review Board rather than that of your department. If you do include subject's signatures, the bottom of the informed consent form is as follows:

_____   _____
Participant's Signature   Date

_____   _____
Researcher's Signature   Date

Further Clarification: To further clarify the rule regarding the use of names of subjects, the federal government has ruled that if you require the names of participants, the human subjects review must be done by the university and cannot be done by a subcommittee or a departmental committee alone. While you can see that not requiring names increases the likelihood that a participant will agree to take part in the study, there is considerable concern that by not requiring names, some researchers may make up their own data or fill out forms themselves. This is highly unethical and is viewed in the same way that plagiarism is viewed and could result in a person's dismissal.

The Debriefing Statement

The debriefing statement is given to the subject upon completion of his or her role in the study. The debriefing statement is a way of informing the subject about what you have attempted to find out in the study and to clarify how the results will be used. In essence, the debriefing statement tries to answer questions the subject might have after taking part in the study. Include the following in any debriefing statement:

1. An explanation of what the study was actually about. If methods were used that were possibly misleading (as in the case of the researcher who asks questions about one topic when the study is actually about something very different), the deception must be explained along with the reason it was done. An example of a deception is the student who asked therapists to use the DSM-4 (American Psychiatric Association, 1994) to diagnose clients with certain emotional problems. The student created vignettes describing a client, but three different versions were given identifying the client as being either Christian, Jewish, or Muslim. The purpose of the study was to determine if the religion of the subjects somehow affected the diagnosis given by the therapists. The student found that Christian clients in the vignette had the least serious diagnosis, Jewish subjects were given a more serious diagnosis, and Muslim subjects were given the most serious diagnosis. Had the student told the subjects beforehand what she was doing, she may have received very different results. She explained the research method in her debriefing statement and the reason she used it, but might the research subjects think they had been mislead? You be the judge.

2. A description of where a subject can get help and who will pay for it in the event the subject has an unexpected physical or emotional response to the study. We have to anticipate potential risks to subjects and make certain that subjects are aware of where they might obtain the needed help to treat the problem. To be absolutely correct, ethically, treatment for all problems that result from involvement in a study should be paid for by the researcher. Of course, determining if we're actually liable can be difficult. Most researchers don't include the issue of payment in the debriefing statement believing that subjects will seek unneeded help if they do. Other

researchers contract with an organization to provide free help if a subject requires it. Again, we should be guided by the principle of doing what is right.

3. The name of a person whom a subject can contact to receive the results of the study. That person must be a member of the organization under whose auspices the research was conducted. Your research instructor is a good example. Some researchers provide the anticipated results in the debriefing statement. If you do this, frame the anticipated results in a way that doesn't suggest that something negative may happen to the subject. For example, the statement "all people who have experienced abuse as children will be abusers as adults" might have a very negative impact on our subjects. The statement isn't correct, and it may not apply to all the subjects.

4. A statement asking subjects not to reveal the predicted outcomes of the study to other potential subjects because revealing outcomes of the study may bias its final results. Including this is a good idea, but it's one that may be difficult to enforce. Consequently, some researchers state in the debriefing statement that final results of the study cannot be reported until all data are tabulated. Subjects sharing the predicted results or the purpose of the study with other participants can give misleading information and may unduly influence later participants. It's worth trying, but subjects knowing what a study is about before they participate in the study (sometimes called **contagion),** is always a problem for researchers.

A Sample Debriefing Statement

This research study was conducted by Dr. John Edwards, Professor of Social Work and Director of Upper Penninsula University Department of Social Work in Mt. Arctic, Michigan. Its purpose was to find out whether the Master of Social Work (MSW) program you are in has caused you unmanageable levels of stress. The instrument used in the study was the Beck's Anxiety Measurement, an instrument that is frequently used to measure levels of anxiety. The study was approved by the Institutional Review Board at Upper Penninsula University in Mt. Arctic, Michigan.

If any of the questions asked on the Beck's Anxiety Measurement or any aspect of the research causes you any emotional stress, you can contact your local family service agency. You can find the number of the agency in the yellow pages of your telephone book or by calling 1-800-564-8956.

A brief summary of the findings and conclusions of the study will be available after June 1, 2003, and can be obtained by calling Dr. Edwards at 012-434-6711. Thank you for your participation in the study.

Ethical Lapses

From time to time, but all too often, we hear about ethical lapses in research studies: Researchers fake interview data; reported results are not accurate or show a bias in favor of the researcher's hypothesis; controversial findings are released before the results have been thoroughly examined and turn out to be incorrect; damaging, unethical things are done to research subjects without informed consent, or the researcher is paid by an organization whose involvement suggests a conflict of interest. The list of ethical lapses goes on and on. Although some researchers do engage in deception, it's important to remember that researchers, like other professionals in highly competitive fields, are under great pressure to release findings that help promote their careers and lead to funding research that provides additional opportunity to explore a topic in more detail.

When ethical lapses occur, it isn't always because of unethical behavior on the part of the researcher. Highly controversial topics often lead to media reports that turn out to be incorrect. How many times have the newspapers reported a cure for AIDS when the researcher has said nothing of the kind? In complex medical research, how often do we hear about unethical behavior only to find out, after the dust settles, that the behavior is explainable and wasn't unethical at all? As future researchers, it's good to get all the facts before you make judgments about unethical conduct.

Still, there must be guidelines to reduce ethical lapses. People get hurt when data are incorrectly found and reported. In the real world, use of a drug or a surgical procedure that hasn't been fully tested can lead to serious repercussions. Here are some suggestions for reducing ethical lapses:

1. Use the human subjects review board correctly.
2. Have other researchers double check your procedures and your findings before they are reported.
3. Don't agree to complete a research study in less time than it realistically takes. Doing so usually results in compromises that lead to ethical lapses.
4. Don't take shortcuts that can lead to errors. Stay with your original plan even if it takes more time to complete.
5. Rely on someone with high moral and ethical principles that you trust and respect when you need to process any methodological issues that may compromise the scientific method.
6. Don't get caught up in competitive studies in which corners must be cut to beat the competition. This will surely lead to ethical lapses.

Summary

The rights of subjects must be respected in all social research endeavors. Even small studies conducted in your classes must first be approved. This process is called human subjects approval. The many aspects of *human subjects approval* were discussed in this chapter, and guidelines were given to instruct research students in the steps necessary to complete a human subjects review.

REVIEW QUESTIONS

1. Isn't it possible that the legal requirements for anyone to conduct research are so inhibiting that important questions, vital to society, may not be asked because a human subjects committee may find them too legally or political incorrect?

2. The informed consent and debriefing statements should give the subject full information regarding the subject's rights. Can you imagine a way that researchers might provide subjects with informed consent and debriefing statements that leave the subject uninformed?

3. Many studies such as the Milgram study of authority have been criticized as examples of the negative impact of not informing subjects of their rights. Isn't it possible that some research topics are so important that keeping the subject uninformed is justifiable? Can you think of some topics?

4. Writing clear and concise informed consent and debriefing statements can be challenging. Choose a topic you want to study and write the statements for review by your classmates. Remember to write at a simple and readable level. Don't use terms unknown to most potential subjects.

REFERENCES

Adler, P. A., & Adler, P. (1993). Ethical issues in self-censorship: Ethnographic research on sensitive topics. In C. Renzetti and R. Lee (Eds.), *Research on sensitive topics* (pp. 249–266). Thousand Oaks, CA: Sage.
Afidi, R. J. (1971). Informed consent: A study of patient reaction. *Journal of the American Medical Association, 216,* 1325–1329.
American Association on Mental Deficiency. (1977). *Consent handbook* (No. 3). Washington, DC: Author.
American Psychiatric Association (1994). Diagnostic Statistical Manual of Mental Disorders (4th Ed.). Washington, DC: Author.
American Psychological Association. (1973). *Ethical principles in the conduct of research with human participants.* Washington, DC: Author.
Bailey, K. D. (1988). Ethical dilemmas in social problems research: A theoretical framework. *American Sociologist, 19,* 121–137.
Baumrind, D. (1985). Research using intentional deception: Ethical issues revisited. *American Psychologist, 40,* 165–174.

Caplan, A. L. (1982). On privacy and confidentiality in social science research. In T. Beauchamp, R. Faden, R. J. Wallace, and L. Walters (Eds.), *Ethical issues in social science research* (pp. 315–327). Baltimore: John Hopkins University Press.

Capron, A. M. (1982). Is consent always necessary in social science research? In T. Beauchamp, R. Faden, R. J. Wallace, & L. Walters (Eds.), *Ethical issues in social science research* (pp. 215–231). Baltimore, MD: John Hopkins University Press.

Chronicle of Higher Education. (1998, November 2). *Scholars who submitted bogus articles to journals may be disciplined.* (pp. A1, A7).

Diamond, S. (1988). Informed consent and survey research: The FBI and the University of Michigan Survey Research Center. In H. O'Gorman (Ed.), *Surveying social life: Papers in honor of Herbert H. Hyman* (pp. 72–99). Middletown, CT: Wesleyan University Press.

Humphreys, L. (1975). *Tearoom trade: Impersonal sex in public places, enlarged ed.* Chicago: Aldine.

Jones, J. H. (1982). *Bad blood: The Tuskegee syphilis experiment.* New York: Free Press.

Lee, R. M. (1993). *Doing research on sensitive topics.* Thousand Oaks, CA: Sage.

McCabe, D. L. (1992). The influence of situational ethics on cheating among college students. *Sociological Inquiry, 62,* 365–374.

Milgram, S. (1963). Behavioral study of obedience. *Journal of Abnormal and Social Psychology, 67,* 371–378.

Punch, M. (1986). *The politics and ethics of fieldwork.* Beverly Hills, CA: Sage.

Reynolds, P. (1982). *Ethics and social science research.* Englewood Cliffs, NJ: Prentice Hall.

Rosenhan, D. L. (1973). On being sane in insane places. *Science, 179,* 240–248.

Sieber, J. E. (1992). *Planning ethically responsible research: A guide for students and internal review boards.* Thousand Oaks, CA: Sage.

Singer, E., & Frankel, M. R. (1982). Informed consent procedures in telephone interviews. *American Sociological Review, 47,* 416–426.

RECOMMENDED INTERNET SITES

Ethical and Legal Aspects of Human Subjects Research in Cyberspace
<http://www.aaas.org/spp/dspp/sfrl/projects/intres/main.htm>
NASW Code of Ethics
<http://www.socialworksearch.com/html/nasw.shtml>
Guidelines for research ethics in the social sciences, law and the humanities, the Research Council of Norway
<http://www.etikkom.no/NESH/eretn.htm>
Ethics in Social Work Research, University of Illinois, Chicago
<http://www.uic.edu/classes/socw/socw560/ETHICS/ETHICS2_files/frame.htm>
Internet Resources on the Tuskegee Study
<http://www.dc.peachnet.edu/~shale/humanities/composition/assignments/experiment/tuskegee.html>

14 Writing the Research Report

Introduction

The research report is an extension of the research proposal. It is finalized when you have completed your data collection and analysis. The research report usually consists of five parts:

1. the introduction/problem formulation;
2. the literature review;
3. a discussion of the research methods;
4. your findings; and
5. a discussion section explaining the meaning of your findings.

Some reports also include an additional section discussing the implications of the study for a specific population of people or for a specific situation. The suggested page length for each section is arbitrary. Follow your instructor's guidelines.

Following is an outline I use in my graduate classes for research projects. A masters thesis or a senior research paper might be longer and, of course, a doctoral dissertation is normally much, much longer.

The Research Report Outline

1. Introduction/Problem Statement
2. Literature Review
3. Research Design and Methods
4. Findings
5. Discussion of Findings
6. Implications

Let's look at each section of the outline in some detail.

1. Introduction/Problem Statement (problem statement and problem focus)

This section is an expanded version of your research proposal. In most research reports, the problem formulation is at least three to five pages long, while for a thesis or dissertation, it might be an entire chapter. In the problem formulation, you introduce the reader to the problem you are studying, give evidence of the importance of studying the problem, describe your methodology, and briefly describe the hypotheses, research questions, or research objectives that guide the study. A longer discussion of your methodology comes in the methodology section.

2. Literature Review

Your proposal literature review is expanded and revised, if necessary, for the research report. Your proposal literature review may need to be re-checked for relevancy. Fifteen to twenty pages is often an appropriate length for a literature review. In the literature review, you summarize the relevant articles you have read, and you show how they relate to the problem formulation. It is a good idea to briefly describe the sources you consulted during the literature review and, at the end of the review, summarize the major findings. If you are testing a hypothesis, your literature review should support the direction of your hypothesis (neutral, positive, or negative).

3. Research Design and Methods

This section describes what you actually did to collect your data. The sampling process is described as well as the data collection procedures. Describe instruments you used including issues of validity, reliability, and cultural sensitivity. The instrument itself should be placed in the appendix. Over the years, I've come to see this section running approximately five to seven pages. It is important that you write this section very clearly. One thing I've noticed is that students who are unsure of what they did in their methodology tend to over-write this section, frequently using meaningless language. This is certainly an important section in your report, and you may want to show early drafts of your work to your instructor for feedback and help.

4. Findings

The findings section presents the relevant data you've uncovered. At a minimum, this section should include measures of central tendency (mean, median, mode, range, standard deviation), and any meaningful chi-squares or correlations comparing the independent and dependent variables. You need to explain what statistics were run and why. If you're uncertain of what to do on this section, ask someone who knows, and be sure that you *understand* what's been done. This is a section that, when poorly done, raises red flags. Your instructor might doubt that you did the analysis yourself and, more importantly, have questions about whether you really understand what you have written. Many of my students don't understand the meaning of the data they've run. They've been taught to use SPSS and they can easily run the data. However, once the data are run, the results often have very little meaning to them. Because I'm their instructor, I take responsibility for their lack of understanding. But you can see why any instructor wants to know why you ran certain statistics and what the statistics mean. Statistics can be confusing to many students, so don't feel badly if you need to ask someone for help. Most universities have statistical consultants in the computer center who are often very patient and can help you run and understand the appropriate statistics.

The list of research question(s) and/or hypothesis(es) from the proposal are used to guide the presentation of the results. Enough data must be given to justify the findings. Tables, figures, and illustrations can be used to clarify the findings, although some tables can be placed in the appendix and can be referred to by the statement "Additional data are found in appendix (give the letter assigned to the appendix where that material is found)." When reporting data, do not display all the raw data or computer print outs, just the data that are central and have meaning. Use the **APA Publications Manual** to help you decide how to present your findings. This section should present only your relevant findings. It should not include a discussion of the interpretations of findings. That comes after the findings are presented to allow the consumer to read the findings free of any outside interpretations. This is done as a courtesy to the consumer of social research. It's difficult to present this section in less than eight to ten pages.

5. Discussion of Findings

In this section, you briefly state the significant results of your study and whether your findings support or fail to support your research hypothesis(es). You might also note whether your results match the results of other similar studies found in your literature review. In this section, interpretations or speculation about why the results came out as they did are acceptable, even expected. It's perfectly all right to speculate in the discussion section about methodological weaknesses and to provide subjective interpretation of the data. You might want to discuss any possible explanations for your results when the results are unexpected. It's always good, in a political sense, to suggest the need for further research, although you should be specific about those areas of your study that need further evaluation. This section is often twelve to fifteen pages, or longer. I urge you to have your instructor read this section in draft form. Many students miss important findings. Strong researchers can help you see findings you may have missed. This additional outside help could considerably strengthen your findings section.

6. Implications

Social scientists should be grounded in the real world. Which is to say that the results of your study, however limited or small they might be, should have implications for some aspect of life. In this section, you try to connect the findings of the study to some real life problem. Discuss how it helps us better understand ways of dealing with that problem. As an example, a study on the prevalence of sexual harassment in organizations should result in suggestions about how the findings of the study can be used to generate needed change. While the writing should be logical, controlled, and objective, the nature of the problem and your ideas about what to do about the problem you've studied should be done creatively.

The implication section can be as long as five pages and can include references, particularly when you discuss your findings and compare them to findings and implications from other studies. This is a very important part of the study. If your findings fail to suggest a range of implications, then perhaps you don't have a good handle on the meaning of your findings, or perhaps you haven't fully thought through the nature of your problem formulation. My experience is that students often miss a vital opportunity to let their minds run free when discussing the implications of their findings. I suggest that you show this section, in draft form, to your instructor or to other researchers for additional feedback. This section should be the most exciting and enjoyable part of the research report because you have the freedom to say essentially what you want to say as long as it's rational and relevant.

What to Include in a Research Report

Your instructor probably has a suggested outline to follow, but here's one you may find helpful when considering the material essential to your report.

1. *Title Page.* Title and author(s).
2. *Signature Page.* Signatures of project supervisor or members of the thesis committee. This is more for a thesis and other more formal reports. You may not need a signature page for your project.
3. *Assigned Responsibilities Page.* For group projects only. I'm including an assigned responsibility page because some schools are picky, as they should be, about who did what and whether there was a fair distribution of labor in research projects with more than one investigator.
4. *Abstract.* This should be on a separate page. The abstract summarizes the report. It condenses what you did in the project and reports your major findings. The abstract should be about 150 words. Look at the abstracts of published articles to get a sense of how abstracts are writ-

ten. Most published writers have the same problem explaining their work in 150 words that you might have so don't feel badly if you have difficulty condensing a long report into 150 words.

5. *Table of Contents.* List the titles of each section and the major headings in the sections.

6. *List of Tables and their page numbers.*

7. *List of Figures or Illustrations and their page numbers.* (if any)

8. *List of Appendices.* This is just the list of appendices. The actual appendices come after the references.

9. *The Problem Formulation.*

10. *The Literature Review.*

11. *The Methodology Section.*

12. *The Findings Section.*

13. *The Implications Section.*

14. *References.* Format this section according to the writing style you have been instructed to use. Most *style books* are available in your bookstore and should be used consistently throughout your report.

15. *Appendices.* Include research instruments, the consent form and debriefing statement, additional tables and data, and any permission letters allowing you to use an instrument or to do your study in a special setting. The letter from the Human Subjects Review Board approving your study could also be included. Include additional analysis of data that may not have been appropriate for the body of the report. A long list of verbatim responses from your open-ended questions might also be placed in the appendix as well as additional analysis of data that are of secondary importance. Be sure to mention, in the body of your report, in which appendix the reader will find certain information. Assign each appendix a letter, and include under that appendix only the information that should logically be included. For example, in one appendix, you might include verbatim responses from your study while in another appendix, you might include the instrument used.

Assessment of Reports

If you are working as part of a group, each student's contribution is usually assessed to the extent that it contributes to the entire project. Negotiate your individual and group contribution with your instructor before the project begins to avoid any problems when the report is finished. A written contract might be a good idea.

The assessment of a research report is usually based on the following:

1. The clarity with which the research question is formulated.

2. How the research report provides insights into, develops, or expands our understanding of people, places, or events in the social sciences.

3. The breadth and depth of the literature review.

4. The appropriateness of the research methods in addressing the research problem.
5. The appropriateness of the statistics used.
6. The quality of the presentation of findings. Are they clearly written, accurate, and understandable to the reader?
7. The relationship of the implications of the findings to the research questions asked.
8. The overall presentation of the report in terms of clarity of the writing, structure and organization, referencing, grammar, and spelling.

The Research Report: An Example

Remember my proposal using a feminist approach in which I suggested that the reason for low male participation rates in social work programs were the results of anti-male sentiments among female social work faculty? And remember the feminist response? I do. Ouch, it still hurts. Following is an example of a short report which could be the result of that proposal. All six sections of the preceding outline are used to guide the report, plus an example of an abstract. This sample report is shortened considerably and is used for illustrative purposes only.

Title: The Lack of Men in Graduate Social Work Programs
Abstract

Twelve schools of social work were randomly visited to find out why there are so few male students in social work. The schools visited had a mean rate of 9.6% male students in their graduate social work programs, the approximate norm for the country. One-hundred fifteen (115) participants (faculty, students, former students, and administrators) were interviewed in twelve (12) focus groups all composed equally of men and women. In general, the respondents failed to indicate concern for low enrollment rates of male students and said that men were not interested in social work as a career. When men *did* apply, they usually had lower GPA's, less work experience, far less reason to choose social work, and seemed less willing to work with poor, disenfranchised clients than were female graduate students. The subjects in the focus groups did not believe that men had special abilities that would help other male clients and expressed a general sense that men were not likely to commit themselves to social work training until salaries were more competitive with other fields.

Problem Statement

The Council on Social Work Education (2001) reports that Master of Social Work programs in the United States have a male composition of less than 10%. This is very troubling news for the many men who may require the specialized help social work provides and who often require male workers (see references in Chapter 3).

At present, men constitute only 5% of the active participants in any form of voluntary out-patient social work therapy, but constitute 80% of the incarcerated mental health patients, 85% of the incarcerated or residentially treated patients with addictions, and 90% of the incarcerated population of jailed felons in America (Johnson, 2000). One could argue that a reason for the high rates of male dysfunction leading to hospitalization or incarceration is that specialized services for men offered by specially trained male workers are not provided because of the small number of men in social work. If more men offering social work services were available before men experience severe crisis, then men at-risk would be less likely to be confined to hospitals, jails, or involuntary treatment settings for mental illness and addictions.

Hypotheses Guiding the Research Study

1. Men have limited enrollment in MSW programs because of a pervasive lack of concern for their inclusion in social work education.
2. Schools of social work are dominated by females who define social work as a female profession.
3. Men are discouraged from attending MSW programs because they are seldom recruited or offered the special incentives that define most under-represented groups.
4. The lack of men in social work is an example of gender bias.

The Literature Review

Rather than do a complete review, let me summarize this section as follows:

The literature review consisted of a computerized search using the help of the resource librarian at Upper Penninsula University in Mt. Arctic, Michigan. (A blessed lady who will go to heaven on the wings of a snow white dove when her time comes and who put up with my loutish, surly, immature behavior for two weeks and not once told me to "zip it" when I started whining and crying about not having seen my girlfriend in two weeks and why, oh why, did an instructor have to be so miserably mean spirited to make me do this? But that's another story.) The key words I used in the literature search were *social work, males in social work, social work admissions, social work education,* and *schools of social work.* I looked at government documents as well as sources in EpscoHost and PsychINFO and would have looked at more sources except that the librarian started making threatening sounds with her teeth. Four hundred (400) abstracts (short summaries of the articles) were reviewed, forty (40) of which were reproduced or read in their entirety in full text. Thirty-five full-text sources were used for this literature review.

The key findings of the literature review are as follows: Thirteen articles (13) noted the general failure of social work journals to mention issues related to men. Six (6) articles suggested a female bias in the subjects published in social work journals. Eight (8) articles suggested the need for more male social workers. Five (5) articles noted the preference men have for male social workers in treatment. Three (3) articles said that male therapists were neither better nor worse with clients than female therapists. Fit of therapist to patient, it was suggested, is more a class and racial/ethnic issue than a gender issue. I laughed a lot at that one. Ha!

Research Design and Methods

Twelve (12) randomly chosen schools of social work with graduate programs in the United States were visited. The total number of U.S. schools of social work with graduate programs is 150. One hundred fifteen (115) total participants were interviewed in 12 separate focus groups. The participants included faculty members, current MSW students, agency personnel and administrators, and admissions and recruitment coordinators in each school. The distribution of men to women was equal in the groups. The interviews were guided by a protocol (a list of questions scrupulously adhered to) to help discover why men were not being admitted to MSW programs in greater numbers and what could be done to increase the number of men in MSW programs. Because the sample size was small and because the use of focus groups is qualitative in nature, the paradigm used was post-positivist. However, there were three researchers involved in all of the interviews who independently collected data to provide objectivity. Consensus statements were developed for each question asked in each of the focus groups to further ensure objectivity. All questions asked in the focus groups had been developed by a group of male and female social work educators who, working together at a national conference, volunteered to spend a day at the conference developing the questions and discussing the research design. In this sense, there is a constructivist element to the study. Because a question guiding this study relates to what can be done to increase the number of men in MSW programs, and because the findings will be used to encourage greater numbers of men to apply to and be admitted to

MSW programs, there is an element in the study of the use of the critical theory paradigm, as well.

Sampling: To randomly select the twelve (12) graduate social work programs, a document listing all 150 U.S. current programs from the Council on Social Work Education was used. By choosing every twelfth school starting with the fifth school on the list, twelve (12) schools on the list in very disparate locations in the country were selected. These schools were equally divided among private and public and large and small schools of social work. Letters to the deans or directors of all of the schools selected were sent and only one, in the midst of reaccreditations, declined participation in the study. An alternative school was selected using the random selection process described above.

One hundred fifteen (115) faculty members, students, administrators, and former students and admissions coordinators were interviewed, or approximately ten (10) subjects per focus group. Morgan (1997) indicates that the ideal size for focus groups is ten to twelve (10–12). Care was taken not to exceed or go lower than that number. In two schools, we had to recruit several more people to reach the desired composition for focus groups. Each group consisted of an equal number of students (2), faculty, including the dean and admissions director (6), and agency personnel (2). The breakdown by gender was 50% male and 50% female. Race/ethnicity was also fairly evenly divided throughout the 12 schools with representation noted as: 50% Caucasian, 25% African American, 12% Latino, and 13% Asian.

Maintaining Objectivity: Three colleagues accompanied the primary researcher on the visits to the twelve schools. One colleague videotaped each focus group to keep an accurate record of the proceedings to be used for later analysis. A second colleague asked consensus statements and helped the primary researcher in the interview process. A third colleague took careful notes of the proceedings, noting any deviations from the original research protocol or any attempts to manipulate answers. Upon completion of the study, all four researchers reviewed the tapes, question by question, and independently summarized their understanding of the answers to each of the fourteen questions that comprised our protocol. These summaries were compared. When there was a difference of opinion, the tape was viewed again and one of the four researchers helped negotiate an interpretation of the answers acceptable to the other three researchers.

Findings
The responses to our fourteen questions were remarkably similar in each of the twelve schools in which focus groups were held. 84% of the respondents thought that it was wrong not to have more male social work students, but most (92%) noted affirmative action limitation on the use of color, creed, race, and gender in the selection process (this was particularly true of schools in California that operate under new laws eliminating affirmative action in state institutions). Eighty-five percent of the respondents noted that men do not apply to social work programs in large numbers, and that when they do, they usually cluster in the lower quartile of the applicants by GPA, experience, ability to write, and prior experience in social work, either volunteer or paid. The focus groups were split almost evenly on whether recruitment would help increase the number of men. Half of the group members believe that low salaries are the greatest inhibitor to male enrollment. However, 73% of the sample admitted that little effort had been made to selectively recruit men, and that race/ethnicity was still the primary concern in recruitment. Only 25% of the respondents felt that more men on faculty would serve to attract more male students, noting that twenty years ago, when male faculty dominated social work education, rates of male students were still very low. 78% of the respondents lamented the minimal numbers of articles about men in social work journals. There was general consensus that more scholarship related to men is needed in social work.

Finally, the consensus of the four researchers viewing the tapes was that the procedures were adhered to closely, the mood of the respondents was serious, and there were no jokes or anti-male statements made by respondents in the focus groups. It was also thought that the similarity in responses across all twelve schools was an indicator that the sentiments of the respondents probably could be generalized to other schools of social work not in this sample.

Discussion of Findings
Although the research hypotheses were not entirely proven to be either true or false, and perhaps the research approach wasn't exact enough to test hypotheses, the findings suggest that qual-

ified men are not applying to social work programs and that
schools are reluctant to recruit men. The findings also suggest
that men are a low priority in admissions. While there is a recognition of the need for more men in social work, schools have not
recruited among the populations of men ready to return to
school including those burned out in the business world ready to
make career changes and who possess a strong social service interest. Many male social work students come from law enforcement including probation and parole departments, but none of
the schools had recruited these men. It was noted that all schools
have something in their literature urging women and people of
color to apply to their schools but that not one school includes
men in these statements. This is curious because women dominate student bodies of social work schools and more women
surely need not be urged to apply unless they are of color, have
non-traditional life experiences, or intend to work with under-
served populations, including men.

The lack of social work literature on men is troubling.
There is a growing body of literature on men in other fields.
There is nothing to prevent the wise social work academic from
using that literature, and certainly no one has said that all readings in the field must be from social work sources. The sample
was serious about the subject, but there seemed to all four researchers a lack of thoughtful consideration of the lack of men
in social work and what it might mean to clients, or to female
students in social work programs who might benefit from interacting with male colleagues. Men, it seemed to us, just didn't
matter much to the respondents. This wasn't seen so much as an
example of bias as it was a lack of ability to see an issue and deal
with it. The existence of few men in social work seems to be a
given, we felt, accepted by our respondents as a fact of life.

Implications
This study, although limited in its scope, seems to support concerns the researcher had about the willingness of social work
programs to recruit, admit, and train men in social work. The
data on the need for men in the helping professions seem fairly
persuasive. We are not convinced that studies saying that fit in
treatment is more a factor of social class than gender. It seems
clear to us that the needs of youthful male offenders and gang
members require the presence of male workers. We also believe
this to be true of men who have committed sexual offenses
against women, men in crisis who have had bad experiences in
their personal lives with issues of intimacy, and a host of men

who seem to be crying out for an understanding, supportive, and empathic male worker who offers a substitute model of male behavior for the absent, abusive, aloof, and non-functioning men who so often represent fathers in America. We think that more, much more, can be done to encourage males to enter the profession, and that recruitment efforts aimed at men who have a social service drive and are currently in jobs that have created high levels of burnout would result in considerably higher numbers of men in the field. The issue of salary, brought up so often, seems to us to be a capitulation to agencies that pay poorly and suggests that schools of social work are unwilling to fight for higher salaries for both men and women. We also think that such statements tie women in social work to long careers in the profession with limited prospects for decent incomes. We believe that much more can be done to attract men and have submitted and had accepted abstracts for national social work conferences where we will make that argument.

Personal Observations on Report Writing

As someone who spends a great deal of his life writing, I have come to realize that we all have our own ways of creating words on paper. Computers give us an opportunity to easily correct those words and to edit our work until we have a suitable finished product. I taught an expository writing course in California. My main observation from that experience is that most students are accustomed to turning in the first draft they write. It's usually awful, just as my first drafts are pretty awful. It may take four or five re-writes to get most writing in some acceptable degree of order. Perhaps the first draft gives you a 50 percent acceptance rate. Each succeeding draft should increase that rate by 10 to 15 percent. I read my material eight to ten times before I turn it in for publication. Even then, it doesn't make me comfortable.

I was talking to a nationally-known poet about a poem of hers I particularly like. She said that the first time she wrote the poem she had it 80 percent right. However, it took her an entire year to finish the rest of the poem, and only at the urging of others did she even submit it for publication. It's a wonderful poem about the loneliness of life and the imperceptible pain caused by early life traumas. But when she reads it in public, she wants to sit down and change it. The urge to write correctly is one that should define your approach to writing.

The impulse of the writer should always be to edit, correct, and improve the writing. If you're one of those first draft students I just mentioned, it just won't work on a research report. In many universities, even if the instructor thinks your writing is acceptable, the project is read by other academics in the graduate office who may not approve it. One student spent a year at my university before the graduate school approved the project for binding, during which time he was not allowed to graduate. Writing centers can help. If your writing isn't good (and not everyone has that facility), you should take extra classes or a writing tutorial. If you can't write in college, you won't be able to write in graduate school and on the job. And while we now have word processing programs that are voice-activated (I have one on my computer), almost no one organizes, speaks, and creates as well verbally as they do when they write. I'd venture a guess that it would take you more time to edit your voice activated writing than if you wrote it to begin with.

In a recent article by Alter and Atkins (2001), the authors note that 60 percent of the graduate social work students in their sample wrote at less than graduate school level. Of the 60 percent of the students who wrote badly in their sample, only 20 percent sought help from writing centers or took tutorials or special writing classes. Something is not working for students who can't or won't write well. In the applied social sciences, children are taken from parents, elderly people have their savings placed in receivership, and people go to jail based on the reports we write. If the writing is poor, then imagine the harm we might do? So please, put effort into your writing and consider each succeeding review of your work an attempt to improve, refine, and strengthen what you have written.

Summary

This chapter gave an outline for writing a research report. It also provided an example of how an actual research report might be written by expanding the problem formulation. A guideline for the way a report should be presented was also included.

REVIEW QUESTIONS

1. Why is it so important to use unemotional and controlled writing in your research report when you may feel very strongly about the subject matter?

2. Doesn't a section on speculations and recommendations permit the otherwise rigorously objective researcher to go into flights of fantasy that may confuse the consumers of the research report?

3. How can we know with any certainty whether the researcher is making up data and whether the findings reported are, in reality, accurate?

4. The research report follows very strict guidelines in form and content. Doesn't this strictness collide with some of the notions provided in this book that research should be creative and free, and that it can sometimes be very subjective in nature?

5. If a research report is just being done for a class assignment and has no likelihood of being presented as a paper at a conference or of being published, then why the need to follow such strict guidelines in the form and content of the report?

REFERENCES

Alter, C., & Atkins, C. (2001, Fall). Improving writing skills of social work students. *Journal of Social Work Education, 3(7):*493–505.

Becker, H. S. (1986). *Writing for social scientists: How to start and finish your thesis, book, or article.* Chicago: University of Chicago Press.

Johnson, M. R. S. (2000). The lady we used to refer to in North Dakota who had wisdom whenever we couldn't find data to support an argument as in, "Well you know, Mrs. Johnson says . . ."

Lennon, T. M. (2001). *Statistics on social work education: 1999.* Alexandria, VA: Council on Social Work Education.

Morgan, D. (1997). *The focus group handbook.* Thousand Oaks, CA: Sage.

Morris, L., Fitz-Gibbon, C. T., & Freeman, M. F. (1987). *How to communicate evaluation findings.* Newbury Park, CA: Sage.

Pyrczak, R., & Bruce, R. (1992). *Writing empirical research reports.* Los Angeles, CA: Pyrczak Publishing.

Reid, W. J. (1981). Research reports and publication procedures. In R. M. Grinnell, Jr. (Ed.), *Social work research and evaluation* (pp. 553–568). Itasca, IL: Peacock.

Reid, W. J. (1985). Writing research reports. In R. M. Grinnell, Jr. (Ed.), *Social work research and evaluation* (2nd ed.), (pp. 459–475). Itasca, IL: Peacock.

Rosenhan, D. L. (1973). On being sane in insane places. *Science, 179,* 240–248.

Sociology Writing Group, UCLA. (1991). *A guide to writing sociology papers (2nd ed).* New York: St. Martin's Press.

Zinsser, W. (1980). *On writing well: An informal guide to writing nonfiction (2nd ed.).* New York: Harper & Row.

RECOMMENDED INTERNET SITES

Writing and Presenting Your Thesis or Dissertation
<http://www.learnerassociates.net/dissthes/>
Writing a Thesis in the Social Sciences
<http://www.york.ac.uk/admin/gso/wrtgthss.htm>
Writing a Literature Review in the Health Sciences and Social Work
<http://www.utoronto.ca/hswriting/lit-review.htm>
How to Write a Thesis Statement
<http://www.indiana.edu/~wts/wts/thesis.html>
Writing for Social Scientists: How to Start and Finish Your Thesis, Book, or Article, by Howard S. Becker
<http://www.brint.com/papers/writing.htm>

15 Our Role as Social Researchers

Introduction

I recently taught a state licensure workshop on human sexuality for social workers and psychologists. As part of the course, I covered the subject of child molestation. As we began to talk about child molesters, a whirlwind of negativism developed. Many of the workshop participants wanted to put child molesters in prison forever and throw away the key. They felt this way because of their moral indignation and also, they said, because the research showed so little promise in treating perpetrators. I've been hearing this sort of talk most of my professional life. The populations we supposedly can't treat have become legion, and while it's true that child molesters are a tough group to treat, it's also true that efforts to find effective treatment approaches for this group, and for many other groups, have been very limited, largely, I think, because certain subjects are just not "okay" to study. In other words, research suffers from a sort of political correctness, even in the applied social sciences.

A commitment to social research is, to a great extent, a commitment to democracy. Citizens need to be informed before they can make valid decisions. The professionals in my workshop were badly informed, and throwing everyone in jail whose behavior offends us (and child molestation is a very serious, dysfunctional, and offensive problem, to be sure) is a troubling way to solve serious social problems. One always hopes that research efforts will lead to alternative treatments that protect the community and provide needed help to offenders. In a democracy, prisons should be a last resort to be used when there are no other options.

A friend and colleague with a Harvard Ph.D. in history and ethnic studies argued, in a California newspaper, that a study of undocumented workers from Mexico returning to Mexico after working in the United States indicated that they had paid far more in taxes than they had received back in services. I know the study and wondered if my friend was correct. Had he factored in the cost of public education provided free to the children of undocumented workers, perhaps $6,000 a year per child and over $12,000 a year for children needing special services: bilingual education, social and emotional counseling, services for children with special physical and emotional needs? Well, no, he hadn't thought of that. Had he factored in the cost of public services such as road construction and maintenance and school bonds to build more schools? Well, no he hadn't. How about the services provided by the police and fire fighters and the emergency ambulance services available in times of medical crisis to all legal and undocumented residents of America? No, he hadn't factored that in, either. Had he thought to consider the cost of social services and welfare benefits to undocumented workers? No, he hadn't done that either. All he was doing, he told me, was reporting back what undocumented workers had said as they re-entered Mexico having just left jobs in the United States.

This is a good example of the confusing role social researchers so often play. Rather than giving convincing arguments based on very good data, they indiscriminately use data to support their point of view even when the data are methodologically questionable. It confuses people and it makes us look bad as social scientists. That just isn't what research is about. Research should be neutral and researchers should be neutral in their interpretation of the data. This is a misleading study reported over and over again in the literature. I happen to be very sympathetic to undocumented workers. My parents were immigrants, but the study my friend reported on is a very limited study. He should have understood and discussed its limitations. The role of the social researcher is to help people understand the complex and often contradictory nature of research findings. All of us should be sensitive to the plight of undocumented workers and the difficult lives they lead in the United States as they try to provide for their families. But it *is* possible to be politically sensitive and caring and still respond in an objective way to the social and political issues that confront us. That, it seems to me, is the role of the social researcher.

In response to my colleague's article, I wrote an opposing article criticizing the research data my colleague used in his original article. I also called for a much more open policy to temporary immigration than my colleague had proposed. I based my argument on the economic data I found available suggesting that undocumented workers are an important part of our economic prosperity. I further proposed that they be given a legal status in this country that would guarantee government services through the taxes they pay. Because I am the son of immigrants, I want the people who come to America to feel a part of this country, not to live clandestine lives of poverty and fear that they will be caught and deported. If they choose to live here, even temporarily, they should know about this country and its laws and, above all, their rights as residents of America. I made the argument and then I wrote a short piece about the immigrant experience that I am including here. It received hundreds of letters, every single one of them positive in a state that was about to pass Proposition 187, a bill denying government services to undocumented workers. While I didn't convince people of the wrongness of Proposition 187, I did remind them of the immigrant experience and the wonderful Americans that immigrants and their children become.

America

My father came from a small rural town in Russia. Because he was coming of age when the Communists would have forced him into the military—an indignity for any Jew denied Russian citizenship—he, my aunt and grandmother left Russia in the middle of the night. Perhaps he was 14. It took them three years of walking across Europe to earn enough money for their passage to America. When he saw the Statue of Liberty, he and a thousand poor Europeans came from the steerage class at the bottom of the ship, stood on the deck, and wept.

America. My father could hardly say the word without tears welling up in his eyes. America. "Give me your tired, your poor, your huddled masses yearning to breathe free." He knew the words on the Statue of Liberty by heart and he would say them to me until I knew the words as well as he did.

My father had a way of avoiding the down side of this country. I guess his immigrant love of America forced him into a sort of selective perception. When we couldn't move from our slum house across from the railroad tracks because no one would sell us a house in a better part of town—being Jewish meaning that you were something akin to having leprosy—my father said, "So, who wants to live with the bastards anyway? Better we should live among our own people where nobody makes jokes about us."

Which, of course, completely begged the question. While it was true that we lived in a small Jewish ghetto, Jewish children went to public schools and the living, as they say, was not easy. I didn't know until I went to public school that, according to my non-Jewish classmates, we Jews drank the blood of our dead and buried our dead standing on top of one another to save money. I hadn't heard the word "Jewed" until second grade and then I didn't understand what it meant. I thought we were the chosen people and that the Jewish men and women in my community were the best and smartest and most wonderful people I could ever know. It was a mystery to me how people could say such wrong-headed and malicious things about us. I guess it still is.

And yet, America was a wonderful place for me. I could spell swear words on the bridge of my mouth with my tongue and still look decently happy whenever any anti-Semitic person would try and remind me of the failings of the Jewish people. I could co-exist because I had bigger fish to fry. America offered me opportunity and it didn't matter to me what other people thought about Jews.

But ultimately, it *did* matter, because they thought the same way about a lot of other people I found pretty admirable. They disliked Blacks and Hispanics and Asians for reasons I couldn't begin to understand. If someone Black came to my hometown, they were asked to leave by the police. Politely, of course. Hispanic farm workers couldn't sit in the same section of the theater as we did. And this, I want to remind you, was in North Dakota, a place so cold and isolated that you should be *paid* to make a visit.

I'm older now and a little more cynical, but in a place deep within my heart, I still love America. To be sure, the country is full of regrettable social problems that beg for solutions. But my underlying belief system, the sense I have when I leave this country and return, is that this place, this America, is full of wonders and riches. Had I lived in Europe, had my parents not left, I would be lying in a mass grave, the victim of another forgotten atrocity to Jewish people.

For my parents, for my brother and sister, for my people who lived to survive the Holocaust because America offered us a safe haven, God Bless America! May she live to offer generation after generation of immigrants a sanctuary against the barbarism of the world.

On Being a Sophisticated Consumer

I hope that this small book has encouraged you to think larger thoughts and to develop your research skills so that you can make a contribution. Research can be very exciting, particularly if your hope is to use the findings of your studies to make this a better place to live, to work, to raise children, and to be able to reach as far as you can at work and in life. You can help do this by sharing your concerns about published social research studies that may be incorrectly reported in the media. You can certainly interpret data to help educate people in a politically neutral way. And when necessary, you can use your knowledge of social research as a "bully pulpit," to paraphrase Teddy Roosevelt, so that you enter into the debates that rage in this country around issues of abortion, crime, educational standards, and a host of social problems for which most of us who understand research say virtually nothing. It's shameful how passive we've become.

I read a report in a California newspaper (Bartholomew, 2001) entitled, "The Golden State Has a Latino Fate." The title of the article alerts us to what follows. The article tells us that Latinos will become the dominant ethnic group in California. However, the article is primarily about the children born to Latino mothers who contribute to the increasing number of Latinos in the state. The article provides "surprising" evidence that Latino babies are as healthy as other groups even though a high percentage of the babies come from mothers in poverty who often fail to receive adequate pre-natal care. According to the article, healthy babies are a result of the desire of their Latino mothers to "emulate the Lady of Guadalupe. The lower the education rate, the less likely they [Latino mothers] are to smoke, use drugs or drink" (p. C6). Finally, the article notes that Latino mothers in California have high out-of-wedlock rates, rates just slightly lower than that of African American women.

This is an offensive article presented under the guise of research. The author has manipulated the data to suggest that Latino mothers take poor care of their babies while they are pregnant, that they get pregnant out of wedlock at a high rate, and that babies are healthy at birth because their mothers have good personal health habits developed as a result of religious beliefs, not because they use medical services in a sophisticated way. This is the type of biased reporting that takes a positive event and makes it nega- tive. What it suggests is that an increasing number of poor, unmarried Latino women will have babies in California, and as Latinos become the dominant ethnic group in the state, a large number of babies will be born to poor mothers who don't understand or use modern health care. And just so the point isn't lost on the reader, the article ends by telling us that almost 60 percent of all Latino mothers are likely to fund their deliveries through the public welfare system. If you hadn't gotten the point before, here comes the kicker. Latino mothers are poor, use welfare, and don't take care of their babies before delivery. It is a pejorative article because it raises the level of bigotry in a state with strong anti-immigration sentiments and a long his- tory of discriminatory practices against Latinos. The role of research is to in- form, not to offend. This is an offensive article. It paints a negative picture of Latinos by using data to create an argument that smacks of bigotry. When you see these articles you should immediately feel a surge of sorrow. Arti- cles such as this one hurt people and indefinitely prolong stereotypes.

Because of similar articles, I sincerely hope that at this point in your understanding of research you can read a research report and determine if the research is well done. I hope you know when the researcher is hiding data and whether more is being made of the data than can reasonably be assumed. You should have a basic understanding of the construction of a research report and whether the researcher has followed the rules of scien- tific inquiry. Your beginning understanding of statistics should give you a sense of whether the researcher is reporting findings that are warranted or unwarranted by the data. If you find statistics a little difficult to compre- hend, improve your understanding with a statistics course. I know statistics isn't always easy, but knowing how to read and understand statistics is the key to being a sophisticated consumer of research, and it will help you in many ways in the world of work. Knowledge is power and knowledge of statistics is real power.

I suspect that technology will make our lives very different in the fu- ture. As social scientists, we have a responsibility to critically analyze all so- cial movements and their impact on people. My sense is that computers are making people more distant from one another. In a society where aloofness and isolation are growing concerns, far too many Americans are lonely, un- happy, and unable to have their intimacy needs met. As social scientists, we should be concerned. Even small research efforts to understand the lives of people and the way our society functions can have a profound impact on the way our society works. It should be part of our commitment as edu- cated people to continue the research effort and to study, even in very small ways, the social trends that change our world so quickly.

One of my students, a former member of a "sub-culture," is doing a research study on sub-culture members and depression. She thinks Americans have stereotypic views of sub-cultures and that the way people dress, their music, and their life styles are not significantly tied to their level of social and emotional functioning. I suppose I have a bit of a bias about sub-cultures. I see people with pierced noses and tongues, and yes, it bothers me. I'm all too willing to accept a negative view of members of sub-cultures, but I'm thrilled that she's interested in her subject. I wish her well. I think that by challenging stereotypes, she's doing a large service in the battle we fight to make democracy work well. When members of sub-cultures are harassed, it means that our society isn't working. To be able to say that members of sub-cultures make life choices in dress and life style that do not result in harm to themselves or to others would be a very useful finding and I wish her well. It is this type of opportunity we have in research to make our concerns known and to challenge traditional, but untested, views of people, views that frequently lead to prejudice.

I admire the researchers among us. It can be very lonely doing studies that no one seems to care about. But we *should* care; we should care quite a bit. We should support research efforts even when they seem difficult to understand or disassociated from anything practical. Research helps make our world a more thoughtful place. The large problems we face with terrorism and hate groups throughout the world require thoughtful and rational analysis. To react emotionally before we know or understand the problem can't help but hurt people. It certainly won't resolve the problems we face with other people in our larger world who have grievances against us.

The researcher's world of calm and rational thought is one that often offends people when they are responding emotionally to an atrocity or to an act of barbarism. The researcher's way seems overly slow and unresponsive. Many people feel that the endless attempts to seek truth will go on indefinitely and that needed answers will never be provided by social researchers. But that's exactly what the world needs right now, slow and careful consideration with a clear and logical idea of what is happening, and then, when we know and we understand a problem, a clear plan for what can be done to rectify the problem. Rather than being passionless, researchers are very passionate people. They want to make a contribution to the world, but they want it to be a helpful and meaningful contribution, not a quick fix that in a moment will work and in a second moment will cause harm.

I recently attended a conference where I met a young woman whose research is on the female police officers who lure men on the streets into having sex for money. My initial reaction was to say that it seemed highly wasteful to use resources to rid our community of street prostitution, but she had a very different purpose. She believes that law enforcement is going to be asked to take on new roles in the fight against terrorism. Her broader goal, she told me, is to understand the impact certain types of assignments have on law enforcement officers. The techniques she is developing to study the problem will be useful in determining response time, emotional side effects of certain assignments, ways of determining who is good and who isn't good at dealing effectively with certain assignments and, lastly, that the research she is doing will hopefully tell us much more about female law enforcement officers, an area she told me we know very little about. She also said that while it seemed wasteful to put our energies into reducing prostitution, did I know that many street prostitutes are addicted to illegal substances, that often they have sexually transmitted diseases that are passed on to customers, and, finally, did I know that many customers are robbed and beaten by co-conspirators and not a few of the beaten men have died in the past year? Well, no, I didn't know any of that but now that I do know, hats off to her for doing such unpleasant but necessary research.

Much of my initial reaction to her research is the same reaction many of us have to research efforts on subjects that seem unimportant or whose subject matter offends our sensibilities. It takes a tough-minded and self-directed person to continue working on a research problem with little public recognition, minimal financial support, and antagonism from others that make it difficult for the researcher to publish findings.

Researchers, real researchers, are the most ethical and duty bound people I know. As they struggle without money and support to do what gives them passion, they develop creative and subtle ways of working around the lack of funding and the social disinterest in their projects. I was writing about job dissatisfaction five years before the burn-out craze hit us. I couldn't publish an article on job unhappiness for the life of me. However, I kept working at it when everyone around me said it was bunk and that it was a research agenda that would get me nowhere. My father was passionately involved in the labor movement. From his work I had seen what job unhappiness did to people. I grew up and worked around some of the brightest but most emotionally broken people you can imagine, people whose dreams and aspirations were exchanged for alcoholism, domestic violence, fights with co-workers, and lives quickly gone to ruin. I stuck with job satisfaction research because I felt a personal responsibility to honor my father's work, work I admired and believed in. And in time, it paid off for me in articles and in other work that gave me a sense of satisfaction that I can't quite describe. Whenever I write about the workplace, I feel my father's presence. I think he would be proud that I continue the work he started as a Russian immigrant at a time in our history when unions were often considered subversive.

From work on job unhappiness, I began writing about the men I knew when I was growing up. Some of them were badly dysfunctional but others were the heroic men I admired and respected, the men who helped me model my life for public service. In time, that writing lead to work on men's issues at a moment in our history of considerable male bashing and blame that men were responsible for all problems in our society.

These are subjects that come from long-held convictions. I believe that what I write about begs to be heard. And I believe that the research I do, however unpopular the subject matter might be at the moment, is important to me as a researcher and that it gives solace to others. In the same way, I hope you find what gives you passion. It may be something that completely turns others off and it may even offend them. That's all right. In a democracy, those who seek truth at times of greatest risk are the real heroes.

There is a sad need to conform to ideas in America today, and political correctness sometimes determines what can and what cannot be studied. Issues of race, ethnicity, gender, and social class that should be very important to social scientists are often felt to be too risky, too likely to offend. I hope that you don't fall into the trap of political correctness and that the star you choose to shoot for is a star that may not blink as brightly for others. Dissent is the mother's milk of a democracy, and dissent born of rational study is the most sublime form of dissent.

As I finish writing this book, the United States has been attacked by a wave of terrorism. It's a frightening feeling to worry about safety and to think that something awful might happen for which we are all unprepared. The random possibilities of terrorism make everyone just a little more apprehensive and frightened. For this reason, we should be concerned about the plight of the underclass: the poor, disenfranchised, throwaway people we ignore to such an extent that they have become, in a sense, invisible. The terror they experience is not that of exploding airplanes or anthrax but the sheer gut-wrenching fear of being killed because they have no protection from violence. It surrounds them. What more important work could anyone do than to make these citizens and neighbors safe from harm's way? If our social research skills can be used for that purpose, then it will have been worth the effort to learn new and complicated terms and concepts.

Similarly, so many people in this country, this wonderful country of ours, suffer. John Perry Barlow (2001), one of the original lyrists for the Grateful Dead, writing about the American condition during the most affluent period in our history, notes:

> During the year 2000, while many of us were feeding at the greatest economic pig trough the world has ever slopped forth, Americans ate 10.2 billion worth of Prozac and other anti-depressants (up 19.5% from the prior year). Better living through chemistry? I don't think so. I have never heard any of my friends who have become citizens of Prozac Nation claim that these drugs bring them closer to actual happiness. Rather, they murmur with listless gratitude, that antidepressants bring them back from the Abyss. They are not pursuing happiness, they are fleeing suicide. (2001, p. 96)

Even if you don't see things in such a negative way, it doesn't take much effort to notice the great number of unhappy people around, many with every material convenience that money can buy. Why are there so many unhappy people in a nation that has experienced such richness? I have my own opinion, but certainly it should be clear that social research has a great deal to tell us about the American condition as we face a decade that might include terrorism and challenges to our economic prosperity.

Thanks to the Reader

Thank you for reading my book. I hope it has helped to make some of the technical issues related to social research more clear. I also hope that you continue to read research as a knowledgeable and sophisticated consumer and that you continue to use scholarly sources to find information. With the use of the Internet, information is a minute or two away. I hope that you decide important life issues based on rational and reflective thought. That approach is certain to help you see the many sides of an issue and to decide on your positions in life in a way that comes from deep conviction.

We live in a society where feeling too strongly is frowned upon. We somehow believe that it's sentimental and uncool to feel too deeply about issues. But to not believe strongly often makes people feel detached and without purpose. It's a wonderful feeling to know that in large and small ways, you have come to conclusions about life issues, not out of a temporary emotional state or because of someone else's influence, but because you've used reason, consideration, and thoughtfulness in determining your position. That is essentially what the scientific method is about.

I hope that you can use objectivity, rationality, and the convictions of your beliefs to have a wonderful, happy, and productive life. And I hope the security you feel in your beliefs leads you to share your thoughts with others and to enter into the world of the scholar who believes that a rational world can often be a very caring world.

REFERENCES

Barlow, J. P. (2001, December 3). The pursuit of emptiness. *Forbes*, 96–97.
Bartholomew, D. (2001, December 19). The golden state has a Latino fate. *The San Bernardino Sun*, C1.

RECOMMENDED READINGS

Barton, A. H. (1995). Asking why about social problems: Ideology and causal models in the public mind. *International Journal of Public Opinion Research, 7*, 299–327.

Bermant, G. (1982). Justifying social science research in terms of social benefit. In T. Beauchamp, R. Faden, R. J. Wallace, & L. Walters (Eds.), *Ethical issues in social science research* (pp. 125–142). Baltimore: John Hopkins University Press.

Black, T. (1993). *Evaluating social science research.* Thousand Oaks, CA: Sage.

Leedy, P. D. (1981). *How to read research and understand it.* New York: Macmillan.

Rogler, L. H. (1989). The meaning of culturally sensitive research in mental health. *American Journal of Psychiatry, 146(3),* 296–303.

GLOSSARY

AB Design A simple before and after design used in single subject research with a pre-test before the treatment input and a post-test after the treatment input. There may be multiple post-tests to determine how long the treatment input lasts.

ABAB Reversal Designs A single subject design in which a pre-test is given, treatment is provided for a specific length of time, improvement is measured, treatment is applied again for the same period of time and change is then measured. Tries to show the importance of treatment in a more objective way than AB Designs.

Abstract A brief summary of the problem studied, the methodology, and the major findings in a research report preceding the full text.

Acculturation Scale An instrument that determines the extent to which the values, beliefs, and experiences of someone's country of origin still affect their lives today.

Alternative Hypothesis The possibility that a null hypothesis may not be proven and that the result is either a positively or negatively directed result.

Analysis of Variance (ANOVA) A statistical test that calculates variance (the percent of a correlation occupied by a specific variable) between two groups.

APA Publication Manual The stylebook of the American Psychological Association rules. Contains the writing and referencing style used most often for writing research reports in the social sciences.

Applied Research Practical research conducted to find out how something might be applied or used to solve a social science issue or problem.

Association A weak link between two variables that is not considered strong enough to indicate a significant or statistically useable correlation (relationship).

Audit Trail The requirement that researchers keep a precise record of their methodology so that unpredictable events might be better understood and controlled for in future research studies.

Baseline Measure A measurement taken before treatment begins.

Bell Shaped Curve A curve that shows an average distribution of scores and may also be called a normal curve.

Between-Groups T-Test A statistical test comparing two groups to one another for levels of significance.

Bi-Modal Scores When the mode in a measure of central tendency occurs twice.

Chance The tendency of unpredictable and uncontrolled for occurrences to affect the findings in a research study.

Chaos Theory A theory suggesting that even randomly occurring and unpredictable events have an order and logic to them that can be objectively studied.

Chi-Square A statistical test to determine the level of chance between variables. Chi-square is represented by the symbol X^2.

Closed-Ended Questions Questions on an instrument which have a fixed set of answers from which respondents must choose.

Cluster Sampling Using groups or clusters of organizations to draw samples, in lieu of individuals.

Coding Assigning raw data numerical value for the purpose of statistical calculations. For example, giving each increment of income a numeric value. $5,000 to $10,000 might be given a value of 1. Rather than computing actual incomes, for convenience sake, we compute intervals of income.

Concurrent Validity How well an instrument measures current functioning of a subject.

Construct Validity How well an instrument measures theories.

Constructivist Paradigm A paradigm providing the research subject significant involvement and control over the research effort.

Contagion When subjects in a research study have information about the study from other participants so that results are affected.

Content Validity Refers to whether the questions asked on an instrument provide an accurate range of questions to cover the issues to be measured.

Control Group The group in an experimental design that does not receive the treatment input; usually the group against which treatment groups are measured.

Convenience Sampling A sample made up of the available subjects when a larger sample is too difficult to obtain.

Correlation The statistical relationship between variables expressed as a number from −1.00 to +1.00 and represented by the letter r.

Cover Letter The letter included with a mailed instrument that explains to the participants the purpose of the study and provides information regarding the time frame in which to complete and return the instrument.

Criterion Validity A comparison of the questions asked on an instrument against some established normative measure, perhaps a well established, often used instrument with excellent validity and reliability.

Critical Incident Interview An interview where the subject is asked to think about a time when something important happened and to discuss it.

Critical Theory Paradigm In keeping with the critical theory paradigm, a researcher admits that he or she has a bias about the research study and that they hope the findings will support that bias.

Critical Value A number based on the level of chance the researcher has selected as acceptable (the *p* value).

Debriefing Statement A statement given to research subjects after their involvement in the study, that explains the purpose of the study and indicates where they might get more information about the findings and, if needed, help for any problem created by being a part of the study.

Deductive Reasoning Orderly lines of thought that include hypothesis testing.

Degrees of Freedom The number of subjects minus one (n–1). Used in statistical reporting.

Delphi Approach A constructivist approach that uses frequent contact with subjects to frame research questions and gather data using consensus statements.

Dependent Variable The consistent variable that depends on the experimental input to be changed. In the treatment of cancer, cancer is the dependent variable.

Descriptive Research Research that adds to information already known.

Exempt Review A human subjects review term indicating that a study is at such minimal risk for human subjects violations that the chair of the Institutional Review Board Committee can grant the request for approval without consulting the larger committee.

Expedited Review A human subjects review term indicating that the research proposal can be approved by a sub-committee of the larger Institutional Review Board because it presents limited risk.

Experimental Design A research design using a positivist paradigm that attempts to control for internal and external validity, has a probability sample, uses a valid and reliable instrument, and tries to keep controls on the design that allow for conclusions of cause-effect relationships and generalizability to other people, places, and events.

Experimental Group The group receiving the treatment input.

Explanatory Research The type of research that attempts to provide meaningful and accurate conclusions from the considerable amount of information already available.

Exploratory Research The type of research that attempts to break new ground by delving into new problem areas to study.

External Validity The ability to apply findings to other places, people, or situations outside of the experimental or research setting.

F-Score The degree to which chance played a role in the outcomes of an ANOVA test.

Face Validity Whether a question on an instrument appears to measure what it claims to measure.

Feminist Research A critical theory approach to social research that stresses the need for action-oriented research using designs that permit creative studies of social relations, power differentials, and social issues that often reflect male dominance.

Focus Group A randomly selected group of subjects who discuss, in a group context, specific issues determined by the researcher.

Frame of Reference The way we view a particular problem in research based upon our belief system.

Full Board Review A Human Subjects Committee term indicating that the level of risk involved in a particular research proposal is great enough to require a full Institutional Review Board evaluation.

Goal-Attainment Scales Measurement scales that allow the researcher to set goals for treatment and then measure whether those goals have been met. Often used with single subject designs.

Halo Effect The tendency to respond positively to an experimental input, but usually only for a short period of time until the "glow" of the experience wears off. No real change has taken place as a result of the experimental input.

Heuristic Paradigm A paradigm suggesting alternative approaches to research consistent with qualitative designs often used in post-positive research.

Human Subjects Review Board A organizational committee usually comprised of members with strong research skills, who make decisions about the ethics of a research study and therefore have power to grant or refuse a researcher permission to do a study. These boards are also known as human subjects committees and have the right to recommend sanctions for unethical behavior by a researcher.

Hypothesis An educated prediction of what the study will find based on what similar studies have found in the past. May be stated in a neutral way (a null hypothesis) or a positive or a negative way suggesting that the study will either find what other studies have found or the exact opposite of what other studies have found.

Independent Variable The treatment variable within a research design that may affect the dependent variable. In the treatment of cancer, chemotherapy is the independent variable.

Independent Verification Suggests the need for research results to be verified by a second and perhaps third review of the study.

Inductive Reasoning Using intuition, subjective judgments, and creative leaps to reason out research problems. The approach most often used in naturalistic research.

Informed Consent Statement A document, signed by the participants in a study that provides clear, truthful, and relevant information to research subjects about the nature of the study they are being asked to take part in. It assures subjects that their participation is voluntary and that they are able to terminate participation at any point.

Institutional Review Board The group of people who have institutional responsibilities for human subjects review.

Internal Validity The degree to which the independent variable can be shown to be the main cause of change in the dependent variable.

Interval Continuous Data Data that are classified and rank ordered.

Intervening Variables Unpredictable reasons for a relationship between the independent and dependent variable that were not controlled for in the research design.

Level of Significance The degree of chance occurring within a given research design. Reported as a value of *p* and usually considered acceptable as less than five chance occurrences per one hundred.

Likert Scale A scale in which the answers to questions are pre-determined on a continuum of responses.

Margin of Error Refers to the fact that all sampling brings with it a certain error rate explained by the fact that the only totally accurate way to get perfect data is to seek information from every individual member of the larger population.

Maturation Changes in emotional functioning related to biological changes in subjects that are unrelated to any treatment input.

Mean A measure of central tendency; the average score. Obtained by adding all scores together and dividing by the total number of scores.

Median A measure of central tendency. The point at which exactly half the scores are higher and the other half of the scores are lower.

Meta-Analysis A literature review of numerous studies that statistically summarizes the findings to identify common themes.

Methodology Includes your research design, sampling size and procedure, instrumentation and paradigm.

Mode A measure of central tendency. The score that appears most often in a range of scores. It's possible to have more than one mode (see bi-modal scores).

Multiple Analysis of Variance (MANOVA) A statistical test that compares the means of multiple groups.

Multiple-Treatment Interference When subjects receive more than one treatment input making it difficult to determine which treatment creates change.

Naturalistic Research Also called *field research*. A technique used frequently in cultural anthropology to study people in their own contexts without any invasive or artificial experiments. It involves studying the way people interact by using carefully constructed approaches in the observation of people, places, and events.

Negative Correlation A negative relationship between the independent and the dependent variables.

Nominal Data Non-mathematical data that has been assigned a number for the purposes of coding and eventual statistical analysis.

Non-probability Sampling Used when the number or location of the people who comprise the population from which we intend to draw a sample is not known.

Normed When an instrument has been tested with various groups to find out how each of those groups score on the instrument.

Null Hypothesis A neutral hypothesis that makes no claim as to how a study will turn out.

One-tailed Hypothesis Suggests that the hypothesis will have a positive or negative outcome.

One-tailed T-Test A modified t-test measuring levels of significance. Used when the direction of difference between two groups is known.

Open-Ended Questions Questions on an instrument in which the answers are not pre-determined, and the subjects can write anything they believe to be relevant.

Ordinal Data Data in which variables can be rank ordered.

Orthogonal Contrast Test Comparing two or more groups for variance and predicting, in advance, that the groups will be different (or similar).

P **Value** The degree to which chance played a role in the outcomes of a statistical test and whether we can accept the finding as statistically significant.

Paradigm A paradigm framework that helps define and organize our thinking.

Parameters A sampling term used to describe the distribution of variables within the research sample that is then inferred for the entire population.

Placebo Effect When a subject improves even though they've been given a nontreatment such as a sugar pill instead of an actual medication.

Plagiarism Using someone else's words in place of your own without properly recognizing their contribution. Plagiarism may also include representing someone else's work as your own.

Population A sampling term used to describe that portion of the population that is available for study.

Positive Correlation A positive relationship between the independent and the dependent variables.

Positivist Paradigm The assumption that if a problem can be studied in a highly objective and scientific way, the researcher may be able to tell the consumer that there are meaningful connections or relationships between variables, if any are found.

Post Hoc Test When two or more groups are compared for variance and you cannot predict whether the groups will be different or similar.

Post Modernism Post-modernism is concerned with social problems that have developed in society as a result of the belief that there are rational explanations for most issues facing humankind.

Post-positivist Paradigm In post-positivist research, important social science issues are studied using approaches that only suggest weak associations, trends, and directions among variables, but if done enough times will eventually demonstrate compelling connections.

Predictive Validity The ability of an instrument to measure a person's future functioning.

Pre-Test The measurement of a subject's behavior, attitudes, or opinions taken before the experimental input is provided.

Post-Test The measurement of a subject's behavior, attitudes, or opinions taken after the experimental input is provided. May be given numerous times after the experimental input to determine how long the input affects the client.

Probability of Error *See* Level of significance.

Probability Sampling A sampling approach in which every member of the larger population has an equal or random chance of being selected.

Problem Formulation The problem formulation sets the tone for the research study. It explains why the issue you plan to study is important and describes that aspect of the issue you are particularly interested in.

Program Evaluation Studies of the effectiveness of social programs that often use quasi-experimental designs and are intended to determine overall effectiveness of a program rather than individual effectiveness of workers.

Public Domain The permission of the author is not necessary because the author of the instrument has given up copyright privileges.

Pure Research Research done out of a desire to build theories and to prove hypotheses without explicit intent to use findings for a specific purpose.

Purposive Sampling A sampling approach that targets a particular population because those populations have a special quality related to the particular study.

Qualitative Research Research that provides more leeway than quantitative research in the flexibility of designs and sampling. Not felt to permit cause-effect relationships or the ability to generalize to other people, places, or situations.

Quantitative Research Research that uses a positivist paradigm, experimental designs, and the scientific method to produce findings that may show relationships that are generalizable to other people, places, and events.

Quasi-Experimental Designs Designs that are not appropriately experimental because they can't completely control important variables but try, to the best of their ability, to do so. These designs may be used in program evaluation studies.

Quota Sampling A non-probability sampling approach that identifies certain categories needing representation, then tries to choose people for the sample who have those special qualities or characteristics until a predetermined number of people have been filled in each category. May be likened to stratified sampling.

Range Test scores that go from the lowest to the highest score. If the lowest score is 16 and the highest is 95, the range is 16 to 95.

Refereed Academic Journal Articles Articles that undergo a lengthy process of evaluation and revision before they are accepted for publication in academic and professional journals.

Regression Analysis A statistical test that determines correlation and variance of many variables and is assumed to have predictive value.

Reliability Refers to whether an instrument will provide the same results when the same subject uses the instrument more than once.

Replicate To do a study over again the exact way it was originally done.

Research Instrument A way of measuring behavior, attitudes, values, or opinions of subjects by using a valid and reliable test or scale.

Research Objectives A way of posing, in behavioral terms, what you hope to find in the study. May be used in lieu of a hypothesis when not enough data are available to support the use of a hypothesis.

Research Question A way of posing a question to guide a research study. Used in lieu of a hypothesis when not enough prior data is available to pose a hypothesis.

Sample A smaller cohort of the larger population that is representative of the population and that may be substituted for the population in a research study.

Sampling The process of selecting a cohort within a population of subjects that while smaller than the population, is thought to accurately represent that population.

Sampling Bias The planned or unplanned changes that take place in the sampling process that may lead to an unrepresentative sample.

Sampling Error The almost inevitable fact that the sample will differ in some subtle way from the population it is drawn from and that a certain amount of error will result.

Sampling Frame A sampling term used to describe that smaller segment of the population that is available for study but is also very much like the larger population.

Scientific Method An approach to problem solving that is highly objective, provides for replicability, and has audit-trails that others can review.

Simple Random Sampling Choosing a large and diverse group of people at random in the hope that we will select a sample that closely represents the larger population.

Single-Subject Research Using a single subject to gather data. Often used in conjunction with goal attainment scales.

Skewed curve A curve whose distribution of scores cluster at one end or the other of the range of scores.

Snowball Sampling By starting out with a small group of people, subjects identify other likely participants who then join the project sample until the sample is complete. This non-probability sampling approach is used when there is no clearly defined population from which to draw a sample.

Social Desirability The tendency of subjects to give answers to researchers that reflect what the subject thinks most people would say to a question. The answer may not reflect the subject's true feelings but his or her assumption that there is a correct answer.

Socio-Demographic Information Descriptive data that usually involves gender, age, educational background, income level, marital status, or other data about the subjects.

Solomon Four-Group Design An experimental design that uses one group (experimental and control) that receives the same pre-test and post-test and another group (experimental and control) that receives just the post-test. Used to minimize the impact of test wiseness.

Split-Half Method Dividing the questions on an instrument into two parts with each part measuring roughly the same thing, and then giving each half to different people.

Spurious Refers to relationships that are unpredicted in a study and that tend to be meaningless.

Standard Deviation A measure of central tendency that allows us to determine how far a score is from the mean.

Statistic A sampling term used to describe the identifying variables or characteristics that may be present in a sample. Examples include race, ethnicity, gender, and age.

Steady State The period of time before the treatment input when a subject's behavior remains constant or deteriorates. Used to see if the treatment input can reverse the steady state.

Stratified Random Sampling Making sure that a sample includes the many elements of a larger population by race\ethnicity, gender, and so forth.

Surveys A way of collecting data from a large number of people using an instrument that garners the same type of information from each subject.

Systematic Random Sampling A type of sampling that uses a formula to select the sample. For example, if we want to choose 50 names from a list of 500 names we would divide 500 by 50 giving us the number 10. We would then arbitrarily choose a number between one and ten as our starting point (let's say the number is 5) so that our first name would be number 5 and then, using 10 intervals between names, our second name would be number 15, then 25 and so on until we have 50 names.

T-Test A statistical test that compares the means of two groups and computes the degree of chance involved in the differences between the groups.

Test-Retest Method To help establish reliability of the instrument, the subject is given the same test several times.

Test-Wiseness The concern that once having used an instrument that subjects choose answers they believe are correct rather than answers that reflect their real opinions.

Testing Interference When the test used in a research design creates changes in the research outcomes that are not related to the treatment.

Theory Connecting hypotheses in an attempt to explain relationships. A theory offers a strongly suggested reason as to why something occurs.

Time-Series Designs Experimental designs that attempt to vary the length of the treatment input to determine if time is a factor in outcome of a study.

Turkey's LSD Test A type of post hoc test that permits the researcher to compare multiple groups against one another.

Two-Tailed Hypothesis A hypothesis that predicts a relationship but doesn't indicate if it will be positive or negative.

Two-Tailed T-Test A modified t-test measuring levels of significance that is used when the direction of difference between two groups is not known.

Type-One Error An error of rejecting the null hypothesis and concluding that there will be a relationship between variables when there won't be.

Type-Two Error An error of failing to reject the null hypothesis and predict that no relationship will exist when, in fact, one will exist.

Universe A sampling term used to describe a group of people who share similar identifying characteristics.

Validity Refers to whether an instrument measures what it is intended to measure.

Variance The percent of a correlation occupied by a variable determined by multiplying the correlation times itself.

Within-Groups T-Test A statistical test that compares a group to itself, usually with pre-tests and post-tests, for levels of significance.

Z-Score The number of standard deviations an individual test taker might score from the average score of everyone taking the test.

INDEX